GOOD NEWS STUDIES

Consulting Editor: Robert J. Karris, O.F.M.

Volume 9

The Unity of Luke's Theology

An Analysis of Luke-Acts

by

Robert F. O'Toole, S.J.

Michael Glazier, Inc.

Wilmington, Delaware

ABOUT THE AUTHOR

Robert F. O'Toole, S.J., is Professor of Theology and Chairman of the Department of Theological Studies at St. Louis University. He is internationally known for his scholarly research on Luke-Acts. His publications have appeared in such learned journals as *Biblica, Revue Biblique, The Journal of Biblical Literature* and *Biblische Zeitschrift.*

First published in 1984 by: MICHAEL GLAZIER, INC., 1723 Delaware Avenue, Wilmington, Delaware 19806

Library of Congress Cataloging in Publication Data

O'Toole, Robert F.
   The unity of Luke's theology.
   (Good News Studies; v. 9)
   Bibliography: p. 270
   Includes index.
   1. Bible. N.T. Luke—Theology. 2. Bible. N.T. Acts—Theology. 3. Luke, Saint.
I. Title. II. Series.
BS2589.J87 1984   226'.406   84-81246
ISBN 0-89453-438-6 (pbk.)

Printed in the United States of America

CONTENTS

For my Mother
and in memory of my Father

INTRODUCTION

This book attempts to synthesize Luke's theology in Luke-Acts. The claim is that this book represents something new in Lucan studies, for it asserts that Luke has one dominant theme and subordinates his other theological concerns to that theme. It also shows how Luke achieves this synthesis. This is not to say that much that is in this book has not been pointed to by other scholars, but that the present synthesis explains in greater detail and makes better sense of all the evidence. The book is not directed only to the college theology student but to students and scholars of Luke's thought.

A very concerted effort has been made in this book to base the presentations and arguments on Luke's text. This is due to the convictions that the actual task of an exegete is to listen to the text and that the reader wants to know what *Luke* thought. It is a presentation which demands that the reader continually refer to Luke's text to check for himself or herself the validity of the assertions made. Thus, the presentation places the dialogue where it truly should be, between Luke and the reader, whether past or present. The numerous biblical citations provided are intended to promote this dialogue and should be so used.

The biblical citations in this volume follow the *Revised Standard Version* unless that translation be judged incorrect or sexist. Also, biblical references have a singular or plural verb, depending on whether the verses are viewed as a unit or not.

This volume does not address in detail the relationship between Luke-Acts and Hellenistic literature. Much of the research in that area is in initial stages and not yet sufficiently refined to allow for precise conclusions. Presently, the evidence does not affect the positions adopted here.

My particular thanks are due to my colleagues and good friends, Father William T. Miller, S.J. of Regis College and Dr. Pauline Viviano of Loyola University of Chicago, for reading over the entire manuscript and making stylistic and exegetical suggestions which make the reading of the book a much more pleasant and informative experience. Nonetheless, whatever errors occur in this book are mine. Special thanks are also owed to Mr. Kevin Phalen who typed this manuscript in its rough draft, to Mrs. Elise McGrath and Sr. Ann Mitchell for proofreading and typing, and to Miss Barbara Douglas who did the final draft. I am grateful to Mr. Michael Glazier for the opportunity to offer you my interpretation of Luke's theological themes, to which topic I have dedicated the last twelve years of my life. A debt of gratitude is also owed the faculty members of the Department of Theological Studies of St. Louis University who over the years have listened to my theories and, sometimes, tolerated my distracted administration. Thanks are due, too, to the members of both the Catholic Biblical Association's Luke-Acts Task Forces who have helped me clarify my interpretation of Luke's theology. Last, but far from least, I thank both my graduate and undergraduate students who over the years have challenged me to think Luke's thought through more carefully and who have shared with me their enthusiasm for God's word.

If this book gives even a few readers a deeper appreciation of Luke and his theology, I shall be more than content.

PRESUPPOSITIONS

Any book has to start somewhere, and not everything that is stated can be proved in detail. So this book, too, has its presuppositions. It will take for granted that Luke's Gospel must be studied with his Acts of the Apostles, and to consider the one book without the other would only truncate Luke's thought. Also, Luke did use sources for Luke-Acts. Few doubt that he used Mark and the *Quelle* for his Gospel, and almost all scholars will also grant that Luke used sources for his Acts of the Apostles. The problem arises when one tries to determine and delineate these sources in Acts. Much labor has been expended in this effort, but little agreement has been reached. Thus, the dominant methodology in this book will be a form of redaction criticism which might more properly be called composition criticism. Obviously, redaction criticism, which considers how an author modified his source(s), proves extremely useful in studying Luke's Gospel where we know the sources he used, but it would be much less useful in Acts. Luke did compose both his Gospel and Acts, and he wove his ideas throughout these two works. Therefore, the use of composition criticism, which like literary criticism analyzes the whole of an author's work, seems often to be the better method.

Luke did not write for non-Christians. He wrote for Christians to assure them of the reliability of the things about which they had been informed (Lk 1:1-4). This Lucan purpose does not entirely eliminate the possibility of non-Christians reading Luke-Acts but these books were not written primarily for them.

One should not draw a rigid distinction between Judaism and Hellenism. Rather, by the time that Luke wrote, Hellenism and Judaism had merged to a considerable extent. Nonetheless, the acceptance of this fact should not lead us to seek the principal influence of Luke's thought in Hellenistic literature. The main influence on Luke comes from the Bible which he used, the Septuagint, the Greek translation of the Hebrew Old Testament. This does not deny that Luke was acquainted with the rhetorical norms of Hellenistic literature and that he used them. It does claim, however, that any effort to interpret Luke's double work principally in terms of Hellenistic literature is mistaken.

Also, if the contention that Luke in Luke-Acts continues to present for Christians the salvation that God brings to Israel be accurate, then "salvation history" is the most correct description of how Luke characterizes this salvation. Nonetheless, Luke reaches out to a universal audience, and he has some expressions and phraseology which reflect those of Hellenistic historical writers. Notable are, of course, Lk 1:1-4 and Acts 1:1 whose closest parallel is probably the pair of prefaces to the two volumes of Josephus' *Against Apion*. Yet Josephus was a Jew. Other claims for the influence of Hellenistic historians may be overstated. For instance, the name and year of the emperor, of the king, or of other governing officials (Lk 1:5;2:1-2;3:1-2,19;9:7) do not differ greatly from how the Books of Kings introduce the reign of each king or from passages like Ezra 1:1;4:6-7;7:1-9; Neh 2:1;5:14; Dan 1:1;2:1;7:1;8:1;9:1-2. Of import for the present study is that both Jewish and Hellenistic history do have a strong bias toward dealing with individuals. Thus, we read of Eli-Samuel-Saul-David, Sulla-Pompey-Caesar-Anthony-Augustus, and John-Jesus-Peter-Paul.

Something should be said about the theory of *Sitz im Leben*, "situation in life," as regards Luke-Acts. Recent scholarship had led to the insight that an author's audience is fictional. A writer constructs in his imagination, clearly or vaguely, an audience cast in some sort of role. Secondly, the reading audience must correspondingly fictionalize itself. So, the consideration of the *Sitz im Leben* of a given work tells us less about the situation a writer finds himself in, than about his interpretation of this situation and his consequent response to it. Moreover, the *Sitz im Leben* of a given text may well be better found in the realization of concerns developed over years of experience and not now directed to any given community but to humanity itself. In addition, the earlier theory of a *Sitz im Leben* tends to presuppose a writer who lives in a given community and writes about its needs. It does not seem amiss to doubt that even the life of an author of biblical times was a little more complicated than this. Luke seems to be such an author. All attempts to tie Luke-Acts to one community and to its concerns have failed. Therefore, this book assumes a more general interpretation of *Sitz im Leben* and refuses to limit the Lucan audience to any one given community.

Some scholars maintain that Luke wrote as a pastoral theologian. This is certainly true, but such a claim does not provide any exceptional insight into Luke-Acts. Every New Testament writer can be designated a pastoral theologian; each of them wrote to encourage and to strengthen the faith of their readers. "Pastoral theologian" proves too vague a term to be very useful. More insight can be gained by a thorough analysis and synthesis of a given author's main theological concerns. Nonetheless, the claim that Luke is a pastoral theologian merits attention if for no other reason than it challenges us to contemporize Luke's thought. Everyone who reads Luke-Acts must realize that this double volume is also addressed to him or her and calls each one to respond to God's saving actions and to imitate Jesus.

The terms, "Christian," "disciple" and "follower" are used in this book as synonyms since they designate someone who has responded in some positive manner to God's saving action. When mention is made of Luke's "reader," the referent is not only to Luke's idealized audience but also to anyone who has or is reading Luke-Acts. However, the emphasis is on the reader whom Luke felt he was addressing. Of course, "apostle" for Luke is a technical term (cf. Acts 1:21-22).

PART I

GOD CONTINUES TO BRING SALVATION TO HIS PEOPLE

PART I

GOD CONTINUES TO BRING SALVATION TO HIS PEOPLE

This book contends that Luke's main theological theme is that God who brought salvation to his people in the Old Testament continues to do this, especially through Jesus Christ. Other authorities speak of Luke's main concern as "promise-fulfillment" or "proof from prophecy." Both of these descriptions create problems. First of all, they overemphasize Luke's use of scripture, especially prophetic texts, but as will be shown, Luke has numerous ways of portraying God's saving action among his people. Secondly, neither "proof from prophecy" nor "promise-fulfillment" sufficiently bring out the fact that Luke does not see any break between the true Jews and the Christians. Christianity just continues the Old Testament. For Luke, as will be seen, the Christians are true Pharisees. Up to the passion narrative, the Pharisees are among Jesus' enemies, but thereafter they even defend Christians.

This chapter will first attempt to establish that the Christians are the Pharisees who are the true Jews. The Christians are the people of God. After that, it will be demonstrated that God continues to bring his salvation to his people who are now the Christians of all times.

The Christians Are the True Israel

The Christians are the true Israel. Luke writes for Christians (cf. Lk 1:4) and wants to show that the crowds, which Jesus had addressed, were gathered after Pentecost into the true Israel and, that as a result, the people of God, the Church, stem in an unbroken and continual process from the people of God of the Old Testament. Of utmost importance to this whole discussion about the Christians as the true Israel is to remember that Luke's readers are Christians. Whether the reader be contemporary with Luke or with ourselves, he or she is the one addressed in Luke-Acts.

"Israel" and related concepts play a surprisingly large role in the Infancy Narrative (Lk 1-2). These passages say that salvation comes for *Israel*. Yet Luke's readers are Christians, and sometimes they are brought into the narrative by his use of "we," "us," and "our." John the Baptist will turn many of the sons of Israel to the Lord their God and make ready for the Lord a people prepared (Lk 1:16-17). God has helped his servant Israel in remembrance of his mercy (Lk 1:54) and raised up a horn of salvation for us in the house of his servant David (Lk 1:69). This thought Luke later puts in the mouth of Paul, "Of this man's (David's) posterity God has brought to Israel a savior, Jesus, as he promised" (Acts 13:22). Blessed be the Lord God of Israel, for he had visited and redeemed his people (Lk 1:68). The Israel spoken of here is the Israel that exists after Jesus' resurrection, that is, the Church. For Christ will reign over the house of Jacob forever (Lk 1:33). Luke is speaking of the eternal reign of the risen Christ. The "house of Jacob" in this passage must mean the Christians, the Church.

But not all Israel belongs to the Church, for Jesus is set for the fall and rise of many in Israel (Lk 2:34; cf. Acts 3:22-23). Those who reject Jesus fall from the people of salvation history who form the true Israel. They are not few, but many. Many, too, believe in Jesus and constitute the true Israel.

The rest of Luke's Gospel and the Acts of the Apostles confirm the contention that the Christians are viewed as

Israel by Luke. Jesus, for Luke, does not address individual crowds, as in Mark, but the whole people of Israel. Luke, in sixteen passages, introduces "people" (*laos*) into his source. His reference is to the Septuagint where "people" appears in positive contexts and means the community which God called and leads to salvation. Luke (3:21) at Jesus' baptism alone writes, "Now when *all* the people were baptized." Luke extends Jesus' activity to all the Jewish cities (Lk 4:43;8:1; cf. Mk 1:38). Luke also is the only one who described Jesus' activity as "teaching throughout all Judea from Galilee even to this place" (Lk 23:5) and "a prophet mighty in deed and word before God and all the people"(Lk 24:19). Luke relates the people to Jesus in an open and sympathetic manner. The people hang on Jesus' words (Lk 19:48), glorify him (Lk 4:15), and rejoice at all the glorious things done by him (Lk 13:17). Fear of the people keeps the scribes and the chief priests from laying hands on Jesus (Lk 20:19).

Luke distinguishes between the people and their leaders so that later he can more easily identify the Christians as the chosen people. It is true that during Jesus' appearance before Pilate, the people do shout, "crucify him" (Lk 23:13,18,21,23; cf. 4:16-30). But after that, no negative redactional statements about the people are recorded until after the Stephen story. A great multitude of the people follow Jesus on the way of the cross (Lk 23:27), and the people look on at the crucifixion in silence (Lk 23:35). Only the rulers and soldiers mock Jesus (Lk 23:35-38; cf. Mk 15:29-32). Finally, the multitudes are apparently repentant, for they return home beating their breasts (Lk 23:48). Therefore, in contrast to Mark, Jesus, for Luke, addresses all the people in favorable contexts. Luke distinguishes the people from their leaders, and he almost always associates them with Jesus in positive contexts.

The quote from Joel (3:1-5 LXX; cf. Acts 2:17-21) demonstrates that all the people, sons and daughters, young men and old men, male and female slaves all receive the Holy Spirit. In Acts 2-5, as in Luke's Gospel, the people are present. They listen (Acts 2:22,37;3:12) and are well-disposed to the Apostles. They are again distinguished from the leaders of the people who fear their reaction (Acts 5:26). The number of them who join the Apostles grows daily. On the first day there are 3000, then 5000. A new criterion is established for belonging to the people of God; those who listen to Jesus, the prophet like Moses, belong to the people.

> Moses said, "The Lord God will raise up a prophet from your brethren as he raised me up. You shall listen to him in whatever he tells you. And it shall be that every soul that does not listen to that prophet shall be destroyed from the people" (Acts 3:22-23).

Christians are represented, through the Twelve (the Apostles). Luke insists that the Twelve (the Apostles) must be preserved (Acts 1:15-26) so that his readers know that Israel which this number reflects continues in the Christian community.

The early chapters of Acts 1-5(6?) present us with the perfect people, the ideal Israel. What is said in these chapters corresponds to the Old Testament description of the ideal Israel. Israel will then receive the Spirit of the Lord (Acts 2:1-42; cf. Isa 63:10-14; Joel 3:1-5 LXX) and experience remarkable growth (Acts 2:41;4:4;5:14;6:1,7;9:31; 11:21,24;12:24;14:1;19:20; cf. Ezek 36:10-12; Jer 3:16). It will be a time of fear of the Lord (Acts 2:43;5:5,11; cf. Dt 10:12,20;31:13) and of recognition of the mighty works of God (Acts 2:11; cf. Dt 11:2-3; Ps 71:19). No one will be in want (Acts 2:45;4:34-35; cf. Dt 15:4). Finally, the Lord will raise up a prophet like Moses (Acts 3:22-23; cf. Dt 18:15-19).

Only after he has pictured this gathering of Israel, does Luke change his tack. This change takes place after the story of Stephen. The people are now seen as hostile and on the side of their leaders. Luke uses "people" (*laos*) less often and calls the unbelieving people "the Jews." But, earlier in Acts, "Jews" appeared only at Pentecost (Acts 2:5,11,14).

Luke's use of "church" in Acts also indicates this change. "Church" first occurs in Acts 5:11 and then in the summary, Acts 8:1-3. Thereafter it is evenly distributed over the rest of

Acts. Apparently, the development of the Church for Luke begins with John the Baptist, continues with Jesus and at Pentecost but has not yet ended. Moreover, Luke begins to distinguish more clearly betweeen "the Jews"and the Christians from Acts 8 onward.

As was seen in the Lucan Infancy Narrative, Israel's redemption and glorification takes place in the Church. This Lucan idea appears again in the Acts of the Apostles (Acts 15:16-18).

> "After this I will return, and I will rebuild the dwelling of David, which has fallen; I will rebuild its ruins, and I will set it up, that the rest of men may seek the Lord, and all the Gentiles who are called by my name, says the Lord, who has made these things known from of old."

James quotes this passage to justify the entrance of Gentiles into the Church. But the passage reports God as claiming that he will rebuild the dwelling of David. This "dwelling of David" must refer to Israel, and it is precisely in this dwelling of David that the rest of humankind will seek the Lord and in which all the Gentiles will be called. Israel, which now embraces the Gentiles, continues in the Church. A similar thought is reflected in the earlier question of the apostles; "Lord will you at this time restore the kingdom to Israel" (Acts 1:6)?

For Luke, Christianity is true Pharisaism. This becomes evident from Paul's trial scene before Festus and Agrippa II. Luke defends Paul by indicating that he has lived all of his life as a Pharisee and is on trial for no other charge than the Pharisaic belief in the hope of the promise of a resurrection of the dead (Acts 26:4-8). Later in the same defense, Paul identifies himself as a Christian (Acts 26:28-29). In fact, in these verses Paul wishes that everyone would be like him, a Pharisee and a Christian, except for the chains he bears. Consequently, Paul in this scene stands for all Christians who are the true Pharisees. Since he identifies the Christians with the true Pharisees, Luke, during Jesus' passion and throughout Acts, does not name Pharisees among Jesus' and the Christians' opponents. In fact, the Pharisee Gamaliel defends the apostles; and Paul, too, finds defenders among the Pharisees (Acts 23:6-10). After the fall of Jerusalem, the Sadducee party, to which the high priests belonged, for all practical purposes disappeared. Thus, Luke identified the Christians with the Jews of his day, the Pharisees.

CHAPTER ONE

GOD WHO BROUGHT SALVATION TO ISRAEL CONTINUES TO DO THIS FOR THE CHRISTIANS

Once it has been established that the Christians are the true Israel, it is more easily seen why the present author maintains that Luke's main theological theme is that God who brought salvation to Israel continues to do this for the Christians. Salvation history (*Heilsgeschichte*) continues, and Luke's concentration on this topic explains in part why and how we can call him an historian. In view of this main theme it is clear why many scholars see a continuity throughout Luke's double work. Moreover, this salvation is always present as Luke's use of "today" (Lk 2:11;4:21;5:26;19:5,9;23:43; Acts 26:29) testifies. Of course, we Christians are to accept this salvation.

Luke has many ways in which he sketches how God continues to bring salvation to Israel. Doubtless, his favorite portrayal consists in the statement that a given event has fulfilled the scriptures (the Law, Psalms, and/or the Prophets). Or he will point to God's foreknowledge, will, plan or purpose. Compound verbs which often begin with "before" (*pro*) and the verbs, "to do" (*poiein*), "to fulfill" (*plēroun*), "to determine" (*horizein*), "to set" (*tithenai*), "to

23

stand or set up" (*histanai*), "to appoint" (*tassein*), and "to be destined" (*mellein*) all point to God's salvific will. "It is necessary" (*dei*; cf. Acts 13:46: *anankaios*) does, too. God directs the Christians through the Holy Spirit, angels, prophets, dreams, and visions. Finally and most importantly, God works through Jesus, our only savior, and subsequently through the word of his salvation. Space does not allow us to study every instance of God's salvific will in Luke-Acts. But at least some indication must be given of the extent of this theme. Moreover, throughout the course of this book, an effort will be made to demonstrate the relationship between Luke's other theological concerns and his theme of God's salvific will.

A. *The Scriptures: the Law of Moses, the Prophets, and the Psalms*

Luke refers to the Old Testament in three different ways: Law, Prophets, and Psalms (Lk 24:44); (Law) of Moses and Prophets (Lk 16:16,29,31; 24:27; Acts 13:15?; 24:14; 26:22; 28:23) or simply Prophets (Acts 26:27). Luke can refer to the whole Old Testament as "Prophets," for he views Moses (Lk 16:29,31;24:27; Acts 3:22-23;7:37;26:22) who wrote the Law and David (Acts 2:30) who wrote the psalms as prophets.

The scripture citations which Luke has are from the Old Testament. He does not cite the apocrypha (but see Lk 11:49). The exegetes who lament the fact that Luke does not often demonstrate explicitly how Jesus fulfills the Old Testament fail to perceive that for Luke the most important relationship to establish between Jesus and the Old Testament is the general principle that all the hopes, promises, and salvation of the Old Testament have been realized in Jesus. This is why Luke almost always speaks of faith in Jesus, not faith in the Old Testament (but cf. Acts 26:27). The whole of the Old Testament becomes fair territory for the discovery of proofs which show who Jesus really was (Acts 17:2-3,11; 18:24,28; cf. 9:22). The Pauline practice of beginning the preaching of the Christian message in the synagogue where the Law and the Prophets were read is thus rendered intelligible. The Christian preachers were confident of their ability to illustrate that the whole of the Old Testament finds its fulfillment in Jesus.

Jesus himself, as portrayed by Luke, began the practice of using the Old Testament to explain the salvation that God was working through him. At the beginning of his career, Jesus expounds on his mission (Lk 4:18-21). Later, he uses Scripture to predict his passion (Lk 18:31-33). When risen, he gives his followers the capacity to understand the Scriptures (Lk 24:27,32,45).

Luke does not employ "Law" by itself to show God's salvific will for Christ and Christianity. The same is true of "Moses" (but see Acts 15:21) when Luke makes him the equal of "Law" as he often does. But Moses does predict that God will raise up a prophet like himself (Acts 3:22-23;7:37). Jesus does refer to passages from the Law to explain his conduct during his temptation (Lk 4:4,8,12), and his comments on the greatest commandment (Lk 10:27) and to the rich ruler (Lk 18:20). Peter quotes the Law (Acts 3:13, 23, 25-26) in his exposition about the cure of the cripple.

The Prophets play a bigger part than Law in establishing God's salvific will in Luke-Acts. One should listen to the Prophets (Lk 16:29-31; Acts 3:22; 26:27), for God speaks through them (Acts 3:18-26) and what they say will happen (Acts 13:29). In particular, the Prophets predicted Jesus' passion and resurrection (Lk 18:31-33; 20:17; 22:37; 22:69; 24:25,27,44; Acts 3:18 etc.); but they also serve to explain other events in salvation history (e.g. Lk 3:4; 4:17; 7:26-27; 8:10; 19:45; 23:30; Acts 2:16-21,25-28,30,34-35; 7:48-50; 8:28-35; 13:40-41,47; 15:15-17; 28:25-28). The Jews are the heirs of the Prophets (Acts 3:25) in that they have the first right and duty to accept the Christ-event as the means of salvation. In spite of all this, the Jews and even the apostles for some time (Lk 13:28; 16:31; 18:34; 24:25; Act 13:27) do not understand or accept what Moses and the Prophets say; if one does not listen to them, he will not listen if someone should rise from the dead and speak to him (Lk 16:31).

Luke rarely refers to a psalm or to the psalms alone as

scriptural proof of God's saving action (but see Lk 20:41-44; Acts 1:16,20;13:33,35). Attestations from the psalms, however, appear in the Lucan presentations of Jesus' temptation (Lk 4:10-11), of his triumphant entry into Jerusalem (Lk 19:38), and of his passion (Lk 22:69;23:46). Thus, Luke demonstrates through the Law of Moses, the Prophets, and psalms that God continues to work in the history of the Christians as in that of the Jews of old.

B. God's Foreknowledge, Will, Plan, or Purpose

Our attention is directed to God's foreknowledge or purpose by verbs which begin with the prefix, "pro-" (e.g. Acts 2:39; 3:18,4:28). God made humankind to live on the face of the earth, and determined allotted times and boundaries of their habitations (Acts 17:26). God selects Jesus to be the Christ (Acts 3:20), Paul to know his will and to see and hear the just one (Acts 22:14), and witnesses to testify to Jesus' resurrection (Acts 10:41). God calls Paul to preach the Gospel to the Macedonians (Acts 16:10), and his grace leads to conversion and faith (Acts 11:23; 13:43). God adds to those being saved (Acts 2:41,47; 5:14; 11:24). He gives heaven and more to the Christians (Lk 12:31).

Jesus is delivered up according to the definite plan and foreknowledge of the Father (Acts 2:23). He had prayed in the garden that not his will, but that of his Father be done (Lk 22:42). This is the prayer of all Christians (Lk 11:2). In summary, God's plan predestines what will or, at least, should take place (Lk 7:30; 22:42; Acts 2:23; 4:28; 5:38; 13:36; 20:27).

C. Certain Verbs Reflect How God Continues to Bring Salvation to the People of God

Luke uses certain verbs to show how God brings salvation. Barnabas and Paul declare to the church at Antioch all that God had "done" with them, and how he had opened a door of faith to the Gentiles (Acts 14:26). God "fulfills" and brings to pass events and the promises of Scriptures (Lk 1:20; 4:21; 21:24; 22:16; 24:44; Acts 1:16; 3:18; 13:27; 14:26). For instance, Jesus has an exodus which he must fulfill in Jerusalem (Lk 9:31). As was seen above, God "determines" allotted periods and geographical boundaries for human-kind (Acts 17:26). The Son of Man goes as it has been determined (Lk 22:22; Acts 2:23). God has determined this, and he has also determined Jesus as the judge of the living and the dead (Acts 10:42; 17:31). God "set" the times and seasons which govern the restoration of the kingdom (Acts 1:6-7). He sets Jesus and Paul as the light of the Gentiles (Acts 13:47; cf. 26:23). He even puts Jesus' enemies as his footstool (Lk 20:43, Acts 2:35). God "appoints" the things which Paul will be told to do (Acts 22:10) and those who are destined for eternal life (Acts 13:48).

Luke predicates "to be destined" of an action which necessarily follows on a divine decree (Lk 9:31; 19:11; 21:7,36; 24:21; Acts 11:28; 17:31; 22:10; 23:3). The Son of Man is destined to be delivered into the hands of men (Lk 9:44). Moses and the prophets tell us what is destined to happen (Acts 26:22). The Christ must suffer, be first to rise from the dead, and is destined to proclaim light both to the people and to the Gentiles (Acts 26:23). There are destined to be a resurrection of the dead (Acts 24:15), the judgment (Acts 24:25) and wrath for some (Lk 3:7).

Luke uses "it is necessary" or "it must" more than any other verb as a means of expressing how God continues or is thought to continue to work among his people (e.g. Lk 11:42; 13:14; 21:9; 22:7). Scriptures must be accomplished (Lk 22:37; 24:44; Acts 1:16). Jesus must be in his Father's house (Lk 2:49) and later preach the good news of the kingdom of God to other cities also (Lk 4:43). He must heal the infirm woman (Lk 13:16). The older son in the parable of the prodigal son must make merry and be glad, for his brother was dead, and is alive; he was lost, and is found (Lk 15:32). It is necessary that Jesus stay at Zacchaeus' house (Lk 19:5) and that he endure his passion (Lk 9:22; 13:33; 17:25) and rise from the dead (Lk 24:7,26; Acts 17:3). It is

necessary that heaven receive the Christ until the Parousia
comes (Acts 3:20-21). Everyone must be saved in Christ
(Acts 4:12; cf. 16:30)! The Holy Spirit will teach the Chris-
tians what they must say when being persecuted (Lk 12:12).
But it is necessary that they pray always (Lk 18:1) and obey
God rather than humans (Acts 5:29). Someone who had
been with Jesus from the baptism of John until the day when
Jesus was taken up must take Judas' place (Acts 1:22).
Barnabas and Paul must first speak the word of God to the
Jews (Acts 13:46). Subsequently, the Ephesian elders were
shown by Paul that by toiling they must help the weak (Acts
20:35). It is necessary that the Christians through many
tribulations enter the kingdom of God (Acts 14:22). It will
be told to Paul what he must do and suffer for Christ's name
(Acts 9:6,16). Paul must be tried before Caesar's tribunal
(Acts 25:10); he must appear before Caesar (Acts 27:24).
Therefore, it is necessary that Paul go to Rome (Acts 19:21;
23:11; 25:10; 27:24).

All of the verbs treated here have in one way or another
shown that God continues to bring his salvation to his
people, who are now the Christians. Jesus and the Christians are to act in accord with God's will. Thus, we, too, are
to act.

D. The Holy Spirit

The best way of describing the Spirit in Luke-Acts is that
the Spirit represents the Father and/or Christ. At times, the
Spirit shows that either the Father or the Son is working or
will work in someone, or calls an individual to a given
position, task, or mission in the Church. For instance,
throughout the Infancy Narrative the Spirit relates to everyone with whom God interacts. It is commonly admitted that
according to Luke, only Jesus, during his early ministry,
had the Spirit. After his resurrection Jesus pours out the
Holy Spirit on those who call on his name and through
whom he works (Acts 2:33). But, as will be seen, the Spirit

does not exhaust the ways in which the risen Christ remains present to the Christians.

Luke calls the Spirit, "gift" (Acts 2:38; 10:45). Ultimately the giver is the Father, but he does this through Christ. The Spirit means power (e.g. Lk 4:14; Acts 1:8; 10:38). Apparently, this power equips one for the mission or task to be performed. Christian baptism finds its distinction in the reception of the Spirit (Lk 3:16,22; Acts 1:5; 10:38,44,45,47; 11:15,16; 15:8; 19:6). The Spirit in Luke should never be separated from Christian baptism which initiates Christians into the community and imitates Christ's own baptism. As the Spirit introduced Jesus' ministry, so he introduces the Christians to theirs.

Christians, and even Jews in the Infancy Narrative, are said to be full of the Spirit (Lk 1:15,41,67; Acts 2:4; 4:8,31; 6:3,5; 7:55; 9:17; 11:24; 13:9,52; 18:25?). Somehow they are instruments of God in his plan for humankind. One should not separate being "full of the Spirit" from the implication that the Spirit in some way dwells in the Christians. "Full of the Spirit" can hardly be only an external determination. Those who are full of the Spirit are the most apt agents of carrying on God's work in history.

The Spirit certainly plays a significant role in deciding the nature and extent of the mission (e.g. Acts 1:8; 8:29,39; 10:19; 11:12; 13:2,4; 16:6-7; 19:21; 20:22-23). However, some scholars have so stressed the connection between the Spirit and the mission that they have obscured other Lucan views of the Spirit. The Spirit speaks through the scriptural and community prophets (e.g. Acts 1:16; 2:17-21; 4:25; 11:28; 21:11; 28:25) and is in the community and protects it (Acts 5:3,9; 15:28). The same Spirit places overseers over the flock to care for the Church (Acts 20:28). He witnesses and provides the Apostles with the capacity to witness (Acts 5:32; cf. 1:8). He teaches the disciples what to say when they are being persecuted (Lk 12:12; cf. Acts 6:10; 7:51). The Spirit comforts the Church (Acts 9:31). If one keeps the above analysis in mind, to maintain that the Spirit in Luke primarily directs the mission can only be true when one understands "mission" in a very broad sense. The Spirit designates the people of God and their Messiah and aids the Christians in their life, community, and mission. He is one of the many ways that the risen Christ is present to the Christians.

E. Angels

Angels appear to Jews and Christians to announce what God has already done or will do; they aid and support Jesus and the Christians and punish evil. Moses saw the angel in the bush who gave him his mission (Acts 7:30-38). Angels delivered the law to the Jews (Acts 7:53). An angel appears to Zechariah and tells him of the birth of John the Baptist (Lk 1:11-20), and, in a parallel appearance, Gabriel comes to Mary and foretells the birth of Jesus (Lk 1:26-38; 2:21). Angels announce Jesus' birth. (Lk 2:9-15). If the reading is correct, an angel supports Jesus during his agony in the garden (cf. Lk 22:43). When the women return from the tomb, they say that they saw a vision of angels who said that Jesus was alive (Lk 24:23; cf. vv 4-8). Angels free the Christians from prison (Acts 5:19; 12:7-15). An angel directs Philip (Acts 8:26) and instructs Cornelius (Acts 10:3,7,22;11:13) to send for Peter and to hear what he has to say. An angel appears to Paul on his sea journey to Rome, and encourages him not to fear, "You must stand before Caesar; and lo God has granted you all those who sail with you" (Acts 27:23-24). Herod Agrippa is punished by an angel because he did not give God the glory (Acts 12:23). Finally, the proper home for angels is heaven (Lk 12:8-9; 15:10; 16:22); so they will appear with the Son of Man when he comes in his glory (Lk 9:26). Angels, then, also reveal God's salvific will. They manifest the importance of given individuals to salvation history, communicate what God wants done, and vindicate God and his people.

F. Visions

Luke tells us through Peter at Pentecost that in these last days young men shall see visions and that old men will dream dreams. God will show wonders in the heaven above and signs on the earth beneath (cf. Acts 2:17,19). Of course, this was true in the Old Testament, too. For instance, the God of glory appeared to Abraham and told him to leave his native land and go to a land which he would show him. (Acts 7:2-3). Moses wondered at the vision which he saw in the bush (Acts 7:31), and made the tent of witness according to the pattern he was shown (Acts 7:44). As noted above, salvation history continues in the New Testament, and so do visions. When Zechariah comes out of the temple and cannot speak, the people know that he has seen a vision (Lk 1:22). We know that this vision dealt with his son John the Baptist, and his place in salvation history. Moses and Elijah appear in glory, and Jesus' countenance is altered at the Transfiguration when they speak of Jesus' *exodus*, which he must accomplish at Jerusalem. The voice from the cloud proclaims, "This is my Son, my chosen, listen to him" (Lk 9:28-36)! Jesus, like the people of Israel, experiences an exodus, and the Christians are to listen to him as the Jews were to listen to Moses.

At Jesus' Ascension, the two men clothed in white robes who showed themselves there let the apostles know that they should not spend their time waiting for the Parousia (Acts 1:9-11). They are to live their Christian lives. Tongues as of fire are seen at Pentecost when the disciples are filled with the Holy Spirit and begin to speak in other tongues (Acts 2:3-4). The symbolism is obvious. Both Cornelius (Acts 10:3) and Peter (Acts 10:11-19; 11:5-10) see visions which ultimately lead to the mission to the Gentiles. Not only does the Holy Spirit forbid Paul to preach the word in Asia and Bithynia, but Paul sees in a vision a man of Macedonia who beseeches him, "Come over to Macedonia and help us" (Acts 16:9-10). Hence, Paul concludes that God has called them to preach the Gospel to the Macedonians. Visions, then, are yet another way in which God directs the salvation history of christianity.

CHAPTER TWO

JESUS, THE SAVIOR

Luke does not have any theoretical discussion on the nature of salvation, but he does show us salvation happening. Salvation, as Luke sees it, designates a present reality, and physical salvation can be symbolic of eternal salvation. This is particularly clear from Acts 4:7-12. Peter in these few verses at first speaks of the physical healing done in the name of Jesus to the cripple. He then concludes that Jesus is the stone which is the head of the corner and leaps to the general conclusion about salvation on both a physical and spiritual level: "And there is salvation in no one else, for there is no other name under heaven given among humankind by which we must be saved." We, Luke's readers, are to remain open to the salvation which Jesus brings.

In order to see more clearly Luke's presentation of salvation in Jesus, we will consider three areas: Jesus as savior in the Infancy Narrative, Jesus as savior during his earthly life, and, finally, the neglected area of the activity of the risen savior. However, as a matter of fact, Luke-Acts was written after Jesus' resurrection, and Luke frequently assumes in his Gospel the saving activity of the risen Jesus.

A. *Jesus as Savior in the Infancy Narrative*

Luke in the Infancy Narrative definitely identifies Jesus as savior. Of course, the Father, too, is called savior (Lk 1:47), for God works in Jesus. Jesus' conception occurs because of the action of the Holy Spirit, and thus Jesus will be called the Son of God. Zechariah, three times in the *Benedictus*, refers to what God has done in Jesus as "salvation" (Lk 1:69,71,77). For God "has raised up a horn of salvation for us in the house of his servant David . . . that we should be saved from our enemies and from the hands of all who hate us." John the Baptist will go before the Lord (Jesus) to prepare his ways, to give the people knowledge of salvation in the forgiving of their sins.

Later, the angels tell the shepherds that "to you is born this day in the city of David a savior, who is Christ the Lord" (Lk 2:11). Simeon, inspired by the Spirit, comes into the temple and says of the child Jesus who is in his arms:

> "Lord, now let your servant depart in peace, according to your word; for my eyes have seen your salvation, which you have prepared in the presence of all peoples, a light for revelation to the Gentiles and for glory to your people Israel" (Lk 2:27-32).

Simeon also contends that Jesus is set for the fall and rise of many in Israel, and for a sign that is spoken against (Lk 2:34). Finally, probably Luke like Matthew (1:21) was aware of the popular etymology of Jesus' name as "Yahweh saves."

Luke says other things about Jesus in his Infancy Narrative but the points made above are what concern us. God brings salvation to his people through his son the Davidic Jesus, who saves. Christians will be saved from their enemies and realize the forgiveness of their sins. Jesus' salvation will be universal and include both the Jews and Gentiles. In fact, he will determine who really belongs to the people of God, for some will reject him and fall from the people. In brief, Luke has given in his Infancy Narrative a general description of Jesus as savior in the whole of Luke-Acts.

B. *The Earthly Ministry of Jesus, the Savior*

The same general description of Jesus as savior occurs in the story of rejection of Jesus at Nazareth (Lk 4:16-30). This rejection story is programmatic for the whole of Luke-Acts. The Spirit anoints Jesus:

> "...to preach good news to the poor. He has sent me to proclaim release to the captives and recovery of sight to the blind, to set at liberty those who are oppressed, to proclaim the acceptable year of the Lord."
>
> (Lk 4:18-19)

These words fulfill Scriptures, and, at first, the people respond in a positive manner. But then they ask, "Is not this Joseph's son?" Their doubt leads Jesus to observe that no prophet is acceptable in his own country. He confirms this observation with the stories about Elijah and the widow of Zarephath and about Elisha and Naaman the Syrian. These Gentiles accept Israel's prophets even though Israel herself did not accept them. Jesus' audience, like their forefathers, rejects him and fulfills his prophecy about the fate of a prophet in his own country by attempting to kill him. The scripture passages in this story leave no doubt that Jesus as savior cares for the poor, captives, blind, and oppressed. Because of rejection he, too, will go to the Gentiles.

Luke explicitly returns to this description of Jesus as savior in the story of Zacchaeus:

> "Today salvation has come to this house, since he also is a son of Abraham. For the Son of Man came to seek and to save the lost." (Lk 19:9-10).

Luke, in fact, throughout his Gospel has introduced narratives in which Jesus "saves" the weak and oppressed. A consideration of these narratives will furnish much insight into Luke's interest in Jesus as savior.

Jesus raises from the dead the only son of the widow of Nain (Lk 7:11-17). This unfortunate woman has already lost her husband and was now deprived of her only son and her most immediate means of support. Jesus forgives a sinful woman (Lk 7:36-50). He forgives her many sins because she has loved much. He gently reassures her, "Your faith has saved you; go in peace." The parable of the Good Samaritan (Lk 10:25-37) shows that a Samaritan, a member of a race despised by the Jews, can prove to be a better "neighbor" than some supposedly religious Jews. Jesus in the healing of a crippled woman (Lk 13:10-17) cares for a woman, a second-class citizen, on the Sabbath. He shames his opponents with the words:

> "You hypocrites! Does not each of you on the sabbath untie his ox or his ass from the manger, and lead it away to water it? And ought not this woman, a daughter of Abraham whom Satan bound for eighteen years, be loosed from this bond on the sabbath day?" (Lk 13:15-16).

The Sabbath provides yet another occasion for a miracle of Jesus which again benefits someone who is weak. In the miracle story of the man with dropsy (Lk 14:1-6), Jesus argues that anyone on the Sabbath would immediately pull his son or ox out of the well into which he has fallen. The implication is, of course, that this man should be healed from the dropsy on the Sabbath.

One of the lessons to the host and guests (Lk 14:7-14) is that they are to invite the poor, the maimed, the lame, and the blind to their banquets. The same care for the weak takes place in the parables of the lost coin and the prodigal son. These parables (Lk 15:8-32) stress God's joy over a repentant sinner. Probably, in view of the audience and their criticism of Jesus (cf. Lk 15:1-2), the last of these parables corrects the attitude of the elder brother who does not have the decency or love to make merry and be glad, for his brother was dead and is alive, he was lost, and is found. We are reminded in another parable, that of the rich man and Lazarus (Lk 16:19-31), of Luke's considerable interest in the rich and the poor. Certainly, this theme belongs to his presentation of Jesus as the savior of the weak. The rich man is not reported as actually doing Lazarus harm; he simply does not pay any attention to him. For this he is condemned, but angels carry Lazarus to Abraham's bosom.

Lepers were unclean. By Jewish law they were not to enter villages or cities and were to let the "clean" know their presence by ringing a bell. Jesus has mercy on ten of them and heals them (Lk 17:11-19), but only one of them, and this a foreigner, a despised Samaritan, returns to thank him. As in the case of the sinful woman, Jesus assures him, ". . . your faith has made you well." The parable of the widow and the unjust judge (Lk 18:1-8) again introduces a disadvantaged member of society, and according to Luke serves to instruct the disciples that they ought to pray always and not lose heart. The determination of this widow, a poor woman apparently without any other defender than the judge, brings him finally to do justice. A sinner in the parable of the Pharisee and the Tax Collector (Lk 18:9-14) once again appears as a hero. The tax collector realized that his only hope lay in throwing himself on God's mercy. On the other hand, the Pharisee in his misguided piety looks down on the tax collector and his kind and exalts himself, not God. Jesus himself exalts the tax collector for his attitude toward God. Luke alone during Jesus' passion repeats the dispute over greatness (Lk 22:24-27; cf. 9:46-48) and calls the apostles to humble service. Finally, Jesus himself is reckoned with transgressors (Lk 22:37-38).

All of these narratives, proper to Luke, show us Jesus as savior. He helps and praises widows, forgives a sinful woman, and heals a crippled one. Samaritans provide examples of virtues. He cures a man with dropsy and recommends humility. He shows that God rejoices over a repentant sinner, and that humankind should imitate him in this. He encourages the poor and condemns the indifferent rich. He heals lepers, associates with criminals, and makes sinners the heroes of his stories. So, nothing need separate us from Jesus' saving activity.

Significantly, Luke in his Gospel speaks a number of times of "Lord," a title of the risen Jesus. He anticipates Jesus' role as saving Lord of the Church. Jesus, the Lord, frees his followers from the obligation of the Jewish law (Lk 11:39; 13:25), invites the believers to repentance (Lk 22:61) and to faith (Lk 17:5-6). As perfect disciples, they hear the word of the Lord (Lk 10:39,41) who exhorts them to distribute their goods (Lk 19:8). The Lucan eschatological parables also have parenetic and ecclesial dimensions. The Lord (Lk 12:41-42;14:23; 16:8; 18:7) whose return the believers await is present in the Church, and in faith they already live in communion with him. Thus, the parables of the Lord and his servants acquire their deepest meaning.

C. Activity of the Risen Jesus Who is the Only Savior

Few scholars have shown much interest in one aspect of Lucan Christology, the amount of activity which the author of Luke-Acts assigns to the risen Christ. Of those who have studied the problem, one author speaks of an "absentee Christology" by which he means that the risen Jesus does little in this world; he is in heaven at the right hand of the Father. This book claims, on the contrary, that the risen Jesus is active in Luke-Acts. Since up to this point no attempt has been made to list all of the activity of the risen Christ in Luke-Acts, all the clear instances of such activity are listed here; this procedure will provide an overall view of Luke's position on this topic. But, first of all, it must be established that Luke views the risen Christ as savior.

Luke in Acts (cf. 13:23) maintains that Jesus is savior. Probably, one should ultimately attribute salvation to the Father (Acts 2:47?) although Lucan scholars are a great deal more concerned about this than Luke himself was. Luke predicates salvation of both the Father and the Son. Peter and the Apostles definitely assert that the risen Christ was savior: "God exalted him to his right hand as Leader and Savior, to give repentance to Israel and forgiveness of sins" (Acts 5:31). As was seen above, this passage should be understood in the sense that only Jesus brings salvation and makes it available to everyone, "And there is salvation in no one else, for there is no other name under heaven given among men by which we must be saved" (Acts 4:12). Peter later says much the same thing when he relates of both Jews and Gentiles, "But we believe that we shall be saved through the grace of the Lord Jesus, just as they will" (Acts 15:11). This understanding of salvation explains the answer that Paul and Silas give to the jailer at Philippi when he asks what he must do to be saved: "Believe in the Lord Jesus, and you will be saved, you and your household" (Acts 16:31). Salvation becomes a concrete experience in baptism when people heed the instruction: "And it shall be that whoever calls on the name of the Lord shall be saved" (Acts 2:21). Originally, "Lord" in this passage surely referred to the Father, but now "Lord" refers to the risen Christ whom the Christians call upon at baptism (Acts 2:38-41).

The message of Christianity, the message about the risen Christ, is one of salvation (Acts 11:14; 13:26); in fact, Paul and his companions are called, "...servants of the Most High God, who proclaim to you the way of salvation"(Acts 16:17). Since the Jews reject this message, the Lord commands Paul and Barnabas, "I have set you to be light for the Gentiles, that you may bring salvation to the uttermost parts of the earth" (Acts 13:47). Although Paul actually performs this mission, Luke sees no inconsistency in predicating this same mission of both Paul and of the risen Christ except that it is preached to everyone, "that the Christ must suffer, and that, by being the first to rise from the dead, he would proclaim light both to the people and to the Gentiles" (Acts 26:23; cf. 26:16-18). Paul at the end of Acts testifies to the kingdom of God and tries to convince the Jews about Jesus both from the law of Moses and from the Prophets (Acts 28:23). When the Jews disagree among themselves about this message, Paul declares, "Let it be known to you then that this salvation of God has been sent to the Gentiles; they will listen" (Acts 28:28). The "salvation of God" from the context can only be the kingdom of God and Jesus.

Luke, then, continues in Acts to present Jesus as savior. Only the risen Christ brings salvation, and this to everyone. The message about the risen Christ is one of salvation.

Sometimes, the mission is carried out by the Christians, but God's salvation through Christ remains the constant throughout the whole of Luke-Acts. An effort will now be made to list all the clear instances of the activity of the risen Christ in Acts. These instances of the risen Christ's activity will help us to perceive further how God persists in bringing salvation to his people, that is, among others to us.

1. ACTIVITY OF THE RISEN JESUS AS LORD

Luke uses "Lord" in various ways which are relevant here. Luke predicates "Lord" of the Father or Jesus as the source of the events of salvation. As noted above, Luke does not differentiate between his application of "Lord" to Jesus in his Gospel and in Acts. Luke sees the kingdom as a present reality, and Jesus is the Lord of the present. In other words, if the resurrected and exalted Lord and Christ, who now acts in the community, stands in the center of Luke's presentation, the question about the time of the Parousia becomes irrelevant.

The following applications of "Lord" to Jesus in Acts deserve consideration and will now be studied in some detail. Probably, Jesus picks Judas' replacement. It could be that Luke speaks of the Father, for the phrase, "Lord who knowest the heart of all men..." (Acts 1:24) does parallel the expression, "And God who knows the heart..." (Acts 15:8). On the other hand, it is Jesus who chooses the Twelve (Lk 6:13; Acts 1:2). Jesus also selected the witnesses (Acts 1:21-22; cf. 1:8; 26:16) about whom the narrative concerning Judas' replacement speaks. Thus, it is possible to maintain that the risen Jesus selects Matthias as Judas' replacement. Needless to say, whether it is the Father or Jesus who appoints Judas' successor, God's salvific will continues to rule the pages of Acts.

Stephen sees Jesus as the Son of Man standing at the right hand of God (Acts 7:55-56). This vision apparently prompts Stephen to call on the Lord Jesus to receive his spirit and shout in a loud voice, "Lord, do not hold this sin against them" (Acts 7:59-60). At the very least, this passage shows the risen Lord as active in a supportive vision to Stephen since Stephen knows that the risen Lord will act to receive his soul and not hold this sin against his opponents.

The Lord in a vision tells Ananias to go to Paul. Ananias objects, but the Lord explains that Paul is his chosen instrument and orders Ananias to lay hands on Paul so that he may see again and be filled with the Holy Spirit (Acts 9:10-17).

The risen Lord appears to Paul in a vision (Acts 9:3-7,17,27; 22:6-10, 14-16; 26:13-18) which follows a pattern similar to the vision of Ananias. Jesus appears to Paul, identifies himself, and gives him a task. In Acts 26 (cf. 9:15; 22:14-15) the risen Lord personally designates Paul as his servant and witness. He promises to rescue Paul from the people and the Gentiles to whom he sends him (Acts 26:17; cf. 20:24). The Lord's promise to rescue Paul includes a guarantee of continual protection and the force of the present participle may mean that the risen Jesus will continually rescue Paul.

The Lord instructs Paul while in a trance in the temple to leave Jerusalem, since the people will not hear his testimony about him, and to go far away (Acts 22:17-21). For Luke, "testimony" relates to the risen Lord, not to the Father. Thus it is the risen Lord who directs Paul's mission. In Acts 18:9-10, the risen Jesus tells Paul that he will be with him, but this passage will be considered more extensively in the section which studies Luke's notion of witness. The risen Lord stands by Paul during his stay in Caesarea and encourages him: to witness to Jesus in Rome as he did in Jerusalem (Act 23:11). Again, it is Jesus who directs Paul's mission.

Paul and Barnabas appointed elders and with prayers and fasting commended them to the Lord in whom they believed (Acts 14:23). This passage probably has a double meaning: the elders' lives and work ought to belong exclusively to the Lord, and, at the same time they are entrusted to his protection and leadership (Acts 14:26; 15:40;20:32). Luke takes for granted that the risen Lord will protect and lead these newly appointed elders.

The grace (Acts 15:11) and salvation (Acts 16:31) brought by the Lord Jesus appear in the next section.

Three other passages very probably relate post-resurrectional activity of Jesus. The Lord commands Paul and Barnabas to be a light to the Gentiles (Acts 13:47). The parallels (Acts 26:17-18,23; cf. 22:21) indicate that the Lord here is Jesus. Acts 26:17-18,23 constitute the closest parallel in Luke-Acts and based, at least in part, on the same OT text (Isa 49:6) relate how the risen Christ assigned this mission to Paul. Elsewhere (Acts 22:21), the risen Jesus missions Paul to the Gentiles.

Acts 14:3 says of Paul and Barnabas: "speaking boldly for the Lord, who bore witness to the word of his grace, granting signs and wonders to be done by their hands." The following parallel indicates that "Lord" in Acts 14:3 should refer to Jesus:

> But Barnabas took him (Paul), and brought him to the apostles, and declared to them how on the road he had seen the Lord, who spoke to him, and how at Damascus he had preached boldly in the name of Jesus. So he went in and out among them at Jerusalem, preaching boldly in the name of the Lord (Acts 9:27-28).

In fact, Luke does not ever make the Father the direct object of preaching. Speaking of the Father, Luke prefers expressions like "word of God" and the "kingdom of God." More importantly, if "Lord" in Acts 14:3 means the Father, the Jews would have had no reason for rejecting the preaching of Paul and Barnabas. It is the risen Lord here witnessing to the word of his grace and granting signs and wonders through the hands of Paul and Barnabas.

Lastly, Acts 21:13-14 reads:

> "...'For I (Paul) am ready not only to be imprisoned but even to die at Jerusalem for the name of the Lord Jesus.' and when he would not be persuaded, we ceased and said, 'The will of the Lord be done'".

Again, one correctly sees the "Lord" in this passage as the risen Lord. The proof lies in the parallel (Acts 20:24) where

Paul tells the Ephesian elders about his trip to Jerusalem:

> "But I do not account my life of any value nor as precious
> to myself, if only I may accomplish my course and the
> ministry which I received from the Lord Jesus, to testify
> to the gospel of the grace of God."

Paul says that his going up to Jerusalem and all that
happens to him there is the accomplishment of the course
and ministry assigned to him by the Lord Jesus. It is natural,
then, to see Acts 21:14 as referring to the risen Jesus actively
determining Paul's trip to Jerusalem. Interestingly, the
Holy Spirit (Acts 19:21?; 20:22-23; 21:4?,11) clarifies Jesus'
will for Paul.

Luke's frequent lack of concern to distinguish carefully
between "Lord" as applied to the Father and to Jesus tells us
something about his view of the activity of the risen Christ.
For Luke, Jesus acts as does the Father, and Jesus can do
what the Father does. Although in heaven, the Father has
acted and acts here below; the risen Christ, although
"located" (Acts 2:33-35; 5:31; 7:55-56) at the Father's right
hand, continues to act here below. Both the Father and
Jesus continue to bring salvation to Israel.

Finally, consider Luke's use of the terms, "being added
to" (Acts 5:14; 11:24), "turning to" (Acts 9:35; 11:21b) and
"believing in" (Acts 5:14; 9:42; 11:17; 14:23; 16:15,31; 18:8; 20:21)
the Lord. To dismiss these expressions as communal and
confessional hardly does justice to Luke. In a culture which
emphasized activity rather than abstractions these expressions also indicated a confidence that the Lord Jesus would
act in the lives of those who joined themselves to him. To
prove this solely from these expressions themselves would
be forcing the texts but the activity of the risen Christ which
has and will be demonstrated shows that these phrases are
best understood in a context of interaction between the risen
Christ and the Christians.

2. THE RISEN LORD AND HIS WITNESSES

Does the Lucan concept of "witness" portray any post-resurrectional activity of Jesus? An affirmative answer is found in Lk 21:12-19 and Acts 3:22-23; 18:5-11; 26:23. This answer does not deny a connection between the Holy Spirit and "witness"; but simply affirms that Luke asserts a direct connection between the risen Jesus and "witness."

It is common knowledge that in Lk 21:12-19 Jesus predicts the persecution his disciples will have to endure. He tells them that these persecutions ". . . will be a time for you to witness" (Lk 21:13). This verse introduces Luke's concept of witness; the passage continues:

> "Settle it therefore in your minds, not to meditate beforehand how to answer; for I will give you a mouth and wisdom which none of your adversaries will be able to resist" (Lk 21:14-15).

Luke has redacted this passage with Acts in mind; the other Synoptics do not have an exact parallel to "I will give you a mouth and wisdom." Only here does Jesus appear as the subject. Elsewhere (Lk 12:12), in a parallel prediction of the persecution of his disciples, Luke writes, "for the Holy Spirit will teach you in that very hour what you are to say." According to Lk 21:15, Jesus promises to be with his disciples when they are persecuted and that this will be a time for them to bear witness. The importance of this promise for understanding the salvific activity of the risen Christ becomes evident when one reflects on how many times in Acts Jesus' witnesses are persecuted and forced to give a response; persecution of Jesus' witnesses occurs throughout most of Acts. Acts provides some examples of Jesus' fidelity to his promise. Acts 3:22-23 reads:

> "Moses said, 'The Lord God will raise up for you a prophet from among your brethren as he raised me up. You shall listen to him in whatever he tells you. And it shall be that every soul that does not listen to that prophet shall be destroyed from the people.'"

Earlier, this passage was used to demonstrate that a new criterion has been established for belonging to the people of

God. It is enough to note here that unless Jesus somehow speaks through Peter, his witness (Acts 3:15; cf. 1:8,21-22; 2:32), there is no way in which the Jewish audience (fictional though it be) can listen to the prophet and thus not be cut off from the people. Peter's word is the word of Jesus; to hear Peter is to hear Jesus.

Acts 18:5-11 provides the next example. Paul is at Corinth and has just been joined by Silas and Timothy who have come down from Macedonia. In additon to the somewhat generic descriptions, "preaching," "speaking," and "teaching the word of God," Luke specifically describes Paul's activity as "witnessing." In this pericope, the Jews oppose and revile Paul who then goes to the Gentiles. Crispus, his household, and many of the Gentile Corinthians believe and are baptized. One night in a vision, the risen Lord says to Paul, "Do not be afraid, but speak and do not be silent; for I am with you, and no man shall attack you to harm you; for I have many people in this city" (Acts 18:9-10). Consequently, in a context of persecution and witnessing which recall the predictions of Lk 21:12-19, the risen Jesus promises Paul his presence and protection. Once again, it is the risen Lord who promises he will be present, protecting those who are witnessing to him (speaking and preaching).

Acts 26:22-23 provides our final example. These verses read:

> "To this day I have had the help that comes from God, and so I stand here witnessing both to small and great, saying nothing but what the prophets and Moses said would come to pass: that the Christ must suffer, and that, by being the first to rise from the dead, he must proclaim light both to the people and to the Gentiles."

In these verses, Paul witnesses; shortly before (Acts 26:16), Paul has reported his appointment by the risen Jesus to be a witness. In this scene of his last apology, Paul literally fulfills Jesus' prediction (Lk 21:12) because only he in Luke-Acts is led before a king (Agrippa II) and a governor (Festus). Most importantly, as was seen above, Luke predicates of the risen Christ the mission of proclaiming light both to the people and to the Gentiles. In actual fact, Paul himself performs this mission (Acts 26:17-18; cf. 13:47); most often he is the subject (Acts 13:5; 15:36; 16:17,21; 17:3,13,23, cf. 13:38) of the post-resurrectional word, "proclaim" (*katangellein*), which Luke uses only in Acts. Paul fulfills the mission which Luke assigns to Christ. Consequently, the risen Jesus cannot only be at the right hand of the Father in heaven; for in Paul he is proclaiming light to the people and to the Gentiles.

Acts 26:23 certainly demonstrates that Jesus was present in his witness and spoke through Paul. Acts 18:5-11 does not say that Jesus speaks in his witness but it does speak of the risen Jesus' presence with and protection of Paul. Lk 10:16, "He who hears you hears me, and he who rejects you rejects me, and he who rejects me rejects him who sent me," addresses the Church and recalls the union between Christ and his messengers and the importance of hearing their word. In this passage, only Luke speaks of hearing; the parallels (Mt 10:40; Jn 13:20) speak of receiving (cf. Lk 9:48). Those who do not hear the word which the risen Jesus speaks through his witness will be cut off from the people (Acts 3:22-23). Since Jesus himself speaks through his disciples, their word naturally grows (Acts 6:7; 12:24; 19:20).

3. THE RISEN LORD AND THE EUCHARIST

Does the story of the two disciples on the road to Emmaus (Lk 24:13-35) mean that the risen Jesus is present to the community through the Eucharist? Surely, this story speaks of the Eucharist, for the Greek of "he took the bread and blessed, and broke it, and gave it to them" (Lk 24:30; cf. 24:35: "in the breaking of the bread") parallels that of "And he took bread, and when he had given thanks he broke it and gave it to them..." (Lk 22:19) of the Institution·Narrative.

In the story of the disciples on the road to Emmaus, Luke addressed the Christian community. Several aspects of the story show this Lucan community-concern. In the first place, the disciples are journeying to Emmaus; this journey reminds us that Luke calls Christianity "the Way" (Acts 9:2; 16:17; 18:25-26; 19:9,23; 22:4; 24:14,22; cf. 8:39). Nor can anyone deny the importance Luke attributes to Jesus' journey to Jerusalem and the importance of Paul's journey to Jerusalem and Rome. Jesus' journey to Jerusalem apparently is meant to be an example for Christians and in this central section of his Gospel Luke gathers a good deal of didactic-parenetic material. Secondly, although Luke gives Cleopas' name, these two disciples can evidently stand for all Christians. Thirdly, the passage contains Christian summaries (Lk 24:19-23,26-27) of a confessional and liturgical nature. Statements such as these could have been used in the Lucan communities' prayer and liturgical life. Fourthly, the passage portrays the disciples' failure to understand and believe (Lk 24:25) what the Scriptures said about Jesus. The discussion that occurs on the way to Emmaus helps to give the journey meaning. Such discussions as that between the disciples themselves and then with Jesus about the Scriptures and the Christ-events are recurrent in the stories of Acts (cf. 17:2-3; 18:24-28) as portrayed by Luke. Fifthly, the assumption that what happened to Jesus was well-known (Lk 24:18-20; cf. Acts 26:26) comes from Luke and better describes what would be truer of Luke's community and later Christianity than of that immediately after Jesus' death. Finally, Lk 24:28-29 seems to recommend the Christian virtue of hospitality which was so important in the early Church.

In view of the above observations, "he was known to them in the breaking of bread" (Acts 24:35) which ends the Emmaus Story reminds the Christian community that Christ is present to them on their Christian journey; in the midst of their misunderstandings and weak faith, they still confess Jesus as the fulfillment of Scriptures and encounter him in the Eucharist.

4. THE HOLY SPIRIT AND THE RISEN JESUS

Earlier, a general presentation of the Holy Spirit's part in salvation history was proposed. However, the question of the connection between the risen Christ and the Spirit has occupied scholars for years. This section attempts to answer this question because this answer bears directly on how the risen Christ continues to be a source of salvation to the Christians. The Church for Luke lives under the rule of Jesus Christ the Lord, who works through the Spirit. The risen Jesus, then, acts directly among his people. Since the Spirit does not exhaust the ways in which the risen Lord remains present to his people, Luke binds the activity of the risen Lord less rigidly to the activity of the Spirit than the reader might at first anticipate. Some authorities admit a connection between Jesus and the Spirit but do not believe that the Spirit renders Jesus present. The majority of scholars, however, maintain that the risen Lord is present through the Spirit. In an effort to show that Luke views the risen Jesus as also present in the Holy Spirit, this section reviews a number of passages from Acts.

According to Acts 2:33 the risen Jesus exalted at the right hand of the Father receives and pours out the promise of the Holy Spirit which the viewers of Pentecost see and hear. The last words of Jesus in the Gospel (Lk 24:49), "And behold, I send the promise of my Father upon you; but stay in the city, until you are clothed with power from on high," make it clear that in Acts 2:33 it is Jesus who sends the Spirit, for the promise of the Father is the Spirit (cf. Acts 1:4-5; 2:38-39). The risen Lord sends the Spirit to Paul, too, as Ananias tells Paul, "the Lord Jesus...has sent me that you may regain your sight and be filled with the Holy Spirit" (Acts 9:17).

The Spirit sent by the risen Lord gives the Apostles power for their witness and mission: "You will receive power when the Holy Spirit has come upon you; and you shall be my witnesses in Jerusalem and in all Judea and Samaria and to the end of the earth" (Acts 1:8). The concept of "witness" in this verse recalls Lk 21:12-15 and its parallel, Lk 12:11-12. The fact that in these verses the words "Jesus" and "Spirit" can be interchanged is best explained if Luke holds that the Spirit stands for Jesus. Other Lucan passages support this interpretation. In Acts 26:16-18, no mention of the Spirit occurs; Jesus personally appoints Paul as his witness and gives him his mission. Earlier, it was shown that Acts 20:22-24 parallels 21:11-14. Both passages speak of Paul's trip to Jerusalem. Acts 20:22-23 leaves no doubt that Paul makes this journey under the direction of the Spirit, but Acts 21:14 calls it the will of the Lord who most reasonably is the Lord Jesus (cf. Acts 20:24).

This suggests another passage, Acts 1:2: ". . . until the day when he was taken up, after he had given command through the Holy Spirit to the apostles whom he had chosen." This translation correctly takes "through the Holy Spirit" with "had given command"; grammatically it could also go with "has chosen" but this interpretation is less likely. Nor should one explain this verse by referring to Lk 24:44-49; its explanation should be sought in its own context (Acts 1:1-11). Acts 1:8 also mentions the Spirit and includes something of a command inasmuch as the Apostles are given a task and promised power to carry it out. The Spirit will bring this power for witnessing and for the mission. Consequently, Acts 1:2 looks forward to what happens in the rest of Acts. The Spirit communicates Jesus' command to his apostles to witness and carry on their mission, and the Spirit continues to do this for the whole of Acts. This relationship which Luke sees between Jesus and the Spirit allows him to write:

> And they went through the region of Phrygia and Galatia, having been forbidden by the Holy Spirit to speak the word in Asia. And when they had come opposite Mysia, they attempted to go into Biythynia, but the Spirit of Jesus did not allow them (Acts 16:6-7).

Here, Luke writes of the "Spirit of Jesus." This cannot be only a stylistic change from the "Holy Spirit" of the previous verse. One does not make stylistic changes which involve a wholly different theology. Rather, at this significant change in the direction of the mission, Luke writes what he has maintained all along: the Spirit is the Spirit of Jesus.

5. THE NAME OF THE RISEN JESUS

The main literary and theological influences on Luke come from the OT LXX. This holds true of "the name." For Luke "the name" can indicate the presence of the risen Jesus; on the other hand, "the name" permits Luke to keep before his readers the reality of Jesus' resurrection and exaltation to the Father's right hand. It is rather well agreed that Jesus' presence is implied in Luke's use of the name, and the contexts in which "the name" appears treat of preaching and spreading the word and witness of the Lord.

Certain Lucan passages which we have already studied from a different angle help us set the stage for a correct understanding of "name" in Acts. Acts 2:21 (cf. Joel 3:5 LXX) reads "whoever calls on the name of the Lord will be saved." As was seen above, in the LXX this passage obviously referred to God the Father but in its present context the reference has to be to Jesus. For when the Jewish audience asks Peter what they should do, he instructs them, "Repent, and be baptized everyone of you in the name of Jesus Christ for the forgiveness of sins; and you shall receive the gift of the Holy Spirit" (Acts 2:38). Acts 4:12 generalizes this claim of salvation in the name Jesus, "And there is salvation in no one else, for there is no other name under heaven given among men by which we must be saved." The Father remains the ultimate source of salvation, yet these passages make the point that without the name of Jesus no one receives salvation. Moreover, as will be seen later, salvation for Luke mainly designates a present reality. Luke is thus claiming that salvation which is a present reality cannot be had without Jesus. The risen Christ is active, saving all through the power of his name.

In the section on "The Holy Spirit and the Risen Lord" the risen Lord was shown to be the one who sends the Holy Spirit. Much the same must be said of the name of Jesus Christ in Acts 2:38 (cf. 19:5-6). The risen Lord, designated by "the name of Jesus Christ," sends the Spirit; reception of baptism in this name brings the gift of the Spirit.

Acts 2:38 also introduces the topic of forgiveness of sins in the name. Needless to say, forgiveness of sins represents another Lucan way of speaking of salvation. "For the forgiveness of your sins" in Acts 2:38 clearly shows the purpose of being baptized in the name of Jesus Christ. With this conviction, Ananias tells Paul, "Rise and be baptized, and wash away your sins, calling on his name" (Acts 22:16). A baptismal context (cf. Acts 10:44-48) apparently lies behind Luke's thought in Acts 10:43: "To him all the prophets bear witness that everyone who believes in him receives forgiveness of sins through his name." Whether the reference in Acts 10:43 is to baptism or not, those who believe in Jesus of Nazareth receive forgiveness of sins through his name. The risen Lord himself told the Eleven and those with them that the Scriptures had foretold that repentance and forgiveness of sins should be preached in his name to all the nations (Lk 24:47). Without the risen Jesus, sins are not forgiven.

Acts mentions miracles performed in Jesus' name. These miracles promote the spread of the word. In these miracle stories, the name stands for the risen Jesus (compare Acts 4:10-12 and 9:34 with 3:6,16) and can be identified with power (Acts 4:7). This power cannot be merely that which Jesus during his earthly life gave his apostles (Lk 9:1) and his disciples (Lk 10:19), for this power is continually received (cf. Lk 24:49; Acts 1:8; 3:12; 4:7,33; 6:8; 8:13; 19:11), and Peter insists that it is not to be attributed to himself nor John (cf. 3:12-16; 4:7-12). Moreover, there would be no reason for Luke to mention the name. Finally, the miracles performed by Paul (Acts 16:18; 19:11-17) would still have to be explained.

Not only does Luke insist that the credit for these miracles should not be given to Jesus' witnesses, he also asserts that magic has nothing to do with this miraculous power. Luke condemns the magical attitude of Simon (Acts 8:9-13,18-24), the magician Elymas (Acts 13:6-12) and the magical use of Jesus' name (Acts 19:13-20). The miracles recorded in Acts occur in a context of faith and this might explain why Luke accepted in his Gospel the account found in Mk 9:38-40 (cf. Lk 9:49-50) where John tells Jesus that they prevented a man from casting out demons in Jesus' name because he was not following them. Although Luke drops Mark's "...for no one who does a mighty work in my name will be able soon after to speak evil of me," he keeps "Do not forbid him... For he that is not against us is for us." Luke rejects the magical use of the name and of things Christian but not miracles done in Jesus' name.

The Acts of the Apostles provides three clear instances of miracles performed in Jesus' name. The healing of the lame man in Jesus' name (Acts 3:6) spans two chapters (Acts 3-4); it serves as a summary of all miraculous activity in Jesus' name and symbolizes salvation on every level (Acts 4:12). Peter and John do not achieve this miracle through their own power or piety (Acts 3:12); the Father does it and glorifies his son (Acts 3:13). Yet, Jesus, too, performs the miracle, for the name strengthened the man, and faith in the name gives the lame man perfect health (Acts 3:16). Thus, Jesus' name is power (Acts 4:7), and his name saves (Acts 4:10,12).

The early Christians in prayer ask the Father to stretch out his hand to heal and to perform signs and wonders through the name of his holy servant, Jesus (Acts 4:30). Again, the Father achieves the miracles, but he does this through the name of Jesus (cf. Acts 3:13). Luke places in Acts 4:30 his theme of "signs and wonders" (Acts 2:43; 5:12; 6:8; 8:13; 14:3; 15:12; cf. 2:19) which runs through the first part of Acts. In accord with Acts 4:30, the Father (Acts 2:19; 15:12) and Jesus (Acts 14:3) bring about these signs and wonders.

After the slave girl possessed by a spirit of divination had followed Paul and his companions for many days and shouted out who they were, Paul finally charged the spirit in the name of Jesus Christ to come out of her. The spirit immediately left her (Acts 16:18). This passage demonstrates the powerful presence of Jesus' name in the life of his witness, Paul. It also pictures Paul's hesitancy in working miracles. Only after Paul became exasperated, did he call on the name of the Lord.

The passages which create the most difficulty for the

interpretation of "the name" of Jesus in Acts are: "to speak in the name" (Acts 4:17-18; 5:40,42; 8:12; 9:15?,27-28), "to teach in the name" (Acts 4:18; 5:28,40; 9:27-28), "to suffer for the name" (Acts 5:41; 9:16; 21:13; cf. Luke 21:12,17), "to risk one's life for the sake of the name of the Lord Jesus Christ" (Acts 15:26), and "to do things against the name of Jesus" (Acts 26:9; cf. 9:14-21). As the treatment of "witness" has indicated, it is the presence of the risen Lord in the proclamation of the word which provides the clue to the correct interpretation of "the name" of Jesus in the above passages. All of the above passages in some way involve the proclamation of the word. For "to suffer for the name," "to risk their lives for the sake of the name of the Lord Jesus Christ," and "to do things against the name of Jesus" look to the suffering which promotes the spread or proclamation of the word. The risen Christ becomes present in the proclaimed word. This explains why it is that when Paul was opposing the proclamation of the resurrection of Jesus, the risen Lord asks him, "Saul, Saul, why do you persecute me?" (Acts 9:4; 22:7; 26:14). Thus, all of the passages in this paragraph include the name of Jesus because the risen Lord manifests himself in the proclamation of the word (cf. Lk 21:12-19).

6. FURTHER SALVIFIC ACTIVITY OF THE RISEN JESUS

This section will consider other examples of the salvific activity of the risen Lord. This includes the topics of Jesus as "leader" and "cornerstone," of miracles, of repentance, of forgiveness of sins, of grace, of justification, and of the resurrection.

Christ as savior is called "leader" and "cornerstone." Luke predicates "leader" of the risen Christ twice (Acts 3:15; 5:31), and both times the term is used in short passion narratives. The best interpretation of "leader" is one who reaches his goal and guides his followers to do the same. (This interpretation incidentally helps us to understand Luke's emphasis on Jesus' journey to Jerusalem and his designation of Christianity as the "Way.") Acts 3:15, the first text where "leader" is found, relates to the resurrection and will be treated very briefly below. The most acceptable interpretation of "Leader and Savior" in Acts 5:31 is to take the expression as an hendiadys; that is, Jesus is the one who leads to salvation. Basically, Luke conveys the same message in his designation of Jesus as "cornerstone" (Acts 4:11). Acts 4:12 explains this designation, "And there is salvation in no one else, for there is no other name under heaven given among men by which we must be saved."

In all probability Luke attributes Paul's cure of the cripple from birth (Acts 14:8-10) to the risen Lord. For in the passage immediately preceding, the risen Lord bears witness to the word of his grace by granting signs and wonders through the hands of Paul and Barnabas (Acts 14:3). This miraculous activity becomes specific in Acts 14:8-10. The closest parallel to Paul's cure of the cripple is in Peter's and John's healing of the lame man at the Beautiful Gate (Acts 3:1-10) where it is the name of the risen Lord that works the cure. Another parallel where the risen Lord definitely performs the miracle is also relevant. In Lydda, Peter orders the man paralyzed and bedridden for eight years: "Aeneas, Jesus Christ heals you; rise and make your bed" (Acts 9:34). The man immediately rose. This passage is the clearest illustration of Luke's teaching that the risen Lord is active performing miracles among his followers. It also provides the best interpretation of Acts 14:8-10.

The risen Lord brings repentance and forgiveness of sins. The Scriptures say that repentance and forgiveness of sins should be preached in his name to all the nations (Lk 24:47). Peter does precisely this when he instructs his Jewish listeners, "Repent, and be baptized everyone of you in the name of Jesus Christ for the forgiveness of your sins..." (Acts 2:38; cf. 10:43; 22:16). Ultimately, the Father accomplishes this, for he exalted Jesus to his right hand as Leader and Savior "to give repentance to Israel and forgiveness of sins" (Acts 5:31). Paul too, proclaims forgiveness of sins in Jesus' name (Acts 13:37-39); and Stephen prays "Lord, do not hold this sin against them" (Acts 7:60).

Two other passages (Acts 3:26; 26:18) should be considered. Acts 3:26 speaks of the risen Jesus in a portrait similar to that of Jesus at his ascension (cf. Lk 24:50-51). Jesus, the servant, blesses Peter's audience and turns all of them from their wickedness. Acts 26:18 occurs within the context of the risen Lord's appearance to Paul; in this verse, the resurrected Christ details Paul's mission:

> "...delivering you from the people and the Gentiles — to whom I send you to open their eyes, that they may turn from darkness to light and from the power of Satan to God, that they may receive forgiveness of sins and a place among those who are sanctified by faith in me" (Acts 26:17-18).

Does "by faith in me" go only with "sanctified" or with the whole description of Paul's mission? The latter solution is the more natural one, but even if the phrase goes only with "sanctified," faith in the risen Christ achieves sanctification. If it goes with Paul's whole mission, faith in the risen Lord brings light, a turning to God, forgiveness of sins, and a place among those who are sanctified. The effects mentioned in Acts 26:18 do not come from the faith of the convert but from Christ in whom this faith is had. No matter what one decides about Acts 3:26 and 26:18, the passages found in Lk 24:47; Acts 2:38; 5:31; 7:60; 13:37-39 (cf. 10:43; 22:16) leave no doubt that for Luke the risen Jesus brings repentance and forgiveness of sins.

"Grace" in the writing of Luke means the divine benevolence or favor which achieves the marvels of salvation. It is a quality of the Father (Lk 2:40; Acts 11:23; 13:43; 14:26; 15:40; 20:24,32) but it is also proper to the risen Lord (Lk 4:22; Acts 4:33?; 14:33; 15:11). Speaking in defense of the Gentile converts who were not circumcised Peter says to his fellow Jewish Christian officials of Jerusalem: "But we believe that we are saved through the grace of the Lord Jesus, just as they" (Acts 15:11). In this verse which stresses universality, the grace of the risen Lord saves both Jewish and Gentile Christians.

"Grace" also is a quality of the evangelical message. Luke-

Acts provides two examples (Lk 4:22; Acts 14:3). In the synagogue at Nazareth, the audience all spoke well of Jesus and wondered at the "gracious words" (Lk 4:22) which proceeded out of his mouth. Lk 4:16-30 calls for several observations. In this pericope, Jesus preaches about himself and brings salvation. "Today (Lk 4:21)" indicates the fulfillment of God's promise in the OT (Isa 61:1-2; 58:6; cf. Lk 4:18-19). "Today," Jesus personifies this promise for his hearers. Each individual is personally addressed by word and called to a decision. Thus, Luke speaks on two levels. The people of Nazareth hear only on the human level. But the reader of Luke's Gospel should hear it as the message of God's grace (Acts 14:3; 20:24,32). In other words, the resurrected Christ fulfills Scripture and becomes present in his word which can be termed "gracious" because the Father and Christ grant their salvific grace to those who hear. The other relevant text (Acts 14:3) summarizes this activity on the part of the risen Lord: "So they remained for a long time, speaking boldly for the Lord, who bore witness to the word of his grace, granting signs and wonders to be done by their hands."

Luke writes of the justification which the risen Lord brings only in Acts 13:38-39:

> "Let it be known to you therefore, brethren, that through this man forgiveness of sins is proclaimed to you, and by him everyone that believes is justified from everything from which you could not be justified by the law of Moses."

"Through this man" and "by him" express some kind of present agency (thus, activity) on the part of Jesus who, as this speech (cf. Acts 13:30-37) earlier asserted, was risen. According to Luke, justification through the risen Christ accomplished what the Law could not; and Paul offers this justification to his Jewish audience (actually, Luke's readers) at Pisidian Antioch as a present reality available to him who believes in the risen Christ.

Luke views the resurrection as part of salvation and maintains that there is a connection between Jesus' resurrection and that of the Christians. This Lucan understanding of our resurrection is clearest in Acts 13:13-52, but a detailed exegesis of this passage is required to show this. Several factors indicate the unity of this pericope. It follows a set pattern, which can be modified, (Acts 13:13-52; 14:1-6; 17:1-11; 18:4-18; 19:8-10; 28:17-32), of how Paul enters a village and is treated by the Jews:

1. Paul and his companions go to the synagogue and preach to the Jews first.
2. The Jews reject the message.
3. The preaching then turns to the Gentiles.
4. The Jews become jealous and cause a disturbance.
5. Paul (or another Christian preacher) leaves or is thrown out of the city.

"Word" (Acts 13:15,26,44,46; 48-49), "to hear" (Acts 13:16b, 44,48), and the concept, "salvation" (Acts 13:23,26,38-39,47), support this unity. Moreover, Acts 13:42-43 connect the speech with its aftermath through the phrase, "the people begged that these things might be told them the next sabbath." Things are not yet settled. This unity of Acts 13:13-52 cannot be disturbed by any claim of different audiences since the real audience of these verses consists in Luke's readers. Therefore, whatever is said about a connection between Jesus' resurrection and our own must depend on this unity of Acts 13:13-52.

True, the speech does not begin to speak of Jesus' resurrection until Acts 13:30, but, if one accepts that Acts 13:32-33 deals with Jesus' resurrection, then the major portion (Acts 13:30-37) of the remainder of the speech has to do with this topic.

But should one understand here Jesus' resurrection? In Acts 13:22-23 it states:

> "And we bring you the good news that what God prom-
> ised to the fathers, this he has fulfilled to us their children
> by raising Jesus; as it is written in the second psalm, 'You
> are my Son, today I have begotten you.'"

Data favor a resurrectional interpretation of "raising,"

instead of understanding it of Jesus' being brought into this earthly life. If these verses do not report Jesus' resurrection, then, the train of thought is broken because Acts 13:30-31,34-37 speak of the resurrection of Jesus. Also, "promise" could refer back to Acts 13:23 where it deals with Jesus' earthly ministry; but, more probably, one should relate it to Acts 26:6-8,22-23 which describe a promise of the resurrection of the dead realized first in Jesus just as the Scriptures claimed. Certainly Luke intends to quote Ps 2 in Acts 13:33. This quote, however, must be understood in relationship to Heb 1:5;5:5, which according to the majority of scholars treat Jesus' exaltation, because Luke and the author of Hebrews rely on a common tradition. Luke quotes Ps 2 in Acts 13:33 with the exact same Greek words as in these verses from Hebrews. Finally, Luke in Acts 2:25-36; 13:34-37 (cf. Ps 15 LXX) relates Jesus' resurrection to his descent from David, and Lk 1:32-33 interrelates sonship, the throne of David his father, and a kingdom which will last forever. But Jesus must be raised from the dead or he cannot reign forever. Nor could his kingdom last forever. Further, Acts 13:33 calls Jesus "Son" with the words of the Davidic Ps 2. Consequently, Acts 13:32-33 speaks of Jesus the Son of God who was raised from the dead and who rules over his eternal kingdom.

How does this theme of Jesus' resurrection fit with Acts 13:44-52? "Eternal life" in Acts 13:46,48 must include more than just Jesus' resurrection; we are dealing with the resurrection of those who believe (cf. Acts 13:48). So, in Acts 13:32-33 Luke demonstrates the connection he sees between Jesus' resurrection and our own. Luke views the resurrection of the dead, and so our resurrection, as the promise made by God to us (the children of Abraham and Sarah) and fulfilled in Jesus' resurrection. Although Luke has Paul speak of the salvation which Jesus brings, a large portion of the speech (Acts 13:30-37; cf. 13:46-48) considers the major aspect of that salvation: Jesus' resurrection and its effect on our own.

Finally, Acts 13:13-52 does not constitute the only *locus* where Luke claims a connection between Jesus' resurrection

and our own. Three other Lucan passages make this assertion. Acts 26:4-23 forms a diptych: the first panel of the
diptych tells us of Paul's life (Acts 26:4-5) and of the resurrection of the dead (Acts 26:6-8), and the second panel
continues the first with further information on Paul's life
(Acts 26:9-21) and Jesus' resurrection (Acts 26:22-23). So,
the second part of each panel treats the resurrection. First,
we are told that the promise made to Israel's ancestors
consists in the resurrection of the dead, and then that Christ
must suffer and, by being first to rise from the dead, proclaim light both to the people and to the Gentiles. "First" for
Luke is not to be understood primarily chronologically, for
Christ's resurrection is first because he leads Christians to
their resurrection.

The other two passages which draw a connection between
our resurrection and Jesus' are:

> And as they were speaking to the people, the priests and
> the captain of the temple and the Sadducees came upon
> them, annoyed because they were teaching the people and
> proclaiming *in Jesus the resurrection from the dead.*
> (Acts 4:1-2).
>
> The times of ignorance God overlooked, but now he
> commands everyone everywhere to repent because he has
> fixed a day on which he will judge the world in righteous-
> ness by a man whom he has appointed, *and he kept faith
> with everyone by raising him from the dead* (Acts 17:30-
> 31; the translation of the italicized portion is my own).

Therefore, although one does not find the lucidity of Paul or
John on the topic of the extent to which Jesus' resurrection
affects ours, Luke does view the resurrection as part of
salvation and holds for a connection between Jesus' resurrection and that of the Christians.

7. SUMMARY OF THE SALVIFIC ACTIVITY OF THE RISEN CHRIST IN LUKE—ACTS

Luke wrote both his Gospel and Acts of the Apostles after
Jesus' resurrection and both volumes mutually influence

each other. Christ's post-resurrectional activity is extensive, far more so than many have acknowledged, even though, quite naturally, Luke has no systematic listing of such activity. The overall OT framework of salvation history allows Luke considerable freedom in determining who (Father, Son, or Holy Spirit) performs a given action. Once he has established that the Father brings salvation in Jesus Christ, Luke introduces into the various narratives whatever divine agency suits the occasion. Certainly, the Father and the Spirit are both active in the world. But to affirm this does not mean that one must deny activity to the risen Christ Jesus, "located" at the right hand of the Father and not visibly present in this world. Moreover, only the clear instances of such activity of the risen Jesus are summarized here.

That the risen Jesus acts among Christians is an essential feature of Luke's portrayal of him. Luke can write of Jesus as the risen Lord who is present in his Church and in his word. In both books Luke predicates repeated activity of the risen Jesus in a number of areas: the Eucharist (Lk 24:30-33, 35), the Holy Spirit (Lk 24:49; Acts 1:2, 8; 2:33, 38-39; 16:6-7), in the preaching of his witnesses (Acts 3:22-23; 18:5-11; 26:23), in his name (Acts 2:21,38; 3:6,16; 4:12; 10:43; 16:18), salvation in the present (Acts 4:12) which embraces repentance, forgiveness of sins, grace, and resurrection, visions (Acts 7:55-56; 9:1-19a par.; 22:17-21), and, finally, signs and wonders (Acts 4:29-30). The best understanding of phrases like "being added to the Lord" and "to speak in the name" is in a context of the presence of the risen Lord in the proclaimed word and interaction between him and the Christians. Lastly , if the discussion of the topic turns to causality (not explicitly a Lucan concept), Jesus in Luke-Acts functions as both efficient and exemplary cause during both his earthly and heavenly existence.

The result of this investigation also affects the study of Luke-Acts a number of ways. For instance, the term, "absentee," proves unacceptable as a description of the christology of Acts. Nor does Luke hold that the time of the Church is exclusively the time of the Holy Spirit. Rather, he maintains that the risen Christ reigns and acts in many ways among the Christians one of which is through the Holy Spirit. This continued presence of Jesus in Acts explains Luke's statement, "In the first book, O Theophilus, I have dealt with all that Jesus began to do and teach (Acts 1:1)" and thus justifies the scholars who have claimed that there is a continuity between Luke's Gospel and Acts of Apostles. This continuity means that more weight has to be given to the assertion that scholars must investigate Luke-Acts as a whole. Finally, Luke did not generally draw rigid distinctions in the activities he attributed to the Father, the risen Christ, and the Holy Spirit.

Luke's christology shapes his ecclesiology. The risen Lord acts and is present to the whole life of his church, that is, to us. He leads us. Our mission is Christ's mission. He gives us our mission and directs us. When we are persecuted, he encourages, supports, and protects us. His power enables us to perform miracles. When we preach, he preaches; when we are heard he is heard. Our salvation, a present experience and reality, comes only from him. We are baptized in his name and realize his presence in the Eucharist. Certainly, the Father and the Spirit are active, but a church without considerable activity on the part of the risen Christ is not Lucan.

CHAPTER 3

THE DISCIPLES CONTINUE THE WORK OF JESUS

Numerous parallels exist between Luke's portrayal of Jesus and that of the disciples in Luke-Acts. What do these parallels tell us about the relationship between Jesus and his disciples? Above it was pointed out that the risen Christ works in his disciples. Christ gives them speech and wisdom which none of their adversaries will be able to resist (Lk 21:15). Whoever does not listen to Peter has not listened to the prophet Jesus and will be cut off from the people (Acts 3:22-23). The risen Christ assures Paul,

> "Do not be afraid, but speak and do not be silent; for I am with you, and no man shall attack you to harm you; for I have many people in this city" (Acts 18:9-10).

Later, the risen Christ is said through Paul to proclaim light to the people and to the Gentiles (Acts 26:23; cf. 26:18). Such is the union between Christ and the Christians that Jesus says to Paul who is persecuting Christians, "I am Jesus whom you are persecuting" (Acts 9:5; cf. 22:8; 26:9-11,15).

Finally, while the Synoptics all show a concern for the unity of the Christians with Christ, only Luke has twice expanded this theme of unity by the notion of hearing.

Jesus, in the woes over the unrepentant cities, concluded, "He who hears you hears me, and he who rejects you rejects me, and he who rejects me rejects him who sent me" (Lk 10:16; cf. 9:48). When the woman from the crowd raises her voice and says, "Blessed is the womb that bore you and the breasts which you sucked," Jesus replies, "Blessed are those who hear the word of God and keep it" (cf. Lk 11:27-28).

Doubtless, these parallels between Jesus and his disciples call the disciples to imitation of Jesus and serve as an apology for them. As Jesus went about doing good, enduring rejection, and yet was innocent, so his disciples continue his good deeds, suffer persecution, and are innocent.

But these parallels particularly demonstrate that Luke wants to show that what Jesus began to do and to teach, he continues through his disciples (Acts 1:1-1). Jesus' disciples continue his salvific activity. He saves, but they through their words and deeds make that salvation available. This section will consider the disciples and their words and deeds. In order to establish that Luke draws numerous parallels between Jesus and his disciples, the narratives about Stephen and Paul will first be studied. Then the more important parallels that Luke records between Jesus and his disciples will be noted.

A. Parallels Between Jesus and Stephen

The following parallels exist between Jesus and Stephen. When the same Greek words or cognates appear in these parallels, the corresponding words will be italicized:

Jesus	*Stephen*
1. And all *spoke well* of him ... (Lk 4:22).	"Therefore, brethren pick out from among you seven men who are *spoken well of* ... (Acts 6:3).
2. And Jesus, *full of the Holy Spirit* ... (Lk 4:1).	... and they chose a man *full* of faith and *of the Holy Spirit* ... (Acts 6:5; cf. 6:3,10; 7:55).

3. And Jesus increased in *wisdom* and in stature ... (Lk 2:52; cf. 2:40).

But they could not withstand the *wisdom* and the Spirit with which he (Stephen) spoke (Acts 6:10; cf. 6:3). And Stephen, full of *grace* ... (Acts 6:8).

4. ... and the *grace* of God was upon him (Lk 2:40; cf. 2:52).

5. And Jesus returned in the *power* of the Spirit into Galilee, ... (Lk 4:14; cf. 4:36; 6:19; 8:46; 21:27; 22:69).

And Stephen, full of grace and *power*, ... (Acts 6:8).

6. ... with mighty works and *wonders and signs* which God did through him (Jesus) in your midst, ... (Acts 2:22).

And Stephen ... did great *wonders and signs* among the people (Acts 6:8).

7. And they were not able in the presence of the people to catch him by what he said; but marveling at his answer they were silent (Lk 20:26).

But they could not withstand the wisdom and the Spirit with which he spoke (Acts 6:10).

8. The charges brought against Stephen parallel those brought against Jesus in Mark's Gospel, which Luke used as a source. Apparently, Luke did not feel that these charges were appropriate during Jesus' trial but he did use them of one of his followers.

For many bore *false witness* against him ...
And some stood up and bore *false witness* against him, saying, "We heard him say, 'I *will destroy* this temple made by hands' (Mk 14:55-58) ..."
You have heard his *blasphemy* (Mk 14:64; cf. Lk 5:21).

Then they secretly instigated men, who said, "We have heard him speak *blasphemous words* against Moses and God" ... and set up *false witnesses* who said, "This man never ceases to speak words against this holy place and the law; for we have heard him say that this Jesus of Nazareth *will destroy* this place ..." (Acts 6:11-14).

9. ... the chief priests and *the scribes* with the *elders came upon* him and said ... (Lk 20:1).

...and they stirred up the people and *the elders* and *the scribes*, and they *came upon* him and seized him ... (Acts 6:12).

10. ... and they *led him* away *to their council* ... (Lk 22:66).

... and *led him before* their *council* ... (Acts 6:12)

11. ... and the eyes of all in the synagogue *were fixed* on him (Lk 4:20).

And all who sat in the council *fixed their eyes* (on him; Acts 6:15).

12. ... the appearance of his *countenance* was altered ... (Lk 9:29).

... saw that his *countenance* was like the *countenance* of an angel (Acts 6:15).

13. Woe to you! for you build the tombs *of the prophets* whom *your fathers killed.* So you are witnesses and consent to the deeds *of your fathers*; for *they killed* them, and you build their tombs. Therefore also the Wisdom of God said, "I will send them *prophets* and apostles, some of whom *they will kill* and *persecute* that the blood of all the *prophets*, shed from the foundation of the world, may be required of this generation ... (Lk 11:47-50; cf. 4:24; 6:22-23).

As *your fathers* did, so do you. Which *of the prophets* did not *your fathers persecute*? And they *killed* those who announced beforehand the coming of the righteous one ...
(Acts 7: 51-52).

14. ... and when Jesus also had been baptized and was praying, *the heaven was opened* ... (Lk 3:21).
(Jesus at his passion) But from now on *the Son of Man*

... and he (Stephen) said "Behold I see *the heavens opened*, and *the Son of Man* standing *at the right hand* of God" (7:56).

shall be seated *at the right hand* of the power of God (Lk 22:69).

15. ... and *cast him outside the city*, and led him to the brow of the hill ... that they might throw him down headlong (Lk 4:29).
And they cast him out of the vineyard and killed him (Lk 20:15).

Then they *cast him out of the city* and stoned him ... (Acts 7:58).

16. Then Jesus, crying *with a loud voice*, said "Father, into your hands I commit *my spirit*." And *having said this*, he breathed his last (Lk 23:46).
And he withdrew from them about a stone's throw, and *knelt down* and prayed, ... (Lk 22:41).

And Jesus said, "Father forgive them, for they know not what they do" (Lk 23:34: a disputed text).

And as they were stoning Stephen, he prayed, "Lord Jesus receive *my spirit*." And he *knelt down* and cried *with a loud voice*, "Lord, do not hold this sin against them." And *when he had said this*, he fell asleep (Acts 7:59-60).

17. Now there was a man named Joseph from the Jewish town of Arimathea. He was a member of the council, a good and righteous man ... This man went to Pilate and asked for the body of Jesus. Then he took it down and wrapped it in a linen shroud, and laid him in a rock-hewn tomb, where no one had ever yet been laid (Lk 23:50-53).

Devout persons buried Stephen, and made great lament over him (Acts 8:2).

18. ... (Jesus) saying, "This cup which is *poured out* for you is the new covenant *in my blood*" (Lk 22:20).
... and the chief priests and the scribes were seeking how *to kill him* for they feared the people (Lk 22:2; cf. Acts 2:23; 10:39).

"And when *the blood* of Stephen your witness *was poured out*, I also was standing by and approving, and keeping the garments of *those who killed him* (Acts 22:20).

The context (Acts 7:51-60) of the vast majority of these parallels further determines that Stephen is an instrument of salvation. The message he proclaims, they reject. They have always resisted the Spirit under whose influence Stephen spoke. They are stiff-necked, uncircumcised in heart and ears; they are just like their ancestors who persecuted the prophets and killed those who announce Jesus' coming. Stephen's audience themselves are said to have betrayed and murdered Jesus, and they prove beyond a doubt that Stephen is like Jesus. They reject and kill him too.

This extensive parallel between Jesus and Stephen manifests that Jesus' words and deeds persist in Stephen. He, too, is full of the Spirit, of wisdom, of grace and of power. He works signs and wonders and speaks of Jesus. Needless to say, Stephen is most like Jesus in his passion. Finally, his vision of the Son of Man standing at the Father's right hand appears to be a foretaste of the resurrection that awaits him.

B. Parallels Between Jesus and Paul

The scope of this book does not permit an exhaustive listing of the parallels between Jesus and Paul. They are truly extensive. However, these parallels seem to reach their high point in Acts 25-26 (Paul's appearances before Festus and Agrippa II) which bears a striking resemblance to Lk 23:1-25 (Christ's appearances before Pilate and Herod Antipas). It was demonstrated above that in Acts 25-26 Paul performs the task which Luke predicates of the risen Christ:

"That . . . , he would proclaim light both to the people and to the Gentiles" (Acts 26:23; cf. 26:18). Not only does this statement summarize Paul's activity since his conversion, but the parallels to this verse in 26:18 and in the *Nunc Dimittis* leave no doubt that "light" in this verse refers to salvation. So, Christ, in the person of Paul, brings salvation both to the people and to the Gentiles. Furthermore, in these appearances Paul clearly identifies himself as a *Christian* (cf. Acts 26:28-29) and fulfills a number of Christ's predictions about the lot of persecuted *Christians* (Lk 21:12-19; cf. 9:23-27; 12:4-12). Paul shows how *Christians* will fulfill these predictions.

THE PARALLEL BETWEEN LUKE 23:1-25 AND ACTS 25-26

Lk 23:1-25 and Acts 25-26 have the same structural elements: an outline of these elements establishes the following:

Introduction

Lk 23:1-25	*Acts 25:1-26:32*
1. Lk 23:1	Acts 25:1

Hearing before Roman Procurator

2. Lk 23:2-5 — Jesus appears before Pilate and Jewish accusers.	Acts 25:2-12 — Paul appears before Festus and Jewish accusers.

Introduction to Appearance before Herodian Prince

3. Lk 23:6-7 — Reasons given why Jesus is sent to Herod Antipas.	Acts 25:13-27 — Reasons why Paul is brought before Agrippa II.

Hearing before Herodian Prince

4. Lk 23:8-11(12) — Jesus before Herod (Pilate plays no part; he is not even there; and only the Lucan Passion Narrative reports this hearing).	Acts 26:1-23 — Paul before Agrippa II (During speech only Agrippa II is addressed, not Festus).

Dialogue

5. Lk 23:13-23 — Between Pilate and Jewish accusers.	Acts 26:24-29 — Among Festus, Paul, and Agrippa II.

Conclusion

6. Lk 23:24-25 — Although he is innocent and should be freed, Jesus is handed over to the will of the Jews; and Barabbas is set free.	Acts 26:30-32 — Paul is innocent and could be freed except for the appeal made to Caesar.

Moreover, the hearings of Jesus before Pilate and Herod Antipas (Lk 23:1-25) appear to be the model for the hearings of Paul before Festus and Agrippa II (Acts 25-26); at least, the following data are true of each episode:

1. Both episodes are structured as hearings.

2. A description of the four main characters is the same: Roman procurator, Herodian prince, Jewish accusers, and defendant.

3. The hearings before the Herodian princes are held at the instigation of the Roman procurator in his own territory (Lk 23:6-7; Acts 25:22-27).

4. The Roman procurator himself thinks that the defendant is innocent (Lk 23:4,14-15,22; Acts 25:18,25a; 26:31-32). After the hearing, the defendant is still found to be innocent; Pilate and Festus each declare the defendant innocent three times; Herod Antipas (by implication) and Agrippa II once each.

5. The defendant is accused by the high priest and the leaders of the Jewish people (Lk 23:2,5,10; Acts 25:2,7,11,15-17; 26:2); they demand death (Lk 23:18,21,23; Acts 25:24bc). The charges are the same: activity against the Jews and Caesar (Lk 23:2; Acts 25:8).

6. The member of the Herodian family (just) happens to be in town at the time; both Herod Antipas and Agrippa II want to see the respective prisoners (Lk 23:8; Acts 25:22).

7. An appearance occurs before the member of the Herodian family.

a. The real audience is not the Herodian prince, but Luke's readers.

b. The main body of the pericope seems to be the work of Luke. He may have reworked data which he found in an unacceptable context in Mk (14:60-61a; 15:3-5,16-20a) and used it of Herod Antipas and his soldiers rather than of the Romans and the high priest. And he could have composed the speech and dialogue in the hearing before Agrippa II. Whatever be the case, this does not say that the Lucan compositions do not contain earlier tradition.

c. Both of these appearances before Herodian princes have possible historical bases although there is a strong temptation to view both as creations of Luke.

8. The defendant could and should be freed except for the fact of the opposition of the Jewish leaders in the case of Jesus (Lk 23:16-25) and the appeal to Caesar in Paul's (Acts 26:32; cf. 28:17).

9. Both episodes have the Suffering Servant motif; Jesus during his passion is suffering as does the servant (Isa 50:6; 52:14; 53:2-12); the Suffering Servant motif is explicitly brought out by the use of the same Greek words for "led" (Isa 53:7,8; Lk 23:1) and "handed over" (Isa 53:6,12; Lk 23:25). Moreover, Jesus is silent before Herod Antipas (Lk 23:9) as is the Lamb in Isa 53:7, and Jesus and the Suffering Servant are both innocent (Lk 23:4,14-15,22; Isa 50:9; 53:9; cf. Acts 8:32-33). The Christ is also seen in Acts 26:23 to be the Suffering Servant who will bring light to the Gentiles (Isa 42:6; 49:6); he shares this task with Paul who is to open the eyes of the Jews and Gentiles (Acts 26:18; Isa 35:5; cf. 42:7; 61:1 LXX) to turn from darkness to light (Isa 42:16). Although he is "handed over" elsewhere in Acts (28:17), in chs 25-26 Paul too is "led" in (Acts 25:6,23; cf. Lk 23:1; Isa 53:7) and declared to be innocent (Acts 25:18-20,25; 26:31-32; cf. Isa 50:9; 53:9).

10. Both episodes (Lk 23:1-25; Acts 25-26) have an illogical aspect about them. During the trial Pilate asks Jesus only one question, and the answer to this question is the only time Jesus speaks; although Herod Antipas asks him

many questions, Jesus does not answer him. Jesus, an innocent man, is handed over to the will of the Jewish leaders; but Barabbas, a man guilty of insurrection and murder, is freed. Paul is also innocent but kept in custody because he appealed to Caesar. (We must assume that even an innocent man could not be freed once he appealed to Caesar). In Acts 25:26-27 Festus says he is holding the hearing before Agrippa II bcause he has nothing to write to Caesar. Why can he not just write up the case as it stands? After all, the Jews had brought up a number of charges. Even more disconcerting is the absence of Jewish accusers at Paul's defense before Festus and Agrippa II (Acts 25:13-26:32).

11. In these two hearings the verses Lk 23:6-12(15) and Acts 25:13-26:32 appear to be inserted into their present position; one could omit them; and the passages still make sense. After Lk 23:5 one could begin reading Lk 23:16-25 if he made certain minor changes. One can say the same about Acts 25:13-26:32 which also appears inserted between 25:1-12 and ch 27 which could easily be read right after Acts 25:1-12.

This detailed similarity of the structure and content of these hearings of Jesus and Paul does not merely demonstrate that Paul is somehow like Christ. Rather, we have a real link between Christ and Paul. Suffering Servant motifs form the main support for this link. Like the Suffering Servant, and despite their personal innocence, Christ, and Paul after him, are "led" before officialdom, suffer, and announce light to the people and the Gentiles (Acts 26:23; cf. 26:18).

Although one may disagree in this or that detail with the above parallels drawn between Jesus and Stephen and Paul, nonetheless, that Luke does draw such parallels and that he shows both Stephen and Paul as carrying on the salvific work of Jesus can hardly be denied. Our study will now turn to some further parallels which Luke draws between Jesus and his disciples. The focus is particularly on those parallels which portray the disciples as continuing Christ's salvific activity. This Lucan material will be organized under the

headings: "Parallel Actions (Performed or Endured)",
"Same Places," "Same Words," "Same Descriptions," and
the "Same Ill-Treatment (Passion)."

C. Parallel Actions (Performed or Endured)

Travel motifs permeate the whole of Luke-Acts. Travel
becomes significant because Jesus and his disciples travel to
achieve God's salvific will or to make it available to all. The
great insertion, Jesus' trip to Jerusalem, appears in Lk
9:51-19:28(?). Before (Lk 9:31,51) and during (Lk 13:32-33;
18:31-34) this trip, Luke proclaims it to be God's will. God
also requires that Jesus' disciples travel. The apostles are
given traveling orders in Acts 1:8 (cf. Lk 24:47). The Lord
instructs Philip to meet (Acts 8:26,29) and leave (Acts 8:39)
the Ethiopian eunuch. Philip, after he has explained the
Scriptures and at the only pause in that travel narrative,
baptizes him. Peter receives clear directions (Acts 10:19-
20,22,28-33; 11:11-14) to go to Cornelius' house in Caesarea. Thus, God makes salvation available to the Gentiles. In
various ways (Acts 13:2; 16:6-10; 19:21; 20:22; 21:13; 23:11)
God sends Paul on his missionary journeys. As Jesus had to
go to Jerusalem, Paul must go to Rome.

Obviously, prayer belongs to Luke's theme of God's salvific will, for as Jesus' own example shows, he prays,
"Father, if you are willing, remove this cup from me; nevertheless, not my will, but yours be done" (Lk 22:42). Luke
depicts Jesus and the disciples as praying before important
events. Jesus (Lk 3:21; 6:12; 9:18,28-29; 11:1; 22:40-46), the
Apostles (Acts 1:24; 6:6), the Christians (Acts 4:31; 12:5,12),
Cornelius (Acts 10:4,30-31), Peter (Acts 8:15; 9:40; 10:9;
11:5), the prophets and teachers at Antioch (Acts 13:3), and
Paul (Acts 9:11; 14:23; 16:13,16,25; 20:36; 21:5; 22:17; 28:8)
all pray before important events. Jesus prays in desert places
(Lk 5:16; cf. 22:44-45); he prays that Peter's faith does not
fail (Lk 22:32). The Apostles cling to prayer (Acts 1:14); they
want to dedicate themselves to prayer (Acts 6:4). Peter and
John go up to the temple at the hour of prayer (Acts 3:1).

Stephen prays at the moment of death (Acts 7:59-60). Simon Magus asks Peter to pray to the Lord on his behalf, after Peter told him to pray that his sins might be forgiven (Acts 8:22,24). The early Christians cling to prayer (Acts 2:42), and Luke described Cornelius as a man of prayer.

Another Lucan theme which relates to God's salvific will and which both Jesus and his disciples perform is "signs and wonders." Certainly, Jesus' miracles look to the faith of his audiences, but they also actualize God's power to overcome evil in this world. Jesus (Acts 2:22), the Apostles (Peter: Acts 2:43; 5:12), the early Christians (Acts 4:30), Stephen (Acts 6:8), Philip (Acts 8:13), and Paul and Barnabas (Acts 14:3; 15:12) perform signs and wonders. Moreover, Jesus and his disciples perform the same kind of miracles. Jesus (Lk 7:22), Peter and John (Acts 3:2), Philip (Acts 8:7), and Paul (Acts 14:8-10) heal the lame. The paralyzed are cured by Jesus (Lk 5:18,24), Philip (Acts 8:7) and Peter (Acts 9:33). Jesus (Lk 7:11-17; cf. 7:22), Peter (Acts 9:36-43), and Paul (Acts 20:7-12) each bring someone back to life.

Above it was noted that the risen Christ was recognized in the breaking of bread and thus was present to the Christian community. Jesus himself breaks bread during the Institution Narrative (Lk 22:19) and at Emmaus (Lk 24:30-31,35). The early Christians devoted themselves to the breaking of bread (Acts 2:42); at Troas the Christians gather to break bread (Acts 20:7) with Paul as the celebrant (Acts 20:11). It may well be that Luke intends us to interpret in the same way Acts 27:33-38, where Paul breaks bread on shipboard. The context is one of nourishment, of encouragement, and of safety.

D. Same Places

Luke associates Jesus and his followers with Jerusalem, the temple and synagogues. Jesus has to go up to Jerusalem, and the Apostles are not to leave Jerusalem but to await there the promise of the Father (cf. Acts 1:4). The relationship of Jesus and his followers to Jerusalem can be presented under the headings of worship, activity, suffering and death. Jerusalem was a place of worship. Jesus at twelve years old (Lk 2:41-43), and the Ethiopian eunuch (Acts 8:26-27) go up to Jerusalem to worship. Paul wants to be in Jerusalem for the day of Pentecost (Acts 20:16). On an earlier return to Jerusalem Paul prays in the temple and falls into a trance (Acts 22:17). In this trance the Lord sends him to the Gentiles. In his defense before Felix Paul asserts that he came up to Jerusalem to worship (Acts 24:11).

Jesus and his disciples are active in Jerusalem. Before and during his passion (Acts 10:39) and after his resurrection, Jesus appears in Jerusalem. The early church lives in Jerusalem. Once, Luke includes Jerusalem in Paul's mission (Acts 26:20). Jesus must endure suffering, persecution and death in Jerusalem (Lk 9:31,51; 13:33-34; 18:31-34; Acts 13:27-28). There Peter and John are imprisoned (Acts 4:3) and persecution breaks out against the Christians (Acts 8:1). In Jerusalem, Paul persecuted (Acts 9:13), imprisoned, and voted for the execution of Christians (Acts 26:10). Yet, as Jesus, Paul has to go up to Jerusalem (Acts 19:21; 21:4,15,17) to suffer (Acts 20:22-23; 21:11,13,31; 23:11). Certain Jews plan to ambush and kill (Acts 23:12-15, 20-21,30) Paul there; and, when Paul was transferred to Caesarea, the chief priest and rulers urged Festus to return him to Jerusalem so that they can ambush him on the way (Acts 25:3; cf. vv 7,9,20,24). From Jerusalem Paul was delivered over as a prisoner into the hands of the Romans (Acts 28:17).

Jesus and his followers frequent the temple. Jesus' parents find him in the temple, and Jesus offers the excuse, "How is it that you sought me? Did you not know that I must be in my Father's house" (Lk 2:49)? Jesus teaches in the temple (Lk 19:47; 20:1; 21:37-38). He can say, "When I was with you day after day in the temple, you did not lay hands on me" (Lk 22:53). The early Christians are continually in the temple (Lk 24:53). On their way to the temple Peter and John heal the man lame from birth (Acts 3:1-7); he goes into the temple with them. The angel of the Lord instructs the Apostles to go to the temple and speak all the words of this life (Acts 5:20-21; cf. v 25). After their release from prison, every day in the temple they did not cease teaching and preaching Jesus as the Christ (Acts 5:42). In the temple, Paul sees the Lord (Acts 22:17-21); later, when in the temple he purifies himself and the four men under vow, some Jews drag him out (Acts 21:26-30; 24:6,12,18) and try to kill him (Acts 26:21). But Paul, like Jesus and Stephen, has done nothing against the temple (Acts 25:8).

Jesus teaches in the synagogues (Lk 4:15-16,20,28,33,38,44; 6:6; 13:10); the same proves true of Paul and companions: Acts 9:20; 13:5, 14, 43; 14:1; 17:1-2, 17; 18:4, 19; 19:8) and of Apollos (Acts 18:26). Christians reach out to the Jews, but they reject the message.

E. The Same Words Describe Jesus' and His Followers' Preaching and Message

Luke describes the preaching of both Jesus and his followers as "teaching (*didaskein*)", "preaching the good news (*euangelizesthai*)", "preaching (*kērussein*)", "proclaiming (*katangellein*)", and "speaking (*lalein*)." They preach about repentance and the kingdom of God and understand much of what they do from the Scriptures. Naturally, this preaching on the part of the disciples carries on the salvific activity of Jesus because his message can still be heard. Luke knew that Jesus, the proclaimer, had become the proclaimed. But, without the preaching of the disciples, the salvation that God brought through Jesus could not be heard. Or, as Luke preferred to phrase it, the risen Christ spoke through his disciples (Lk 21:15; cf. Lk 10:16; Acts 3:22-23; 26:23).

Luke summarizes his Gospel, "all that Jesus began to do and teach" (Acts 1:1; cf. Lk 23:5). Jesus teaches in the synagogues of the Jews (Lk 4:15,31-32; 6:6; 13:10) and the temple (Lk 19:47; 20:1,21; 21:37). He teaches from a boat (Lk 5:3), in the villages (Lk 5:17; 13:22), and in the streets (Lk 13:26). A disciple asks him to teach them to pray (Lk 11:1).

Peter and John teach the people (Acts 4:2; cf. v 18). The

apostles teach in the temple (Acts 5:21,25,42) and in Jerusalem (Acts 5:28); the Christians cling to their teaching (Acts 2:42). Apollos teaches (Acts 18:25); for a whole year Barnabas and Paul teach in Antioch (Acts 11:26; cf. 15:35). The proconsul in Cyprus believes and is astonished at their teaching (Acts 13:12). The Athenians want to know Paul's new teaching (Acts 17:19). In Corinth for a year and a half Paul teaches the word of God (Acts 18:11); he teaches the Ephesians in public and from house to house (Acts 20:20). At the very end of Acts, Paul still teaches quite openly and unhindered (Acts 28:30).

The Holy Spirit anoints Jesus to "preach the good news" (*euangelizesthai*: Lk 4:18; cf. Acts 10:34-38). Jesus must preach the good news of the kingdom to other cities (Lk 4:43; cf. 8:1). He does this in the temple, too (Lk 20:1). The Twelve (Lk 9:6), the apostles (Acts 5:42), Peter and John (Acts 8:25), the Christians scattered from Jerusalem (Acts 8:4; 11:20), and Philip (Acts 8:12,35,40) all preach the good news. Finally, Paul preaches the good news in Pisidian Antioch (Acts 13:32), Lystra (Acts 14:15), Derbe (Acts 14:21), the surrounding countryside (Acts 14:7), Antioch of Syria (Acts 15:35), Macedonia (Acts 16:10), and Athens (Acts 17:18).

The Spirit of the Lord sends Jesus to "preach" (*kērussein*) release to captives ... to "preach" the acceptable year of the Lord (Lk 4:18-19). Jesus preaches in the synagogues (Lk 4:44) and in cities and villages (Lk 8:1). Jesus sends the Twelve out to preach the kingdom of God (Lk 9:2; 24:47). Philip preaches the Christ to the Samaritans (Acts 8:5). Christ commands Peter and the other witnesses to preach to the people (Acts 10:42). At Damascus, in the synagogues, Paul preaches Jesus (Acts 9:20; cf. 19:13) and the kingdom among the Ephesians (Acts 20:25). Again at the very end of Acts (28:30-31), he preaches the kingdom of God quite openly and unhindered.

The risen Christ through Paul "proclaims" (*katangellein*) light (salvation) to the people and to the Gentiles (Acts 26:23). Peter and John proclaim in Jesus the resurrection from the dead (Acts 4:2); also, Paul and Barnabas proclaim the word of God (Acts 13:5,38; 15:36). Paul and his companions are described as men "who proclaim to you the way of salvation" (Acts 16:17). Furthermore, Paul proclaims in Thessalonica (Acts 17:3), in Beroea (Acts 17:13), and in Athens (Acts 17:18,23).

In Luke-Acts, *lalein* has the meaning of "to speak." Beginning with Lk 24 what is "spoken" is almost always something about Christ. So, "to speak" takes on the nuance of "to preach the Gospel." With this meaning of "to speak," Jesus (Lk 24:6-7,32,44), Peter and John (Acts 4:1,17,20; 8:25), Christians (Acts 4:29,31; 11:19-20), the apostles (Acts 5:20,40), Stephen (Acts 6:9-11), Peter (Acts 10:44; 11:14-15), and Apollos (Acts 18:25) appear as subjects. To be sure, it comes as no surprise that Paul is most frequently the subject of "to speak" when it has the above meaning.

F. What Jesus and His Followers Preach

Jesus and his followers preach about the same things. Jesus has not come to call the righteous, but sinners to repentance (Lk 5:32; cf. 10:13; 11:32; 13:3,5). Two of Jesus' parables speak of the joy over one sinner who repents (Lk 15:7,10 cf. vv 22-24,32). Jesus gives repentance and forgiveness of sins (Acts 5:31; cf. Lk 24:47). Peter tells the people to repent for the forgiveness of their sins (Acts 2:38; 3:19; cf. 8:22). According to Paul in Athens, God now commands all men everywhere to repent (Acts 17:30). Paul declares to the Jews and Gentiles "that they should repent and turn to God and perform deeds worthy of their repentance" (Acts 26:20).

Jesus and his followers preach about the kingdom of God. Jesus was sent to preach the good news of "the kingdom of God." Jesus sends the Twelve (Lk 9:2) and the Seventy (Lk 10:9, cf. v 11) to preach the kingdom of God. The would-be follower of Jesus should leave the dead to bury the dead; he is to proclaim the kingdom of God (Lk 9:60). In Samaria Philip preached the good news about the kingdom of God (Acts 8:12). Paul speaks of the kingdom of God in Lystra, Iconium, and Antioch (Acts 14:22), in

Corinth (Acts 19:8), and in Ephesus (Acts 20:25). When Acts ends, Paul is still preaching the kingdom of God (Acts 28:23,31).

Finally, Jesus and his followers understand much of what they do in terms of the Old Testament scriptures. At his temptation (Lk 4:4-13), in the synagogue at Nazareth (Lk 4:16-30; Isa 58:6; 61:1-2), in speaking of John (Lk 7:27; cf. Mal 3:1; Exod 23:20), Jesus appeals to the Old Testament. Jesus explains the Jews' unbelief (Lk 8:10; Isa 6:9-10), inheriting eternal life (Lk 18:20; cf. Exod 20:13-16; Deut 5:17-20) and his cleansing of the temple (Lk 19:47; cf. Isa 56:7; Jer 7:11) in Old Testament terms. Jesus uses Ps 117:22 in the parable of the vineyard (Lk 20:17); his defense of the resurrection of the dead rests on Exod 3:6,15,16 (Lk 20:37-38). Ps 109 shows that the Messiah is superior to David (Lk 20:42-44); when Dan 7:13 comes true, our redemption will be near (Lk 21:27). During his passion Jesus continues to quote Scripture. He is reckoned with transgressors (Lk 22:37; Isa 53:12), and he answers the high priests and scribes in the words of Dan 7:13; Ps 109:1 (Lk 22:69). His response to the women of Jerusalem takes the form of Hos 10:8 (Lk 23:30). At his death, Jesus cries out to his Father with words taken from Ps 30:6 (Lk 23:46).

Peter maintains that Judas must be replaced because of Pss 68:26 and 108:8 (Acts 1:20) and that Pentecost fulfills Joel 3:1-5 LXX (Acts 2:17-21). At Pentecost, Peter supports Christ's resurrection with Pss 15:8-11; 13:11; 2 Sam 7:12-13 (Acts 2:25-28,30-31) and his exaltation with Ps 109:1 (Acts 2:34-35). Peter speaks of "the God of Abraham and of Isaac and of Jacob, the God of our fathers (Acts 3:13; cf. Lk 20:37; Exod 3:6,15)." By combining Old Testament texts (Deut 18:15-16,19; Lev 23:29; cf. Acts 3:22-23) Peter redefines who belongs to the people. He ends this speech with a reference to God's promise to Abraham (Gen 22:18; 26:4; cf. Acts 3:25).

Ps 2:1-2 (Acts 4:25-26) forms part of the prayer of the Christians when Peter and John are released from prison. Stephen weaves numerous Old Testament quotes into his speech before the Sanhedrin. Beginning with Isa 53:7-8

LXX (Acts 8:32-33), Philip tells the Ethiopian eunuch the good news about Jesus. At the Council of Jerusalem, James claims that the words of the prophets (Acts 15:13-17; cf. Amos 9:11-12) agree with Peter's assertion that God has begun to take from among the Gentiles a people for his name.

At Pisidian Antioch, Paul supports the claim of Jesus' resurrection through Ps 2:7; Isa 55:3 LXX; Ps 15:10 LXX (Acts 13:32-25); this speech ends with a warning to unbelievers (Acts 13:41; cf. Hab 1:5). Because of Jewish rejection, the Lord commands Paul and Barnabas to go to the Gentiles (Acts 13:46-48; cf. Isa 49:6). In Jerusalem, Paul agrees that it is wrong to speak evil of the high priest (Acts 23:4-5; cf. Exod 12:28). Finally, at the end of Acts, Paul says the Holy Spirit correctly describes the Jewish rejection of the word (Acts 28:24-28; cf. Isa 6:9-10).

G. Luke Provides the Same Description of Jesus and His Followers

Another way in which Luke shows that Jesus' disciples continue his salvific activity is by describing Jesus and his followers in the same way. Jesus and certain of his followers are full of the Spirit and wisdom, possessed of power (*dynamis*), favor or grace (*charis*), joy (*chara*). Above, it was seen how Jesus and his followers "must" (*dei*) do certain things beause of God's salvific will. People fall at the feet of Jesus and of his disciples, and awe (*phobos*) falls on those who come in contact with them. They are prophets. Luke associates Jesus and his followers with centurions. Finally, Jesus' passion constitutes a model for the suffering and ill-treatment that the Christians endure.

Luke predicates "full of the Holy Spirit" of Jesus (Lk 4:1, cf. vv 18-19), the Seven (Acts 6:3), Stephen (Acts 6:5; 7:55), Barnabas (Acts 11:24), and the disciples (Acts 13:52). As regards wisdom, the child Jesus was "filled with wisdom" (Luke 2:40, cf. v 52). The Seven are picked because they are full of wisdom (Acts 6:3). Stephen's opponents could not resist his wisdom (Acts 6:10). Joseph (Acts 7:10) and Moses (Acts 7:22) constitute the prototypes of the wisdom of Jesus.

"Power" characterizes Jesus in Galilee (Lk 4:14; cf. Acts 10:38) in his command over unclean spirits (Lk 4:36), in his healing of the crowds (Lk 6:19; 8:46; 10:13?; 19:37?). The Son of Man will come with power (Lk 21:27; cf. 22:69). The power of Jesus continues after his resurrection (Acts 3:12; 4:7). Jesus gives the Twelve power and authority over all demons and to cure diseases (Lk 9:1). Power characterizes the apostles (Acts 1:8; 4:33; cf. 24:49) and Stephen (Acts 6:8).

The "favor" or "grace" of God was with the child Jesus; in the synagogue at Nazareth, the people wonder at Jesus' "gracious words." Probably, Joseph (Acts 7:10) and David (Acts 7:46) prefigure Jesus' favor. Christians live by grace (Acts 4:33; 11:23; 13:43; 15:11; 18:27; cf. 2:47). Paul testifies among the Ephesians to the Gospel of the grace of God (Acts 20:24: cf. v 32; 14:3). The grace of the Lord accompanies the activities of Stephen (Acts 6:8), Paul and Barnabas (Acts 14:3,26), and Paul and Silas (Acts 15:40-41).

Jesus, his message, and activity bring "joy" to the recipient. The angels tell the shepherds about the good news of a great joy (Lk 2:10-11). The resurrected Christ brings joy to the Eleven (Lk 24:41,52). Jesus' disciples, their message, and activity also bring joy. The Seventy return from their mission with joy (Lk 10:17). Christian mission activity brings joy to a Samaritan village (Acts 8:8; cf. Lk 8:13), to the disciples at Pisidian Antioch (Acts 13:52), and to Phoenicia and Samaria (Acts 15:3). Finally, Rhoda recognizes Peter's voice with joy (Acts 12:14).

Luke's use of "to rejoice" (*chairein*) parallels that of "joy." At Jesus' conception, Mary is told to rejoice (Lk 1:28). The disciples and the Seventy are to rejoice because they will be in heaven (Lk 6:23; 10:20). The Lucan parables about lost objects all have the theme of rejoicing (Lk 15:5,9,32). The cure of the woman bent with infirmity brings rejoicing (Lk 13:17). Zacchaeus (Lk 19:6) and the disciples in Jerusalem (Lk 19:37) receive Jesus with rejoicing. When the apostles suffer for the name, they rejoice (Acts 5:41). The reception of the word brings rejoicing to the Ethiopian eunuch (Acts 8:39), to Barnabas at Antioch of Syria (Acts 11:23), and the Gentiles in Antioch of Pisidia (Acts 13:48). Even the letter of directives from the apostles and elders with the whole church at Jerusalem causes rejoicing in Antioch of Syria (Acts 15:31).

Luke uses the phrase, "at his feet" in reference to Jesus (Lk 7:38; 8:35,41; 10:39; 17:16), to the apostles (Acts 4:35,37; 5:2), and to Peter (Acts 5:10; 10:25). Apparently, this phrase points to the authority of the one so approached (cf. Acts 22:3).

Actions of Jesus and his followers bring "awe" upon their audiences. Miracles of Jesus create awe among his audiences (Lk 5:26; 7:16; 8:37); the same holds true of the miracles of Peter and the apostles (Acts 5:5,11). On the other hand, when the sons of Sceva abuse the proper use of Jesus' name, they are attacked by the possessed man and wounded, and awe falls on everyone (Acts 19:17). In fact, awe comes upon everyone who meets the early Christians (Acts 2:43; cf. 9:31).

Recent research has focused on both Jesus and his followers as prophets. According to Luke, Jesus identifies himself as a prophet. In the synagogue at Nazareth Jesus retorts, "Truly, I say to you no prophet is acceptable in his own country (Lk 4:24-27)." Later Jesus says of himself, "for it cannot be that a prophet should perish away from Jerusalem (Lk 13:33-34)."

The people accepted Jesus as a prophet. After the raising of the son of the widow of Nain, the people proclaim, "A great prophet has arisen among us (Lk 7:6; cf. 9:7,9,19)." A Pharisee doubts that Jesus could be a prophet because he allows a sinful woman to touch him (Lk 7:39). On the road to Emmaus the disciples assert that Jesus was "a prophet mighty in deed and word before God and all the people (Lk 24:19)." In Acts 3:22-23, Peter identifies Jesus as the prophet like Moses.

Speaking about the persecution of Christians, Jesus refers to the Wisdom of God, "I will send them prophets and apostles, some of whom they will kill and persecute (Lk

11:49)." At Pentecost, Peter maintains Joel's prophecy is fulfilled: "... I will pour out my Spirit upon all flesh, and your sons and daughters will prophesy ... I will pour out my Spirit; and they shall, prophesy (Acts 2:17-18; cf. 19:6)." Prophets exist in the early church, for prophets come down from Jerusalem to Antioch (Acts 11:27); and there are prophets in the church at Antioch (Acts 13:1). Judas and Silas, themselves prophets, exhort the brethren with many words and strengthen them (Acts 15:32). Agabus, a prophet, comes down from Caesarea (Acts 21:10) and predicts Paul's suffering in Jerusalem.

Peter is a prophet; at least, he speaks in the person of Jesus the prophet (Acts 3:22-23) to whom the Jews must listen to belong to the people. Philip, too, may be a prophet. Like the prophets, Philip receives directions from God, moves around, and is carried off (cf. 1 Kgs 18:12). Acts 8:25-40 parallels the Emmaus event in Luke 24:13-35 where Jesus is called a prophet. Also, Philip has four unmarried daughters who prophesy (Acts 21:9). Elsewhere, Luke views Paul as a prophet too. At any rate, in Acts 26:16-18, Paul seems to have the same task as Ezekiel (2:1), Jeremiah (1:7), and Isaiah (35:5; 42:7; 61:1 LXX). In Acts 26:22, Paul maintains that he says nothing but what the prophets and Moses said would come to pass. Shortly thereafter, Paul asks Agrippa II whether he believes in the prophets (Acts 26:27), but Agrippa II has heard only Paul.

"Centurion" (Mt 4xs; Lk 3xs; Acts 13xs; NT 20xs) is mostly a Lucan Word. Luke associates Jesus (Lk 7:6-7; 23:47), Peter (Acts 10-11:18) and Paul (Acts 21:32; 22:25-26; 23:17,23-24; 24:23; 27:1-44) in a favorable context with centurions.

H. Jesus' Passion (Ill-Treatment) Constitutes a Model for the Suffering, Persecution, and Ill-treatment which the Christians Endure

As Jesus and his followers go about proclaiming and actualizing God's salvation, they experience the same ill-treatment. The same opponents appear against them; the opponents "come upon" (*ephistēmi*) them. They are "handed over" (*paradidōmi*), have "hands laid on," are "led" before the Sanhedrin and elsewhere, are beaten (*derein*) and thrown out (*ekballein*). They could be freed (*apoluein*), but are frequently "killed" (*anairein, apokteinein*). Yet all of them are innocent.

Jesus and his followers have the same opponents: high priests, Sadducees, rulers, elders, and the scribes. Jesus predicts that the Son of Man must be rejected by the elders, chief priests, and scribes, and be killed, and on the third day be raised (Lk 9:22); later in the Gospel this prediction finds realization (Lk 19:47; 20:1,19; 22:2,4,52,54,66; 23:4-5,10,13; 24:20). The Christians have the same opponents: the high priest (Acts 7:1; 9:1,14,21; 22:5; 23:2-5; 26:10,12), the high priest and elders (Acts 4:23; 23:14; 24:1; 25:2,15), high priest and council (Acts 22:30), high priest and Sadducees (Acts 5:17), the elders and the scribes (Acts 6:12-13), and the rulers, elders, scribes, and the whole high priestly family (Acts 4:5-7; cf. v 1).

Sometimes, "come upon" or "stand by" portrays the conduct of these opponents. It portrays what they do to Jesus (Lk 20:1-2), Peter and John (Acts 4:1), Stephen (Acts 6:12) and Jason (Acts 17:5). Paul "stands by" and approves the death of Stephen (Acts 22:20).

Jesus and his followers are "handed over" as was the Suffering Servant (Isa 53:6,12 LXX). Jesus predicts that he will be handed over (Lk 9:44; 18:32; 24:7). The scribes and the chief priests watch him so as to hand him over (Lk 20:20; cf. 24:20; Acts 3:13); Judas confers as to how he might hand Jesus over (Lk 22:4,6; cf. vv 21-22) and actually hands him over with a kiss (Lk 22:48). Pilate hands Jesus over to his Jewish opponents (Lk 23:25).

Jesus also predicts that Christians will be handed over to synagogues and prisons (Lk 21:12; cf. v 16). Paul hands men and women over to prison (Acts 8:3; 22:4). Herod Agrippa hands Peter over to four squads of soldiers to guard him (Acts 12:4). Agabus prophesies that the Jews will hand Paul over into the hands of the Gentiles (Acts 21:11). In fact, Paul is handed over to the centurion Julius (Acts 27:1) and subsequently into the hands of the Romans (Acts 28:17).

Luke makes both Jesus and his followers objects of "to lay hands on." The scribes and the chief priests try to lay hands on Jesus (Lk 20:19). Again, Jesus predicts that opponents will lay hands on the Christians (Lk 21:12). And hands are laid on Christians (Acts 12:1), Peter and John (Acts 4:3), the apostles (Acts 5:18), and Paul (Acts 21:27).

Like the Suffering Servant, both Jesus and the Christians are "led" (*agein*: Lk 13xs; Acts 26xs; NT 66xs; and its cognates). The people of Nazareth (Lk 4:29), the crowd (Lk 22:54), and the whole company (Lk 23:1) lead Jesus to some official or to suffering. Philip explains that "As a lamb led to the slaughter (Acts 8:32; cf. Isa 53:7-8 LXX)" refers to Jesus. The chief priests and scribes (Lk 22:66) and the Jews (Lk 23:26) lead Jesus away. The apostles (Acts 5:21, cf. vv26-27) and Stephen (Acts 6:12) are led while Peter will be led (Acts 12:4). Before his conversion, Paul wants to lead Christians bound to Jerusalem (Acts 9:2,21; 22:5); the Ephesians lead the innocent Gaius and Aristarchus into the theater (Acts 19:37; cf. v 29).

Paul fulfills Jesus' predictions that Christians will be led before kings and governors (Lk 21:12). The Jews (Acts 18:12), the tribune (Acts 21:34; 23:10) and the soldiers (23:31) lead Paul. As predicted, Festus has Paul led before him (Acts 25:6,17) and later before Festus and King Agrippa II (Acts 25:23-27).

Jesus and a number of his followers have a hearing before the "Sanhedrin" (Lk 1x; Acts 14xs; NT 22xs). The chief priests and scribes lead Jesus before the Sanhedrin (Lk 22:66-71). Peter and John (Acts 4:5-22), the apostles, (Acts 5:21-41), Stephen (Acts 6:12-15), and Paul (Acts 22:30-23:10; cf. 23:28; 24:20) all appear before the Sanhedrin.

Jesus (Lk 22:63) and his followers (Acts 5:40; 16:37; 22:19) are "beaten." They are "put out." The people of Nazareth put Jesus out of the city (Lk 4:29), and the tenants put the son out of the vineyard (Lk 20:15). The following Christians are put out of a city or region: Stephen (Acts 7:58), Paul and Barnabas (Acts 13:50) and Paul (Acts

16:37). Yet officials "free" or want to "set at liberty" Jesus and his followers. Pilate wants to free Jesus (Lk 23:16,17?,20,22; Acts 3:13). Peter and John (Acts 4:21,23), the apostles (Acts 5:40), Paul and Silas (Acts 16:35-36), and Jason (Acts 17:9) are all freed. Agrippa II declares that Paul could be freed had he not appealed to Caesar (Acts 26:32); the Romans want to free Paul (Acts 28:17-18).

Luke employs *anairein* (Lk 2xs; Acts 19xs; NT 24xs) "to do away with," more than he does *apokteinein* "to kill." The subjects of "to do away with" include the high priests and scribes, Israelites, inhabitants of Judea and Jerusalem, Jews, Hellenists, the Sanhedrin, Herod, and Paul; in short, the opponents of the Christians. The objects of "to do away with" are Jesus (Lk 22:2; Acts 2:23; 10:39; 13:28; cf. Lk 23:32) the apostles (Acts 5:33), Paul (Acts 9:23,24,29; 23:15,21,27; 25:3), James, the brother of John (Acts 12:2), Stephen (Acts 22:20), and the Christians (Acts 26:10).

Similar to the above is Luke's use of *apokteinein* "to kill." Opponents want to kill Jesus (Lk 9:22; 13:31,34; 18:33; 20:14-15; Acts 3:15) and Paul (Acts 21:31; 23:12,14; 27:42?). Jesus instructs his followers not to fear those who can only kill the body (Lk 12:4-5).

Finally, for Luke, innocence characterizes Jesus and his followers. Nowhere in Luke-Acts is Jesus or any of his followers found guilty of any civil crime. Pilate (Lk 23:4,14-15; 22; cf. Acts 3:13-14), the good thief (Lk 23:41), and the centurion (Lk 23:47; the multitude: 23:48?) pronounce Jesus innocent. Paul summarizes it at Pisidian Antioch, "Though they could charge him with nothing deserving death, yet they asked Pilate to have him killed (Acts 13:28)." The Sanhedrin can find no reason for punishing Peter and John (Acts 4:21) and are advised by Gamaliel to let the apostles alone (Acts 5:38-39). Stephen's opponents resort to false witnesses (Acts 6:10-14). Gallio (Acts 18:14-15) and Claudius Lysias (Acts 23:29) regard the charges against Paul as purely religious. Some Pharisees (Acts 23:9), Festus (Acts 25:18-19,25; 26:31), and Agrippa II (Acts 26:31-32) affirm Paul's innocence. According to Paul's statement at the end of Acts, the Romans wanted to free him because they found no reason for the death penalty (Acts 28:18); and the Jews say that they have heard no evil about him.

Earlier, the comment was made that Jesus and his disciples proclaim and actualize God's salvation in the midst of their persecution. A brief reflection on this assertion is in place. Persecution is the result of the failure to accept the Gospel message. This refusal of God's salvific will, of his divine condescension, lies at the origin of that intolerance which becomes persecution. Further, the disciples, the church, aggravate their position by reaffirming their proclamation. But persecution becomes an integral and necessary moment in the church's history. Persecution fails to achieve its objectives but rather causes the church to grow, thus constituting a positive element and a decisive factor in the spread of the word. Paradoxically, persecution itself serves to spread the news of God's saving will.

This section has considered the parallels between Luke's description of Jesus and those of his disciples. Luke with these parallels illustrates that Jesus through his disciples continues his actions and teachings. The disciples have his qualities and, as he, must do certain things because of the Father's salvific will. They have the same effect on their audiences and like him are associated with centurions. Their ill-treatment paradoxically becomes an integral moment in their Christian living and helps to bring the news of salvation to yet more people.

I. The Word and Other Designations of the Salvation that Jesus' Disciples Continue to Proclaim

If Jesus continues to preach through his disciples, their words, as his, make salvation available to their audiences. Any consideration of "word" in Luke-Acts has to depend on the words of Jesus and of his disciples, for it is only through their words and preaching that the various audiences accept or reject God's salvific will. Moreover, "word" is not the only expression that Luke has for the salvation that Christ brings to Israel. Luke rarely uses "gospel," but he has a number of abbreviations for the message of salvation: "Christ" or "Christ Jesus," "Jesus," and the kingdom. Closely connected with all of these expressions for salvation are the basic senses which for Luke are the natural way of coming into contact with the salvation that God brought in Christ: hearing and seeing. Correct hearing and seeing will result in faith which may express itself in repentance or the reception of baptism.

The meaning of the Hebrew *dābār* helps us to understand Luke's use of "word." This Hebrew word can mean "word," but it can also mean "deed." It was especially appropriate as regards God's word because his word automatically becomes a deed. What God says is concomitantly a reality. Luke, in part depending on this Hebrew tradition, uses two Greek words (*rhēma* and *logos*) for "word." Before proposing a study of each of these, it will be well to establish the general context which Luke gives to "word." Luke writes of the first Christians who delivered the Christian message to him (and to his readers) as "eyewitnesses and ministers of the word" (Lk 1:2). Two verses later, Luke gives us his clearest statement of his purpose in writing Luke-Acts: "that you may know the certainty of the words (deeds) you were taught" (Lk 1:4). Luke at the beginning of Acts persists in calling the gospel, "the word," for, although most translators with good reason translate Acts 1:1, "In the First Book, O Theophilus, I have dealt with all that Jesus began to do and teach," the fact is that Luke in this verse uses "word" (*logos*) for "book." Luke does not in this verse resort to a totally different meaning of *logos*. On the contrary, he relates this verse to the considerable development that he has of the "word" for Jesus' message. Luke in the same vein refers to the whole of his gospel as the "first word."

In the consideration of the activity of the risen Jesus, Lk 4:16-30 was cited as an example where Jesus preached of himself and salvation. Some further observations on these verses should be made here. Few Lucan scholars deny that Lk 4:16-30 are programmatic for the whole of Jesus' life. Jesus in fulfillment of scriptures preaches to his fellow Jews.

At first their response seems positive, but ultimately they reject him. Jesus summarizes the situation as follows: "Truly, I say to you no prophet is acceptable in his own country." So, like Elijah and Elisha, Jesus will have to go to the Gentiles. The Jews, when they hear this, try to kill him. What should not be missed here is that in this programmatic narrative Jesus is described as speaking "gracious words" (Lk 4:22). The description of what his "gracious words" promise includes preaching the gospel to the poor, proclaiming release to the captives and recovery of sight to the blind, liberty to the oppressed, and the acceptable year of the Lord. In brief, Jesus' "gracious words" were salvation.

Mary, Jesus' mother, provides the example of how one should respond to the word of God, of Jesus, or of his disciples. She simply says, "Behold I am the handmaid of the Lord; let it be done to me according to your word" (Lk 1:38). She also keeps all these things (words) in her heart (Lk 2:51; cf. 2:9).

Once this background of "word" has been established, a detailed consideration of "word" in Luke-Acts can be more easily understood. One Greek word that Luke employs for "word" is *rhēma*. Luke in his Gospel normally uses *rhēma* in the singular. It indicates some word or action of God or Jesus; the plural is a number of such actions. Only in Lk 24:8,11 do we begin to find the use of *rhēma* which typifies Acts although these two uses should not be rigidly distinguished. In Acts *rhēma* is regularly plural and means the early preaching or a summary of the salvific events which God performed through Jesus; this is also true of the singular in Acts 10:37. The singular in Acts 11:16 indicates a saying of Jesus while that in Acts 28:25 is the "one word" of Paul which includes the quote from Isa 6:9-10.

More to the point presently being made, Luke in many of these passages clearly relates *rhēma* to salvation. The *rhēma* spoken of in Lk 1:37-38 is Mary's miraculous conception of Jesus who will be called holy, the Son of God. The *rhēma* which the shepherds go to see (Lk 2:15,17) is, according to the context, "for to you is born this day in the city of David a Savior who is Christ the Lord" (Lk 2:11). The "word" promised to Simeon was that he would not die until he had seen the salvation God has prepared in the presence of all the people (Lk 2:29-30). The earlier consideration of "it is necessary" indicated that the "word" which Jesus' parents failed to understand, "Did you not know that I must be in my Father's house" (Lk 2:48-50) belongs to the theme of God's salvific will. The same is true of the "word" that the disciples did not understand, namely, "The Son of Man must be delivered into the hands of men" (Lk 9:44-45; cf. 18:34; 24:8). The "words" of Peter (Acts 2:14; cf. 11:16) are that the Pentecost event fulfills Joel 3:1-5 LXX. When the people at the end of the speech ask what they should do, Peter tells them, "Repent, and be baptized every one of you in the name of Jesus Christ for the forgiveness of your sins; and you will receive the gift of the Holy Spirit" (Acts 2:38). When the angel of the Lord frees the apostles from prison, he instructs them, "Go and stand in the temple and speak to the people all the words of this life" (Acts 5:20). "Life," of course, is an alternate expression for salvation. The apostles and the Holy Spirit are witnesses to the *rhēmata*:

> "The God of our fathers raised Jesus whom you killed by hanging him on a tree. God exalted him at his right hand as leader and Savior, to give repentance to Israel and forgiveness of sins" (Acts 5:30-31).

The "word" (Acts 10:37; cf. 10:44) attested by Peter in his speech (Acts 10:34-43) in Cornelius' house actually endorses the main contents of this speech. The following topics in this speech are all various ways of speaking of salvation:

> "... good news of peace through Jesus Christ ... how he (Jesus) went about doing good and healing all that were oppressed by the devil, for God was with him ... he is the one ordained by God to be judge of the living and the dead ... everyone who believes in him receives forgiveness of sins through his name."

Cornelius was told to send to Joppa for Peter who will declare "words" to him by which he and his household will be saved (Acts 11:14). The "words" of Acts 13:42 have to refer to Paul's speech in Acts 13:16b-41, yet above it was pointed out that salvation (Acts 13:23,26,38-39, cf. v 47) forms the main theme of this speech and its aftermath. Paul's answer to Festus in Acts 26:25, "I am speaking words of sober truth," also concerns salvation. The nearest referent and the statement which led to Festus' interruption of Paul is, "that the Christ must suffer, and that by being the first to rise from the dead, he would proclaim light to the people and to the Gentiles (Acts 26:23). "Light" in this passage means salvation, for Acts 26:18 reads:

> "to open their eyes, that they may turn from darkness to light and from the power of Satan to God, and that they may receive forgiveness of sins and a place among those who are sanctified by faith in me."

The parallel of Acts 26:23 to Simeon's *Nunc Dimittis* leaves no doubt that "light" in this verse means salvation. Finally, Paul's "one word" in Acts 28:25 surely refers to Isa 6:9-10, but this citation is immediately followed by the reason why Paul cited this passage, "Let it be known to you then that this salvation of God has been sent to the Gentiles; they will listen" (vv 26-28).

Luke also uses *logos* for "word"; *logos* appears in Luke's Gospel 33 times and 65 times in Acts, that is, a little less than a third of its appearances in the whole of the NT. Like *rhēma*, Luke uses *logos* in his Gospel for some word(s) or action(s) of Jesus or of the Father. In Acts, *logos* is generally in the singular and regularly signifies the gospel. But no ground exists for claiming any fine distinction between the singular and the plural. Finally, one can point to the fact that the proclaiming by Jesus of the gospel becomes the proclaimed Jesus in Acts. However, the more accurate interpretation in this case, as for all the words of proclamation, is once again to realize that the Christians for Luke are seen as the true Israel and that thus the proclamation by and about Jesus is part of the continuum of God's constant salvific relationship with his people. Luke sees no radical change in the nature of the proclamation of God's saving actions for Israel.

Luke usually takes for granted that the word(s) of God or Christ are salvific and that, when *logos* means the gospel, it is a message of salvation. But more than enough evidence exists to show that in Luke's mind "word" was interrelated with salvation. The "word" is a word of salvation (Acts 13:26); the word of God leads to eternal life (Acts 13:48; cf. 13:44,46). Jesus' word can heal (Lk 7:7). His word is one of grace (Lk 4:22; Acts 14:3), and the word of God's grace is able to build up the Christians and give them inheritance among all those who are sanctified (Acts 20:32). Or, as Peter phrases it, "But we believe that we shall be saved through the grace of the Lord Jesus, just as they will" (Acts 15:11; cf. v 7). When the risen Christ tells the disciples that these are the words that he spoke to them, he opens their minds to understand the scriptures. This understanding admits that repentance and forgiveness of sins should be preached in Christ's name to all nations (Lk 24:44-47). Those who receive Peter's word at Pentecost (Acts 2:41; cf. 2:22,40) were baptized, and there were added that day about three thousand souls. Peter's speech at Caesarea can also be designated a "word" (Acts 10:36,44); yet, the consideration of *rhēma* revealed that this speech contains a number of expressions of salvation. When the jailer at Philippi asks Paul and Silas what he must do to be saved, they answer him, "Believe in the Lord Jesus, and you will be saved, you and your household." Then they speak the "word of the Lord" to him and to all who were in his house (cf. Acts 16:30-32). When Paul preaches the word in Corinth (Acts 18:5-11), Jesus tells him in a vision of the night,

> "Do not be afraid, but speak and do not be silent, for I am with you, and no man shall attack you to harm you; for I have many people in this city."

The necessity of listening to Jesus allows Luke to write, "for whoever is ashamed of me and of my words, of him will the Son of Man be ashamed when he comes in his glory and the glory of the Father and of the holy angels" (Lk 9:26). Consequently, the "words" of Jesus must be heard (Lk 5:1; 10:39), and the response to God's word and that of the disciples is faith (Lk 1:20; Acts 4:4). The genuine Christian not only hears the word but does it (Lk 6:47; 8:11-15). He who does so is Jesus' closest relative (Lk 8:21), and blessed (Lk 11:28). Finally, since the word is ultimately God's word and therefore productive, the "word grows" (Acts 6:7; 12:24; 19:20) in the sense that God brings more and more people into Israel.

Luke only avails himself of the word, "gospel," twice (Acts 15:7; 20:24). The first of these instances further establishes that "word" is another expression for gospel: " ... Peter rose and said to them, 'Brethren, you know that in the early days God made choice among you that by my mouth the Gentiles should hear the word of the gospel and believe.'" The second, " ... if only I may accomplish my course and the ministry which I received from the Lord Jesus, to testify to the gospel of the grace of God," bears a striking resemblance to Acts 20:32, "And now I commend you to God and the word of his grace which is able to build you up, and to give you the inheritance among all those who are sanctified." Once again, "word" is the equivalent of "gospel," and this parallel leaves no doubt that Acts 20:24 is in a context of salvation. Moreover, as was shown above, Acts 15:7 is also in such a context (cf. Acts 15:11).

Luke also summarizes the gospel message as "Jesus" (e.g. Acts 9:20,22,27; 17:18; 18:25; 24:24), "Christ" (e.g. Acts 8:5), or "Jesus Christ" (Acts 8:12; 28:31). These summaries, too, naturally imply salvation, but in some cases this is more explicit. When the Jewish officials charge Peter and John not to speak or teach at all in the name of Jesus (Acts 4:18; 5:40,42), Peter had proclaimed, "And there is salvation in no one else, for there is no other name under heaven given among men by which we must be saved" (Acts 4:12). There is not a needy person in the Christian community, for great is the grace upon them while the apostles testify to the resurrection of the Lord Jesus (Acts 4:33-34). Later, Philip tells the eunuch the good news of Jesus, and, shortly thereafter, the eunuch is baptized (Acts 8:35-39). When men from Cyprus and Cyrene came to Antioch of Syria and spoke to the Greeks, preaching the Lord Jesus, the hand of the Lord was with them, and a great number believed and turned to the Lord (Acts 11:20-21). Finally, at the end of Acts, in Rome, Paul is preaching the kingdom of God and teaching about the Lord Jesus Christ (Acts 28:31; cf. v 23) to the Gentiles, for he has just proclaimed to the Jews, "Let it be known to you then that this salvation of God has been sent to the Gentiles; they will listen" (Acts 28:28).

Luke has someone assert that Jesus is the Christ four times (Acts 5:42; 17:3; 18:5,28). Two of these passages are obviously in a context of salvation. Paul in Thessalonica argued from the scriptures proving that it was necessary for the Christ to suffer and to rise from the dead, "This Jesus whom I proclaim to you, is the Christ" (Acts 17:3). The phrase, "it is necessary," leaves no doubt that this passage stands in a salvific context. In Corinth, Paul testifies to the Jews, "that the Christ was Jesus." (Acts 18:5). When they oppose and revile him, he goes to the Gentiles of the city. Afterward, the Lord one night says to Paul in a vision, "Fear not ...; for I am with you, and no one shall attack you to harm you; for I have many people in this city" (Acts 18:10). Finally, when Philip in a city of Samaria preaches the good news about the kingdom of God and the name of Jesus Christ, they were baptized, both men and women (Acts 8:12). So, whether Luke speaks of the gospel message as "Jesus," "(the) Christ," or "Jesus Christ," he views this message as offering salvation to those who hear it.

The same must be maintained for "kingdom (of God)" (Lk 4:43; 8:1; 9:60; 10:11; Acts 19:8) which is another abbreviated phrase for the gospel message. Most of the passages which relate "kingdom" to salvation have already been treated (e.g. Acts 8:12; 20:25; 28:23,31). But the following passages are worthy of note. The proclamation of the "kingdom" is connected to healing (Lk 9:2,6,11; 10:9), and after John the Baptist, the good news of the kingdom is preached, and everyone enters it violently (Lk 16:16).

Luke, then, through a number of abbreviations for the gospel message, "word," "gospel," "Jesus," "Christ," "Jesus

Christ," and "kingdom," lets his reader know that salvation continues to be present. Luke connects these abbreviations for the gospel message with salvation.

Luke addresses these parallels between Jesus and his followers to his readers. These parallels remind everyone that Christ continues to work through us, his disciples. All of Jesus' followers are able to continue his salvific activity. As Jesus went about doing good, preaching and endured rejection, yet was innocent, so should we.

PART II

LUKE'S DESCRIPTION OF HOW GOD MAKES SALVATION IN JESUS PRESENT TO THE PEOPLE OF ISRAEL

PART II

LUKE'S DESCRIPTION OF HOW GOD MAKES SALVATION IN JESUS' PRESENT TO THE PEOPLE OF ISRAEL

Up to this point, the main topic of this book has been how Luke has illustrated his main theological theme that God, who brought salvation to his people in the Old Testament, continues to do this in Christianity, especially through Jesus Christ. However, granted that Christ brings salvation to Israel, how does Luke specify this salvation? Salvation, according to Luke, is universal. Christ appears as the Savior of the weak, downtrodden, and despised, and the parousia is sketched as delayed. Christians live peacefully in a Roman world. Finally, Luke in his presentation of how salvation comes, attends more to the personal than do the other Synoptics.

CHAPTER 4

THE UNIVERSALITY OF SALVATION

No one denies that Luke in both his works sees salvation as universal, that is, as directed to both the Jews and the Gentiles. Nonetheless, no exhaustive effort has yet been made to show how this theme permeates both Luke's Gospel and the Acts of the Apostles. At first, it may seem strange to speak of this theme permeating both Lucan works when everyone knows that Luke does not see the actual beginning of the mission to the Gentiles until the Cornelius event (Acts 10:1-11:18). This fact cannot be denied, yet Luke apparently wanted to stamp God's salvation in Christ as universal even from the very beginning of his Gospel. Nonetheless, he does not violate the literary fiction that his readers do not know about the universality of Christianity until Acts 10. This section, consequently reviews the universal framework that Luke gives Luke-Acts and then considers all the evidence in Luke's Gospel and in Acts for the "universal" specification of salvation.

Almost everyone is familiar with what is called "the universal framework" of Luke-Acts. If one excepts the Infancy Narrative, which would not be unreasonable since it was very likely added last to Luke's Gospel, one finds the following passages at the beginning and end of both Luke and Acts:

> ". . . and all flesh shall see the salvation of God"(Lk 3:6).
> " . . . and that repentance and forgiveness of sins should be preached in his name to all nations, beginning from Jerusalem" (Lk 24:47). ". . . and you shall be my witnesses in Jerusalem and in all Judea and Samaria and to the end of the Earth" (Acts 1:8). "Let it be known to you then that this salvation of God has been sent to the Gentiles; they will listen" (Acts 28:28).

Luke, like any good writer, alerts his reader and then reminds him of a main concern he has in his writing.

Not only is the theme of universality found in the framework, but it is present throughout Luke-Acts. This is also true of the Infancy Narrative. When Mary responds to her cousin Elizabeth's designation of her as "mother of my Lord" and her blessing of Mary for her trust in the Lord, Mary's response, the *Magnificat*, contains the claim, "For behold, hence forth all generations will call me blessed"(Lk 1:48), and probably includes all Christians, Jew or Gentile. The same statement should very likely be made of Zechariah's comment in the *Benedictus*, " . . . to give light to those who sit in darkness and in the shadow of death, to guide our feet into the way of peace" (Lk 1:79); for, as was seen above, Israel in these passages embraces both Jews and Gentiles. Universality should also be seen in, "Glory to God in the highest, and on earth peace among all with whom he is pleased!" (Lk 2:14).

Even if someone is inclined to reject any universality in the above three verses, there is no way one can dissent from the universality in the *Nunc Dimittis*:

> " . . . for my eyes have seen your salvation which you have prepared in the presence of all peoples, a light for revelation to the Gentiles and for glory to your people Israel" (Lk 2:30-32).

Not only does Luke begin his Gospel with a universal statement (Lk 3:6), but he continues this idea, " . . . ; for I tell you, God is able from these stones to raise up children to Abraham" (Lk 3:8). It is common knowledge that Luke's genealogy, unlike Matthew's, does not start with Abraham but with Adam (or, if one prefers with God; cf. Lk 3:38). Doubtless, the emphasis is on "son of God" to reinforce the statement at Jesus baptism, "You are my beloved Son, with you I am well pleased" (Lk 3:22). The baptismal scene immediately precedes the genealogy. But the fact remains that Luke's genealogy, which traces Jesus' lineage back through Adam, is more universal than Matthew's.

Certainly, the programmatic Lk 4:16-30 has universal dimensions. The references to the Old Testament stories about the prophets Elijah and Elisha, prototypes of Jesus, who are sent to a widow in Sidon and cleanse the leper, Naaman the Syrian, are proper to Luke. These non-Jews stand for the universal mission of Jesus, a prophet not accepted in his own country. One is reminded of "The Sign of Jonah" story (Lk 11:29-32) in which once again non-Jews are portrayed as more receptive of Jesus than Jews. Perhaps, the mention of Tyre and Sidon, in " ... and a great multitude of people from all Judea and Jerusalem and the seacoast of Tyre and Sidon, who came to hear him and to be healed of their diseases" (Lk 6:17), betrays a universal audience. The passage does look beyond Israel. While Luke does take it over from Mark (3:8), he includes it, but Matthew leaves it out. Moreover the centurion of Capernaum is a non-Jew. Only Luke mentions the elders, who among other things say of the centurion, " ... for he loves our nation" (Lk 7:5). These words hardly imply that the centurion is a Jew. This impression is further supported by Jesus' amazement, "I tell you, not even in Israel have I found such faith" (Lk 7:9). Certainly, the exact nature of the faith of the centurion remains unclear, but a non-Jew responds positively to Jesus. Much the same should probably be said of the possessed man in the healing of the Gerasene demoniac (Lk 8:26-39), for the presence of a herd of swine suggests a Gentile district. However, the story provides no clear indications as to the Jewish or non-Jewish identity of the demoniac.

Only Luke tells us of Jesus' plan to enter a Samaritan village. Even though the Samaritan village refuses to receive him and his disciples, Jesus will not bid fire to come down from heaven to consume them. Rather, he and his disciples go to another village, which may or may not have been Samaritan (cf. Lk 9:51-56). This same openness to the Samaritans, who were hated by the Jews and surely not regarded as Jewish, can be seen in the parable of "The Good Samaritan" (Lk 10:25-37) proper to Luke. The activity of the hero in this story serves as the answer to the question, "And who is my neighbor?", which results from a feigned attempt to understand a Jewish point of law. So, a Samaritan reveals to Jews the true response to their law. Something similar occurs in another narrative proper to Luke, the cleansing of the ten lepers (Lk 17:11-19). All ten are cleansed, but only the Samaritan, "this foreigner," returns to give thanks. Jesus' words to him, "Rise and go your way ; your faith has made you well," leave no doubt that this non-Jew gave the proper response and thus was healed. These three narratives about Samaritans disclose to Luke's readers the universal aspect of Jesus' mission.

Two banquet scenes also speak of a universal mission. Luke (13:22-30), as Matthew (8:11-12) elsewhere, in the narrative about the narrow door writes of a banquet in the kingdom at which Abraham, Isaac, Jacob, and all the prophets are present, but Jesus' audience is thrust out. However, people from east and west, and from north and south will sit at table in the kingdom of God. Luke briefly concludes this narrative, "And behold some are last who will be first, and some are first who will be last." The scene leaves no doubt that non-Jews will enter the kingdom. The Parable of the Great Banquet (Lk 14:15-24) has the same import. Whether non-Jews are to be included in this banquet depends on how one interprets Lk 14:24, "For I tell you, none of those who were invited shall taste my banquet," a verse proper to Luke. "My" determines that Jesus is speaking of his heavenly banquet. At first, one gets the impression that Luke is thinking only about the oppressed Jewish society, because he speaks of bringing in, "the poor and maimed and blind and lame." But the next instruction proves to be more far-reaching, "Go out to the highways and hedges, and compel people to come in, that my house may be filled." Certainly, a very natural understanding is that those first invited to Jesus' heavenly banquet would be the Jews. As a result of their rejection of his invitation, Gentiles are now invited to the banquet.

The parable of the vineyard and the tenants (Lk 20:9-19) constitutes a parallel to the two banquet scenes. The vineyard stands for Israel (cf. Isa 5:1-7). The scribes and the chief priests perceive that Jesus tells this parable against them, and that is why they want to seize him. The son in the parable is Jesus whom they will kill; yet he will become "the head of the corner." God, the owner of the vineyard, will come and destroy those tenants, and give the vineyard to others. Since Luke views the Christians as Israel, the parable well fits his scheme. The vineyard is taken from the Jewish leaders and given to the Gentiles and Jews who listen to Jesus.

Only Luke in the destruction of Jerusalem foretold reports that the people will fall by the sword and be led captive among all nations and that Jerusalem will be trodden down by the Gentiles, "until the times of the Gentiles are fulfilled" (Lk 21:24). "The times of the Gentiles" cannot mean the capture of Jerusalem because according to the text that has already occurred. "Fulfill" points to God's will. The times of the Gentiles may well look to their being included among the Christians, for the Cornelius event leaves no doubt that this inclusion is God's will. "The times of the Gentiles" would then point to those significant moments when the early Christians realize that their message was to go to the Gentiles too. For example, when the Jews in Corinth oppose and revile Paul, he says to them, "Your blood be upon your heads! I am innocent. From now on I will go to the Gentiles" (Acts 18:6). Luke's Gospel closes on a universal note with the framework statement in Lk 24:47.

Luke opens Acts with another universal statement (Acts 1:8), and develops this universality in the Pentecost story. Of course, Luke preserves the integrity of the Cornelius event as the beginning of the Gentile mission. Yet Jews from every nation under heaven were dwelling in Jerusalem when the Pentecost events occurred and were part of the crowd that came together (Acts 2:5-6). Luke even lists the places from which these Jews came (Acts 2:9-11) so that his readers do not lose sight of the world-wide audience which hears Peter's speech. Peter explains to his audience that the Pentecost event fulfills what the prophet Joel said, and the quotation that Peter gives includes two obvious universal statements: "And in the last days it shall be, God declares, that I will pour out my Spirit upon all flesh ... whoever calls on the name of the Lord shall be saved"(Acts 2:17-21). This citation has other indications of universality. First, a comparatively exhaustive list of people is given: "... all flesh ... your sons and your daughters ... young men ... old men ... menservants ... maidservants;" and, secondly, the whole world is considered, "And I will show wonders in heaven above and signs on the earth beneath." Finally, after the speech Peter assures his audience, "For the promise is to you and to your children and to all that are far off, everyone whom the Lord our God calls to him" (Acts 2:39). Thus, Luke has introduced into the Pentecost story his theme of universality and furnishes his readers with a preview of coming events.

Luke, in Peter's next speech in Acts, has also included some indications of universality. Jesus is called the "author of life." Since this title appears in the phrase, " ... and (you) killed the author of life, whom God raised from the dead" (Acts 3:15; cf. 5:20), "life" looks to the opposite of death, and the title would no longer make sense if Jesus were dead. Thus, "author of life" looks to the resurrection, and not only of the Jews but of everyone. As Luke states it elsewhere, the leaders of the Jews were "annoyed because they (Peter and John) were teaching the people and proclaiming in Jesus the resurrection from the dead" (Acts 4:2). Somehow, Jesus leads humankind to the resurrection. Later, in the same speech, Peter says of Jesus:

> "Moses said, 'The Lord God will raise up for you a prophet from your brethren as he raised me up. You shall

> listen to him in whatever he tells you. And it shall be that
> every soul that does not listen to that prophet shall be
> destroyed from the people.'" (Acts 3:22-23).

As was noted above, this passage redefines Israel. This
definition of Israel, opens membership to anyone who
listens to Jesus. One need no longer be a Jew to belong to the
people. This same openness stands in the statement, "You
are the sons of the prophets and of the covenant which God
gave to your fathers, saying to Abraham, 'And in your
posterity shall all the families of the earth be blessed'" (Acts
3:25). If one understands "first" adverbially, the next verse
explains that the Jews were first, "God, having raised up his
servant, sent him to you first, to bless you in turning everyone of you from your wickedness." The implication follows that the Gentiles would be second. Certainly, "all the
families of the earth" would include the Gentiles, too. Acts
4:12 reads "And there is salvation in no one else, for there is
no other name under heaven given among humankind by
which we must be saved." Jesus is the savior of everyone, not
just the Jews.

Philip proclaims the message to a city of Samaria, and
Samaritans certainly were not regarded as true Jews. These
Samaritans were baptized, and, when Peter and John came
down and laid hands on them, they received the Holy Spirit
(cf. Acts 8:14-24). Nor is there any reason to suspect that the
Ethiopian eunuch was a Jew (cf. (Acts 8:25-40). Eunuchs,
unless the term merely describes one's office, were not to
enter the assembly of the Lord (Deut 23:1). Luke cannot
destroy the harmony of his presentation by having a Gentile
converted prior to Cornelius' conversion, but he did want to
include the beautiful story about the Ethiopian eunuch. To
do this, Luke avoids any clear statement of the religious
stance of the eunuch. Luke through this very lack of clarity
reflects the universal outreach of the Christian message and
prepares his readers for the Cornelius story.

Also prior to the Cornelius event, Luke reports the Lord
as saying to Ananias about Paul, "Go, for he is a chosen
instrument of mine to carry my name before the Gentiles
and kings and the sons of Israel; . . . " (Acts 9:15). This

description of Paul's task as a chosen instrument verifies his Gentile mission.

The Peter and Cornelius story (Acts 10:1-11:17) marks the last in a series of great conversion stories (cf. Acts 8:5-13,25-40; 9:1-19a). Alongside the Stephen story, it is one of the longest individual reports in Acts. Luke has actually constructed the story by repeating a number of times both the vision of Cornelius (Acts 10:3-6,22,30-33; 11:13-14; cf. 15:7) and that of Peter (Acts 10:11-15,28; 11:4-9; cf. 15:14). The reader is certain that God wanted Cornelius' conversion, for Peter says in his explanation to the circumcision party, "If then God gave the same gift to them as he gave to us when we believed in the Lord Jesus, who was I that I could withstand God" (Acts 11:17)? God's will was clear because the Gentiles had received the Holy Spirit just as these early Christians (Acts 10:44-48; 11:15-16; cf. 2:1-4). Luke wants his readers to respond just as did Peter's audience in Jerusalem: "Then to the Gentiles also God has granted repentance unto life" (Acts 11:18). Moreover, throughout the whole story Luke leaves no doubt that the whole event was God's will which is manifested by a vision (Acts 10:3,17,19; 11:5), an angel (Acts 10:3,7,22; 11:13) and the Spirit (Acts 10:19,38,44,45,47; 11:12,15,16). God's salvific will is that the salvation in Christ be universal.

Once the universal nature of salvation in Christ has been established in the Peter and Cornelius story, the message spreads rapidly to the Gentiles. Some men from Cyprus and Cyrene preach the Lord Jesus to Greeks (Acts 11:20), and the Holy Spirit instructs that Barnabas and Paul be set apart for a mission (Acts 13:2). Then Luke in Acts 13-14 relates the missionary activity of Barnabas and Paul in Seleucia, Cyprus, Perga of Pamphylia, Antioch of Pisidia, Iconium, Lystra, and Derbe. From Derbe, they backtrack as far as Perga in Pamphylia, and from there return to Antioch of Syria. Later, according to Luke, Paul and Barnabas have a dispute because of Mark. Barnabas takes Mark and goes to Cyprus while Paul chooses Silas and travels through Syria and Cilicia, strengthening the churches (Acts 15:39-41). Paul and Silas next go to Derbe and to Lystra, where Paul selects Timothy to work with him (Acts 16:1-5). They pass through the region of Phrygia and Galatia. Since the Spirit will not allow them to preach in Asia, they move on to Troas. From there they journey rapidly by way of Samothrace to Neapolis and finally to Philippi (Acts 16:6-40). After their release from prison in Philippi, they pass through Amphipolis and Apollonia to Thessalonica, where the opposition of the Jews forces Paul to move to Beroea and then to Athens (Acts 17:1-34). After he leaves Athens, Paul finds Aquila and Priscilla at Corinth. Despite opposition from the Jews, Paul stays more than a year and a half at Corinth and teaches the word of God (Acts 18:1-17). Paul sails for Syria and on the way leaves Aquila and Priscilla at Ephesus with the promise that he would return if God permits. He goes on to Caesarea, apparently greets the church in Jerusalem, and then travels to Antioch. Next, he again tours the region of Galatia and Phrygia, strengthening all the disciples (cf. Acts 18:18-23). In the meantime, Apollos has come to Ephesus and after receiving instructions from Aquila and Priscilla, he crosses to Achaia and is a great help to the Christians there, because he confutes the Jews by showing in the scriptures that the Christ was Jesus (Acts 18:24-28).

Paul returns to Ephesus and stays there two years (Acts 19:1-20). After the riot of the silversmiths in that city (Acts 19:23-41), he departs for Macedonia; after he encourages them, he goes to Greece and stays there three months. But a plot of the Jews forces him to return through Macedonia to Troas where he remains seven days (Acts 20:1-6). Paul then takes ship for Miletus, and when he arrives there, he calls the elders of the church of Ephesus to him (Acts 20:17-38). After this meeting he sails from there, spends seven days at Tyre, a day at Ptolemais, and some days with Philip and his daughters in Caesarea (Acts 21:1-14). Finally, Paul arrives in Jerusalem where he is attacked and imprisoned (Acts 21:15-23:10). When the Jews plot against him, Paul is moved to a prison in Caesarea where he remains two years until Festus becomes procurator (Acts 23:12-24:27). When Festus desires to return Paul to Jerusalem to stand trial, Paul appeals to Caesar and thus is sent to Rome (Acts 25:1-26:32). After a perilous sea journey (Acts 27:1-44), they arrive in Malta where Paul heals the father of Publius (Acts 28:1-10), and the Christians of Rome come out to meet Paul at the Forum of Appius and Three Taverns (Acts 28:15). When he finally arrives in Rome, Paul lives there two whole years at his own expense and welcomes all who come to him (Acts 28:16-31).

After the reader has worked his way through this extensive development which Luke has of the universal nature of our salvation in Christ, it is beyond dispute that this was a major theological concern of Luke. Yet, most properly, it is subordinated to God's salvific will, since this universality itself was due to that will. Nonetheless, so important was this universal dimension of salvation to Luke that he integrated it into his Gospel and the Acts so that it would always, in some sense, be before the eyes of his readers.

CHAPTER 5

CHRIST, THE SAVIOR OF THE DISADVANTAGED

Many designations have been offered for the conclusion drawn by almost every reader of Luke-Acts, namely, that Luke gives special attention to those who stand in more need. Some of the evidence on this topic is common to Luke, Matthew, and Mark, and some to Luke and Matthew. Nevertheless, Luke himself introduced a substantial amount of material which speaks of Jesus or one of his followers as caring for the disadvantaged. The Lucan concern for the disadvantaged extends beyond the limits that some scholars would permit. For instance, Luke's concerns about the universal nature of salvation, about riches and poverty, and about persecuted Christians relate to his interest in the disadvantaged. This Lucan interest also reveals yet again how Jesus and his followers make salvation available. But, more importantly, Luke's concern for the disadvantaged is a specification of the salvation that God brings in Christ.

Luke does not develop in a vacuum his theological concern about Jesus, the savior of the disadvantaged. After all, the recognition of a need to be saved already involves an admission of one's weakness. An arrogant or self-satisfied person hardly makes a suitable candidate for salvation, since he is not inclined to admit his need of it. So, from a theoretical point of view, the concept of "salvation" includes weakness. Nor was this insight into weakness or poverty absent from the Jewish tradition. For them, the poor (*anawim*) were those who had the good sense to rely totally on Yahweh. This Jewish tradition of "poverty" has influenced Luke. For instance, Mary in the *Magnificat* describes herself with the following words, "the low estate of his handmaid." God's mercy, according to her prayer, is on those who fear him; and he has exalted the lowly and filled the hungry with good things (cf. Lk 1:46-55). The *Benedictus* speaks of being "saved from our enemies" and "from the hands of those who hate us." The Israelites will serve God without fear when God gives light to those who sit in darkness and the shadow of death, to guide their feet in the way of peace (cf. Lk 1:67-79). Moreover, few authorities deny that the Jewish notion of *anawim* forms the background for the narrative of the beatitudes (cf. Lk 6:20-23). Finally, it is not amiss here to indicate that for Luke the whole world is divided into two camps, that of God and that of Satan. The risen Christ characterizes the mission he is giving Paul with the following words:

> "... to open their eyes, that they may turn from darkness to light and from the power of Satan to God, that they may receive forgiveness of sins and a place among those who are sanctified by faith in me." (Acts 26:18)

"Darkness" and "the power of Satan" portray the poverty or weakness in which the unsanctified find themselves. Through faith in Christ, they can come to God and the light, receive forgiveness of sins and a place among the sanctified.

Jesus himself reaches out to the disadvantaged. In the prayer of Jesus, which Luke shares with Matthew, Jesus thanks his Father because, "You have hidden these things from the wise and understanding and revealed· them to babes, because such was your gracious will." (Lk 10:21-22). Further along in the same prayer we discover that no one can know who the Father is unless the Son chooses to reveal him. Apparently, the Father and the Son choose the same recipients of their revelations.

Earlier, Luke's programmatic presentation of Jesus in Lk 4:16-30 was discussed. This directs Jesus' ministry toward the disadvantaged. In the scripture passages which Jesus proclaims as fulfilled the following are singled out for his saving activity: good news to the poor, release to captives, sight to the blind, liberty to the oppressed. Jesus, a prophet rejected in his own country, then compares himself to Elijah and Elisha who in going to a widow and a leper certainly were sent to the disadvantaged, for that matter, to Gentiles. Thus, Luke from the beginning of his Gospel clarifies to whom Jesus would direct his activity.

Jesus also directs his disciples to minister to the disadvantaged. It might be best to consider Luke's overall viewpoint on this topic. Luke in Paul's speech at Athens reminds his readers that God is not far from any of them, " . . ., for, 'in him we live and move and have our being'; as even some of your poets have said, 'For we are indeed his offspring' " (Acts 17:28). God who gives each one his daily bread (Lk 11:3) sustains everyone, and a human being's dignity consists in realizing that he is like him. Christians are loving because they are sons and daughters of the Most High. God is kind to the ungrateful and the selfish. The Christians should be like God, therefore, and love their enemies and do good, and lend, expecting nothing in return (cf. Lk 6:35-36). There must be no mistake. One cannot serve God and mammon (cf. Lk 16:13). This fidelity to God and Christ demands that the disciple renounce everything (Lk 14:33). This call to renunciation explains Jesus' statement to his disciples, "Whoever seeks to gain his life will lose it, but whoever loses his life will preserve it" (Lk 17:33; cf. 9:23-26). Such a stance is what justifies the publican in the parable of the Pharisee and the tax collector. The tax collector knows that he depends on God and that he can gain his life by putting it in God's hands. So he says, "God be merciful to me a sinner" (Lk 18:13). One can phrase this truth in two other ways, " . . . for everyone who exalts himself will be humbled, but he who humbles himself will be exalted" (Lk

18:14) or "Truly, I say to you, whoever does not receive the kingdom of God like a child shall not enter it" (Lk 18:17).

The willingness to admit one's needs provokes the blessings in the beatitudes (Lk 6:20-22). Poverty, hunger, and weeping are blessed because they bring one to depend on God and Christ. Significantly, the same is to be said of those who are hated, ostracized, and reviled on account of the Son of Man — in brief, those who are persecuted. They should rejoice and leap for joy, for their reward is great in heaven. After all, they are like the prophets. This last blessing for the persecuted leaves no doubt that it is expressed in a Christian context. On the other hand, people who are rich, full, laughing, and spoken well of by all, feel no need to go to God (Lk 6:24-26). They mistakenly try to stand on their own.

The Christians are sent out as lambs in the midst of wolves (Lk 10:3). The passages reviewed here are all proper to Luke. When the disciples are invited to a banquet, they are to sit in the lowest place so that their host may say, "Friend, go up higher" (Lk 14:10). At another banquet, the Eucharist meal, Luke records the disciples' dispute as to which of them was the greatest (Lk 22:24-27; cf. 9:46-48). Jesus indicates that Gentile kings lord it over their subjects and that their officials want to be called "benefactors." But for the Christians the greatest is as the youngest, and the leader serves as Jesus serves. When Christians give a feast, they are to do as Christ has done (cf. Lk 14:21-24) and invite the poor, the maimed, the lame, the blind; and the Christians will be blessed because these people cannot repay them (Lk 14:13-14).

The mission to the Gentiles probably belongs to the Lucan theological theme of Christ, the savior of the disadvantaged. There is, after all, a certain elitism in insisting on membership among a given people. It is precisely this elitism which Luke breaks down when he insists that Israel can embrace all humankind. Obviously, the early church had already addressed this question. Traces of Luke's reasoning can be found in Acts. The scope of Peter's vision is to be found in the words, "What God has cleansed, you must not call common" (Acts 10:15). The divisions among humankind which were based on, among other things, dietary regulations cannot stand before God's cleansing action. As Luke himself phrases it a few verses later, "Truly, I perceive that God shows no partiality, but in every nation anyone who fears him and does what is right is acceptable to him" (Acts 10:34-35). Moreover, Luke can picture the Gentiles as weak and standing in need of assistance. In the vision that Paul has which ultimately leads him toward Rome, the Lucan description reads, "a man of Macedonia was standing beseeching him and saying, 'Come over to Macedonia and help us'" (Acts 16:9). Macedonia needs help. The early church has to struggle so that the Gentiles are not once again reduced to second-class citizens within Christianity. Doubtless, the solution strikes us as less acceptable than ideal, but the effort merits our applause. James judges that,

> " ... we should not trouble those of the Gentiles who turn to God, but should write to them to abstain from the pollutions of idols and from unchastity and from what is strangled and from blood" (Acts 15:19-20).

In summary, Luke's universality, like his attitude toward the disadvantaged in general, depends on God's own attitude. God and Christ show no partiality, unless it be toward the disadvantaged, and Christians are to do the same.

Before this introduction to Christ, the savior of the disadvantaged, is brought to a close, something should be said about Professor Frederick W. Danker's *Benefactor: Epigraphic Study of a Graeco-Roman and New Testament Semantic Field*, St. Louis, Clayton Publishing House, 1982. His theory is that for the benefit of auditors with broad Graeco-Roman background Luke incorporates language patterns drawn from the Hellenistic semantic field of the honored benefactor. Danker applies this theory to more New Testament books than Luke-Acts, but for obvious reasons, the response given here will limit itself to these two books. For Danker, the author of Luke-Acts sees God as the chief benefactor. In his earthly life Jesus is a benefactor especially of the oppressed, namely those outside the social and cultural mainstream. According to Danker, numerous terms and formulations are expressive of benefactors and benefactions as perceived in the Graeco-Roman world, and some of these are applied by Luke to Jesus who is then seen as a benefactor in a Graeco-Roman sense.

Several observations should be made about Danker's theory. When Danker speaks of a "semantic field," one realizes that the elements of his theory are not easily organized. The main Greek term in this semantic field, *aretē*, which denotes excellence of a high order, does not even appear in Luke-Acts, and it rarely appears in the New Testament. As was seen above, Luke explicitly rejects the application of "benefactors" in the pagan sense to Christians (cf. Lk 22:24-27), the only time this noun appears in Luke-Acts. The verb is found only once (cf. Acts 10:38). Christians are rather to serve as Christ himself served. Moreover, Luke's main source for his notion of salvation is the Old Testament, which well explains Luke's varied references. Danker must prove that the Graeco-Roman notion of benefactor permeated the Old Testament or really explains passages in Luke-Acts; otherwise his argument remains weak. One does not establish parallels between two passages by pointing to one or two words that they have in common. Finally, it is not easy to determine what would be the advantage of being designated "benefactor" according to the Graeco-Roman-world standard. When Jesus' saving activity is compared to that of God in the Old Testament, much is being said about who Jesus is and what he is doing for humankind. But it is not at all clear that Luke would be enhancing his presentation of Jesus by comparing his activity to the benefactions of a pagan god or to those of a human being whose motivation for his action scarcely reaches the heights of love which characterize God the Father.

A. Jesus and Sinners

The Lucan Jesus associates with sinners. He eats with publicans and sinners (Lk 5:29-32; 15:1-2; 19:7). Only Luke has expanded the call of Peter (Lk 5:1-11; cf. Jn 21:1-11) and included his statement, "Depart from me, for I am a sinful man, O Lord" (Lk 5:8). Jesus calls a confessed sinner to follow him. The healing of the paralytic (Lk 5:17-26) appears to be a combination of a miracle story and a dispute story. The result is a paradigm in which the emphasis falls on Jesus' pronouncement toward the story's end:

> "But that you may know that the Son of Man has author-
> ity on earth to forgive sins"—he said to the man who was
> paralyzed—"I say to you, rise, take up your bed and go
> home." (Lk 5:24; cf. Mk 2:10-11).

With the other Synoptics, Luke quotes Jesus as saying, "I have not come to call the righteous, but sinners to repentance" (Lk 5:32; cf. Mk 2:17; Mt 9:13). Jesus next encounters the woman who was a sinner (Lk 7:36-50; cf. Mk 14:3-9; Jn 12:1-8). Although a similar account exists in all the gospels, Luke's story has a significant number of differences. The other gospels stress the fact that the ointment of pure nard could have been sold and the money given to the poor. Jesus, according to them, corrects this interpretation because the woman is anointing his body for burial, and the people can always help the poor. They mention nothing about the woman's being a sinner and having her sins forgiven. Luke, in contrast to them, explicitly states a number of times that the woman was a sinner. He alone recounts the extent of her repentance and Jesus' forgiveness of her sins. She stands behind Jesus at his feet and weeps. She even wets his feet with her tears. Jesus tells Simon, "her sins, which are many, are forgiven, for she loves much, but he who is forgiven little, loves little." Jesus tells the woman, "Your sins are forgiven," and his table companions wonder, "Who is this, who even forgives sins?" Luke has made the incident into an encounter between Christ and a sinner whose sins are forgiven. Late in Acts (10:43; 13:38-39), Luke guarantees his readers that everyone who believes in Christ will have their sins forgiven.

Only Luke reports the story of the Galileans' blood which Pilate had mingled with their sacrifices, and that of the eighteen persons upon whom the tower in Siloam fell. Luke's conclusion to both these stories is that these people were no different from their countrymen, but unless they repent they would likewise perish (Lk 13:1-5). Luke immediately follows these stories with that of the barren fig tree (Lk 13:6-9). Matthew (21:18-19) and Mark (11:12-14) do speak of a fig tree, but their story is not a true parallel. The owner of the fig tree in Luke has for three years been looking for fruit on this tree and found none, so he tells the vinedresser to cut it down. But the vinedresser asks for permission to dig around it and fertilize it for yet another year in hope that it will bear fruit. There can be little doubt that the point of the parable of the fig tree, given its context of a call to repentance, is that the sinners among Jesus' hearers should not presume on God's mercy but should repent while there is still time. (God is patient with sinners, but they should not abuse his patience.)

Most of Lk 15 (cf. Mt 18:12-14) is proper to Luke. The setting of these three parables about a lost sinner is important. The Pharisees are upset because Jesus receives tax collectors and sinners and eats with them. Jesus in response tells them the three parables about a lost sheep, a lost coin, and a lost (prodigal) son. The first two have an almost identical conclusion when the lost is found: "Just so, I tell you there is joy before the angels of God over one sinner who repents" (Lk 15:10; cf. 15:7). The conclusion of the third parable does not differ much from that of the first two; for the father says to the elder son, "It was fitting to make merry and be glad, for this your brother was dead, and is alive; he was lost, and is found" (Lk 15:32). The whole chapter sets forth the joy that the repentance of a sinner brings in heaven, and should bring on earth. Thus, one should be disposed to forgive his brother who sins if he repents (Lk 17:3b-4; cf. Mt 18:15).

All of the Synoptics report Peter's denial (Lk 22:34,57,60; par.). But only Luke records Jesus' forgiveness of his persecutors, "Father, forgive them; for they know not what they do" (Lk 23:34) which is reflected in Stephen's words, "Lord, do not hold this sin against them" (Acts 7:60). Luke alone also narrates the story of the good thief (Lk 23:39-43). The good thief admits his guilt and asserts Jesus' innocence. He asks for Jesus' intercession and receives an assurance which every Christian would like to hear, "Truly, I say to you, today you will be with me in Paradise!"

The story of Simon the magician (Acts 8:9-13,18-24) allows us to see the disciples interacting with a sinner. Simon considered himself important. The people exalt him, "This man is that power of God which is called great." But when he sees the miracles of Philip, he believes and is baptized. Simon, however, wants to buy from the apostles their power to give the Holy Spirit through the laying on of hands. Peter condemns his action and denies him any part in Christianity because his heart is not straight before God. Simon is in the very bond of iniquity. Peter calls him to repentance and prayer for forgiveness. Repentant, Simon asks Peter to pray for him that he be spared the evils of which Peter speaks. Luke ends the story there. But, since Luke encourages Christians to forgive if one repents and always portrays prayer as efficacious, his reader should take for granted that this story has a happy resolution.

For Luke, a "publican," that is, a tax collector, is synonymous with a sinner. All the Synoptics mention Jesus' calling Levi the tax collector (Lk 5:27-32; Mk 2:13-17; Mt 9:9-13). Only Luke, after Jesus' praise of John the Baptist and his assertion that " ... yet he who is least in the kingdom of God is greater than he," observes that when they heard this all the people and tax collectors justified God because they had received the baptism of John (cf. Lk 7:28-30). The people are fickle in their response to both John the Baptist and Jesus. In the case of Jesus who has come eating and drinking, they say, "Behold, a glutton and a drunkard, a friend of tax collectors and sinners" (Lk 7:34)!

Two stories about publicans are proper to Luke. It was noted above that a publican is the hero of the parable of the Pharisee and the tax collector; the publican does not trust in himself that he is just, nor does he despise anyone (Lk 18:9; cf. vv 9-14). Secondly, Zacchaeus, a chief tax collector, serves as an example of how Jesus brings salvation to the house of a son of Abraham (Lk 19:1-10). Zacchaeus does three things which recommend him to any Christian. He is anxious to see Jesus even to the point of climbing a syca- more tree to do so. When Jesus tells him to hurry and come down so that he can eat with him, Zacchaeus does so and receives Jesus joyfully . Finally, he gives half of his goods to the poor and restores fourfold anything of which he has defrauded anyone.

These numerous examples of Jesus' positive interaction with sinners assure the reader that for Luke Jesus in a special way came for sinners. Luke's intention was not to encourage sinners to sin but to exhort the repentant sinner to trust in Christ's forgiveness.

B. Jesus and Women

The Lucan theme of treatment of women has to be con- sidered along with that of Jesus' being savior of the disad- vantaged. The fact is that in the world as Luke experienced it women did not enjoy the same privileges as did men. The most correct way of evaluating Luke's concern in this matter is to compare and contrast his treatment of women with that of his fellow New Testament authors. A comparison of Luke with Hellenistic and Roman authors on this topic is not out of place, but care must be taken to weigh the evidence very carefully . For instance, the Christian teach- ing about the incarnation, redemption and new creation ultimately must result in attributing an intrinsic dignity to human nature which does not exist in pagan literature.

Luke is fond of parallel pairs, and these pairs help us understand his stance toward women. There is some reason to believe that Luke partially derived this pairing from his sources. Of interest here is that in some cases the pairs involve first men and then women. Mary in the Infancy Narrative corresponds to Zechariah; they both receive the promise of a child and offer a song of praise. Simeon and then Anna, the prophetess, acknowledge the infant Jesus. Jesus during his earthly ministry first heals the demoniac and then Peter's mother-in-law (Lk 4:31-39), and restores the centurion's servant to health, and the widow of Nain's son to life (Lk 7:1-17). Then he raises the only daughter of Jairus from the dead (Lk 8:41-42,49-56). There is the story of Simon the Pharisee and the woman who was a sinner (Lk 7:36-50) and the parable of the Good Samaritan is followed by the story of Mary and Martha (Lk 10:29-42). Luke points to a man (Lk 11:5-13) and to a widow (Lk 18:1-8) to encourage the disciples in steadfastness and confidence in prayer. At first, Luke compares the kingdom to a grain of mustard seed which a man sowed in his garden; next he compares it to leaven which a woman took and hid in three measures of flour until the whole was leavened (Lk 13:18-21). The man who loses his sheep goes after it until he finds it (Lk 15:3-7) and the woman who loses a coin sweeps the house and seeks diligently until she finds it (Lk 15:8-10). When Luke discusses the coming of the Son of Man, he says that there will be two men in one bed; one will be taken and the other left. Next, he talks of two women who are grinding together; one of them will be taken and the other left (Lk 17:34-35). Luke reports the presence of the women at the tomb and next the journey of the disciples on the way to Emmaus (Lk 23:55-24:35).

Luke continues these pairs in Acts. Both men and women in Samaria believe the good news and are baptized (Acts 8:12). Peter at Lydda heals the paralytic Aeneas (Acts 9:32-35). Luke then narrates Peter's raising of Tabitha from the dead (Acts 9:36-43). Dionysius the Areopagite and a woman named Damaris join Paul and believe what he proclaimed at Athens (Acts 17:34). Couples appear in Acts, too. Aquila and Priscilla are the ideal missionary couple; her name is given before his more often than not (cf. Acts 18:2,18,26). Unfortunately, Ananias and Sapphira demonstrate the dishonest use of money in the community. Needless to say, the story about Sapphira (Acts 5:7-11) parallels that of Ananias (Acts 5:2-6) in detail.

Sometimes, Luke in these pairs refers first to the woman and then to the man. Elijah goes first to the widow of Zarephath, and later Elisha to the leper, Naaman the

Syrian. Jesus heals the infirm woman (Lk 13:10-17) and the man with dropsy (Lk 14:1-6) on the Sabbath. In both miracle stories Jesus justifies his action by referring to how people treat their draft animals better than human beings on the Sabbath. Paul in Acts accepts the hospitality of Lydia in Philippi (Acts 16:14-15). When he is in Thessalonica, still located in Macedonia, Jason is his host (Acts 17:5-9). It might be more correct to note that Paul first converts Lydia and then the jailor. Finally, the evangelist Philip has four unmarried daughters who prophesy. In the next verse the prophet Agabus comes down from Judea and predicts Paul's imprisonment (Acts 21:8-11).

These Lucan pairs of men and women suggest an equality. Men and women receive the same salvific benefits. God, Christ, and the disciples act in their lives in similar fashion. Women and men have similar experiences and fulfill similar functions. They believe and proclaim the gospel message. Unfortunately, they are alike in their sins, too.

Women do often enter Luke-Acts. Mary, Elizabeth, and Anna are in the Infancy Narrative. Mary and Jesus are the dominant characters of this Narrative. Luke views Mary as the ideal disciple; her response to God's will, announced by the angel, should be the response of every Christian to God's will in his life, "Behold, I am the handmaid of the Lord; let it be done to me according to your word" (Lk 1:38). God fails none of the women in the Infancy Narrative. Mary becomes the Mother of Jesus, the Son of the Most High; Elizabeth, no longer barren, becomes the mother of John the Baptist, of whom Jesus will later say that among those born of women none is greater than John (cf. Lk 7:28); and Anna, doubtless due to the insights of her prayerful life, thanks God and speaks of Jesus to all who were expecting the redemption of Jerusalem.

Jesus associates and interacts with women during his earthly ministry. Only according to Luke do women accompany Jesus when he preaches in the cities and villages (Lk 8:1-3). Luke further indicates that Jesus had healed these women of evil spirits and infirmities. Three of the women are named: Mary Magdalene, Joanna, the wife of Chuza, Herod's steward, and Susanna. These and other women provided for Jesus and the disciples out of their means. The exact degree to which these women participated in the ministry is not clear, but their activity does not have to be reduced to menial tasks. Probably, Luke eliminates the story of the Syrophoenician woman (cf. Mk 7:24-30; Mt 15:21-28) because its portraiture of Jesus is too harsh.

Luke's presentation of the woman who was a sinner has already been studied. The stories of Jairus' daughter and of the healing of the woman with a hemorrhage are common to all the Synoptics (Lk 8:40-56; cf. Mk 5: 21-43; Mt 9:18-26). But Luke has added details that intensify Jesus' interaction with these women. According to Luke, the girl is an only daughter who is twelve years old. At twelve, she was close to the marrying age of the time; so she was taken away in the prime of her youth. Also, in Luke, Jesus allows the girl's parents to enter the house with him, and Peter, James and John; the girl's parents are amazed at the cure. On the other hand, Luke through the addition of the words of the woman cured from the flow of blood, repeats the immediacy of the cure.

Only Luke has the story of Martha and Mary (Lk 10:38-42; cf. Jn 11:1; 12:1-3). Jesus was a friend of these two women. The thrust of the story is not to criticize the work of Martha but to emphasize that only one thing is supremely important, namely, hearing Jesus' teaching. For that is the only thing which Mary does in this story. To be sure, one can claim that attention must be paid to Mary's "sitting at the Lord's feet," but, since this was the position of a pupil before a rabbi, the phrase probably amounts to "hearing his teaching." Here a woman functions as the example of the ideal disciple because Luke certainly writes the story for his Christian readers. A story which has much the same point also occurs only in Luke:

> As he said this, a woman in the crowd raised her voice and said to him, "Blessed is the womb that bore you, and the breasts that you sucked!" But he said, "Blessed rather are those who hear the word of God and keep it" (Lk 11:27-28)

Again the stress falls on hearing and doing the word of God.

Luke certainly does not want to infer that Mary's hearing of Jesus' teaching should be separated from her actions. Nor does Jesus intend to curse his mother but to state that, if one does not hear and do the word of God, being his mother would be of only secondary advantage. As was noted above, Luke leaves no doubt that Mary heard and did the Father's will. Only Luke speaks of both "the menservants and the maidservants" in Jesus' reflections on the faithful and wise steward (Lk 12:45).

Some observations were made above about the healing of the crippled woman on the Sabbath (Lk 13:10-17). The law of the Sabbath observance was so interpreted that this woman was deprived of an opportunity to be cured. Her lot on the Sabbath was worse than that of a beast of burden which, at least, was led to water. Jesus in Luke powerfully upholds the justice of her being freed from her bond.

Significantly, only Luke speaks of the great multitude of the people and of the women who bewail and lament Jesus as they follow him on the way of the cross (Lk 23:27-31). Jesus, addressing only the women, warns them that they will soon have to weep for themselves and their children. The picture that Jesus paints is one of great despair. The words, "Blessed are the barren, and the wombs that never bore, and the breasts that never gave suck," should not lead us to conclude that Jesus was unreceptive of their sympathy. But he commiserates with them at the fate that waits them. All four evangelists apprise us that women witness Jesus' crucifixion (Lk 23:49; cf. Mk 15:40-41; Mt 27:55-56; Jn 19:24b-27). John specifies that the beloved disciple was present, but of the Synoptics only Luke states that Jesus' acquaintances were there. The Greek Luke employs leaves no doubt that at least one man has to be among them.

All the evangelists also let us know that women came to the tomb after the resurrection (Lk 24:1-11,22-24; Mk 16:1-8; Mt 28:1-8; Jn 20:1-2,11-18). Of course, John's story of Mary Magdalene stands by itself; and, at first, the accounts of the Synoptics seem of one accord. But Luke has two significant differences. The men in dazzling apparel say to the women, "Remember how he told you, while he was still in Galilee, that the Son of Man must be delivered into the hands of sinful men, and be crucified, and on the third day rise." And the women remember. This command to remember recalls the fact that these women accompanied Jesus during his whole ministry beginning from Galilee (cf. Lk 23:49), and their remembering marks them as active hearers of Christ's words. They were not just there to do the menial tasks. Moreover, their remembering reminds Luke's readers of Mary, Martha's sister, who attentively heard the Lord's word. Secondly, Luke does not say that the women were instructed to go and tell the Eleven and the rest. The women easily remember Jesus's words, return from the tomb, and tell them; they do not need to be directed like children as to the appropriate action which should follow on their present realization of the tremendous impact of Jesus' words. Less significantly, Luke (24:10) indicates the presence of more women than either Mark (16:1) and Matthew (28:1). The reaction of the disciples to what the women say, namely that these words were an idle tale, hardly puts the women in a bad light. The reader knows that they are right and that the Eleven and the others are wrong!

Luke shows a concern for widows. Social security or life insurance were not realities in those days, so a widow was often not well provided for when her husband died. A widow was frequently forced to depend on the kindness of her nearest male relative. The prophetess Anna lived seven years with her husband; for the rest of her life she was a devout widow who did not leave the temple, but worshipped with fasting and prayer night and day. She fulfills the definition which the author of I Tim gives of a widow, "She who is a real widow, and is left all alone, has set her hope on God and continues in supplications and prayers night and day ..." (5:5). Jesus in the synagogue at Nazareth compares himself to Elijah who was sent to a widow. He has compassion on the widow of Nain and raises her only son from the dead. Luke, in this story which is proper to him, paints the picture with gentle strokes, "And he gave him to his mother" (Lk 7:15b). A widow functions in the parable of the unjust judge (Lk 18:1) as an example to the disciples that they ought to pray and not lose heart. Her steadfast determination brings the judge to do his duty. Thus far all the examples are proper to Luke. Both Luke and Mark praise the generosity of the widow who puts more into the treasury than anyone else (Lk 21:1-4; cf. Mk 12:41-44). They both also condemn the scribes who devour widows' houses (Lk 20:47; cf. Mk 12:40).

Luke mentions widows in the church in Acts. The Greek-speaking Christians complain about the Aramaic-speaking Christians' treatment of their widows in the daily distribution of food (Acts 6:1). The Greek-speaking widows were being neglected. The narrative reveals that the early church had a support program for needy widows. Unfortunately, the program was marred by prejudice. Steps are taken to correct the injustice, the existence of which Luke does not question in the least. Another example of the early church caring for needy widows is the good deeds of Dorcas (Acts 9:36-42). Widows show Peter the tunics and other garments which Dorcas had made for them. After he had raised her from the dead, Peter gives her back to the saints and widows.

Women play a role in the early church. Mary and other women join the apostles and Jesus' relatives in prayer. Luke thus unites women to his theme of prayer and illustrates that they, like the men, stay in Jerusalem and await the promise of the Father. These verses do not depict a one-time event. They return to where they were staying, and the Greek imperfects imply that their ordinary activity is being described. As women accompanied Jesus, so they are now in the company of the disciples. Attention has already been called to the universal aspects of the quotation from Joel at Pentecost (Acts 2:17-21; cf. Joel 3:1-5 LXX): " . . . upon all flesh ... your daughters ... my maidservants ... and they shall prophesy ... And it shall be that whoever calls on the name of the Lord will be saved."

The most illustrious convert of Philippi is Lydia, from Thyatira, who sells purple goods (Acts 16:14-16). Paul, before he leaves Philippi, returns to visit her. She heeds what Paul says and is baptized. Paul judges her to be faithful, and so he and his companions accept her hospitality. Lydia furnishes Luke's reader with an example of listening, faith, being baptized, and a right attitude toward wealth since she offers hospitality to Christian missionaries and does not let her money keep her from believing. The other woman who plays a role in the Philippi story is the slave girl (Acts 16:16-19) who had a spirit of divination. All we know about her owners is that they profited greatly from her soothsaying, and that they get Paul and Silas condemned because of their anger over the loss of their money. The slave girl's ability allows her to identify Paul and his companions accurately, "These men are servants of the Most High God, who proclaim to you the way of salvation." Luke mitigates Paul's annoyance at this continual, unsolicited heralding by noting that this happened for many days. Moreover, Paul's words are not addressed to the slave girl but to the demon, "I charge you in the name of Jesus Christ to come out of her." Consequently, a slave girl who has been used by her masters only for financial gain is liberated from the demon. Luke in Acts 17:12 mentions that "not a few Greek women of high standing" believed Paul's words in the synagogue at Beroea. Finally, the four unmarried daughters of Philip may provide us with an example of virginity in the early church (Acts 21:9). Obviously, the community at Caesarea benefited from their prophetical gifts.   .

What can be said, by way of summary, about the Lucan presentation of women? Although we have not compared the Lucan evidence to that of all the other New Testament writers, it is true that Luke does enlighten us more about women in the early church than do they. It is naive to read back into Lucan times the precise concern for the equality of women that we have today. But he did see their lot as among the disadvantaged of society and wanted his reader to realize that they were favorites of the Savior. The only limit to their position in the Christian community which Luke records is that women were not listed among the apostles. Doubtless, Luke was bound here by the historical fact that Jesus did not have a woman among his apostles (The Twelve). However, Jesus' mother and other women represent ideal disciples who listen to God and to Jesus and follow this out in deeds. They discover God's will and praise him in their prayer.

Widows, more disadvantaged than other women, were particular favorites of Luke. Their needy and sometimes pitiable circumstances, but also their sense of prayer, determination, and generosity stirred his heart. At least, he calls attention to these experiences and qualities in their regard. Luke reveals a close association between Jesus and women in his ministry. Certain women were close friends of his. Luke likes to add details which enhance the personal interaction of Jesus with women. He draws parallels between men and women to suggest an appropriate equality. Sapphira is the only woman in Luke-Acts who appears in a bad light; all the others are in favorable contexts. Men do not fare as well. Women are instruments of sympathy and examples of courage during Jesus' passion. They are the first to know of this resurrection, and they share in the life of the early church.

C. Jesus and the Sick

The sick and oppressed surely should be numbered among the disadvantaged of this world. This was also true in the time of Luke who sees oppression in anything that keeps one from being able to enjoy human existence and to respond to Christ and God. Consequently, at times, "healing" should be understood metaphorically. When all the Synoptics report Jesus' saying, "Those who are well have no need of a physician, but those who are sick; I have not come to call the righteous but sinners to repentance" (Lk 5:31-32; cf. Mk 2:17; Mt 9:12-13), a parallel already exists between "sick" and "sinner." They quote this passage as Jesus' response to the question why he and his disciples eat with tax collectors. Surely, the passage is ironical, but it determines that sickness means to be in need of Jesus the physician. In Luke's time, the distinction between "sin" and "sickness" is unclear. But it was certain that Jesus could cure all.

The sick are mentioned right from the start of Jesus' ministry as can be seen from the programmatic passage referred to elsewhere. Luke quotes Old Testament passages about giving sight to the blind and liberty to those who are oppressed (Lk 4:18). Immediately following he compares Jesus to Elijah who works a miracle to help a widow and to Elisha who cures Naaman the leper.

When John the Baptist sends two of his disciples to find out if Jesus is the one who is to come or should they wait for another, only Luke describes what Jesus is doing at the time: "In that hour he cured many of diseases and plagues and evil spirits, and on many that were blind he bestowed sight" (Lk 7:21). Then both Luke and Matthew relate Jesus' answer to John's messengers:

> "Go and tell John what you have seen and heard; the blind receive their sight, the lame walk, lepers are cleansed, and the deaf hear, the dead are raised up, the poor have good news preached to them" (Lk 7:22; cf. 4:18, Mt 11:4-5).

Unique to Luke is that this passage corresponds to and repeats the ideas of the programmatic presentation of Jesus in the synagogue at Nazareth. This correspondence and repetition remind Luke's reader that Jesus is doing what he was anointed to do.

Luke follows Mark's summaries (Mk 1:32-34; 3:7-12; Lk 4:40-41; 6:17-19) in which Jesus cures the crowds of sick brought to him and casts out demons. Luke in these summaries seems more personal in that he writes of Jesus laying his hands on everyone of them. The crowd tries to touch him because power came forth from him and he healed them all. Elsewhere, Luke briefly summarizes Jesus' general stance toward the sick: he "cured those who had need of healing" (9:11; cf. Mt 14:14). Peter at Pentecost briefly describes Jesus of Nazareth as " ... a man attested to you by God with mighty works and wonders and signs which God did through him in your midst" (Acts 2:22). At the "Little Pentecost," the persecuted Christians in their prayer to the Father affirm much the same thing of the risen Christ, " ... while you stretch out your hand to heal, and signs and

wonders are performed through the name of your holy
servant Jesus" (Acts 4:30).

Peter, according to Luke, says in his speech in Cornelius'
house (with obvious reference to the event in the synagogue
at Nazareth), " ... how God anointed Jesus at Nazareth
with the Holy Spirit and with power; how he went about
doing good and healing all who were oppressed by the devil
for God was with him" (Acts 10:38). Jesus spent his whole
life doing good and relieving the oppressed.

The disciples continue the healing ministry of Jesus. That
is to say, the risen Christ continues to heal through them.
During his ministry, Jesus gave the Twelve power and
authority over all demons and diseases; he sent them out to
preach the kingdom of God and to heal (Lk 9:1-2). Only
Luke recounts that Jesus appoints seventy others and sends
them ahead of himself into every town and place where he
was to come. They are to heal the sick (Lk 10:1,9). The
seventy return from their mission joyful, for even the demons were subject to them in Jesus' name (Lk 10:17). As was
noted above the Lucan theme of signs and wonders (Acts
2:22,43; 4:30; 5:12; 6:8; 8:13?; 14:3; 15:12) is predicated of
both Jesus and his disciples.

Jesus and his disciples cure numerous types of illnesses.
Never is it said that Jesus lacked the power to heal, he even
heals through the disciples. Jesus heals persons oppressed
by evil spirits (Lk 4:31-37; 11:14). He cures Peter's mother-
in-law's fever (Lk 4:38-39), and Paul does much the same for
Publius' father who lies sick with fever and dysentery (Acts
28:8). Twice Jesus cleanses lepers (Lk 5:12-16; 17:11-19).
Jesus (Lk 5:17-26), Peter (Acts 3:1-10; 9:32-35) and Paul
(Acts 14:8-10) all heal paralytics. Jesus also works cures for
the man with a withered hand (Lk 6:6-11), for an epileptic
child (Lk 9:37-43a), for a man with dropsy (Lk 14:1-6), for a
blind man (Lk 18:35-43), and even for the slave of the high
priest (Lk 22:51) who was a member of the crowd that seized
him. He cures the slave of the centurion without even seeing
him (Lk 7:1-10). Jesus (Lk 7:11-17; 8:40-42,49-56), Peter
(Acts 9:36-43), and Paul (Acts 20:7-12) all raise people from
the dead. Jesus' conduct toward the woman cured of the

flow of blood actually serves to demonstrate that he is concerned about the most personal and intimate kinds of maladies which oppress humankind. Finally, as summary statements were made about Jesus and his healing activity, Luke does the same in the case of Peter (Acts 5:15-16) and Paul (Acts 19:11-12; 28:9).

Jesus and his disciples did go around doing good and freeing people from the physical and spiritual evils which prevented them from responding to Jesus or to the Father. They freed them from oppression. The manner in which Luke portrays these miracles, and their number, assure Luke's reader that Christ can overcome all evil, even death itself. So those who are disadvantaged because of sickness or the activity of the evil spirit truly find in him a savior.

D. Jesus and the Rich and Poor

Luke stresses that Jesus preaches good news to the poor (Lk 4:18; 7:22; cf. Mt 11:5). And Luke writes "blessed are the poor" (Lk 6:20) while Matthew has "blessed are the poor in spirit" (Mt 5:3). However Luke is not naive enough to maintain that riches in themselves were evil, but he perceives that unless riches are subordinated to higher values they can lead one away from God and Christ and his neighbor. The parable of the Sower states it simply "And as for that which fell among the thorns, they are those who hear but are choked by the cares and riches and pleasures of life, and their fruit does not mature" (Lk 8:14; Mk 4:18-19; Mt 13:22). So, "no servant can serve two masters; for either he will hate the one and love the other, or he will be devoted to one and despise the other. You cannot serve God and riches" (Lk 16:13; cf. Mt 6:24). This is the thrust of Jesus' warning which is proper to Luke: "But woe to you that are rich, for you have received your consolation" (Lk 6:24).

Certain Lucan passages are clearly metaphorical. The whole of Luke 12 treats of one's relationship to God and Christ. The parable of the rich fool and the instruction on anxiety (Lk 12:13-34) offer examples of the metaphorical use of riches. Instead of concentrating his efforts on his relationship with God, the fool seeks his security in the storing up of grain and goods. But his plans lead nowhere, for he dies that very night. Luke concludes the parable with the generalization, "So is he who lays up treasure for himself, and is not rich toward God." The instruction on anxiety immediately follows in the Lucan text. This ends with the words:

> "Sell your possessions, and give alms; provide yourselves with purses that do not grow old, with treasure in the heavens that does not fail, where no thief approaches and no moth destroys. For where your treasure is, there will your heart be also." (Lk 12:33-34).

These words definitely repeat the concern in the conclusion to the parable of the rich fool. However, the instruction about anxiety does not concentrate directly on wealth but rather on food and clothing. Thus, we see that money or wealth can stand for what one can buy or acquire with it.

The story of the rich ruler (Lk 18:18-30; Mk 10:17-31; Mt 19:16-30) also witnesses to the metaphorical use of wealth. If one limits himself strictly to the story, its main message is that although the rich cannot on their own enter the kingdom of heaven, their entry becomes possible because God makes it so. The metaphorical understanding of the story follows from Peter's subsequent observation, "Lo we have left our homes and followed you" and from Jesus' response that one who has left house, wife, brothers, parents, or children for the sake of the kingdom of God will receive manifold now and eternal life later. The concept of riches has been expanded to include one's home and personal relationships, and those who are willing to give them up for the sake of the kingdom, will benefit now and in heaven. Consequently, the contexts and Luke's openness to the metaphorical meaning of money or wealth should not escape us nor leave us with overly literal interpretations of passages which may look far beyond just wealth or poverty.

Luke even in the Infancy Narrative weaves a close relationship between Jesus and the poor. His parents could find no place in the inn, and shepherds were first invited to see the child (Lk 2:7-13). The contrast between the shepherds and the exotic, princely Magi of Matthew's Infancy Narrative proves helpful in determining Luke's point: wealth tends to lead one away from God. Jesus' parents offer the sacrifice which Leviticus prescribes for the poor, "And if she cannot afford a lamb, then she shall take two turtle-doves or two young pigeons" (Lev 12:8; cf. Lk 2:22-24). When the Jewish audience in the synagogue at Nazareth wonder, "Is not this Joseph's son?" (Lk 4:22), they imply that there is nothing exceptional about Jesus or Joseph. Jesus does not come from an influential family of wealth and power. John's understanding of this passage, "They said, 'Is not this Jesus, the son of Joseph, whose father and mother we know? How does he now say, I have come down from heaven?'" (Jn 6:42), confirms this interpretation, even if Luke drops "And they took offense at him" of Mark (6:3) and of Matthew (13:56).

Only Luke reports John the Baptist's answers to those who question him. The man with two coats is to share with him who has none (Lk 3:10-14). The one who has food should share too. Tax collectors should only collect the allotted amount, and soldiers are to be satisfied with their pay and not rob anyone by violence or false accusations. In brief, John tells them to share their possessions or not to take more than their due. Neither Luke nor Matthew describes John himself as wealthy, for those who are gorgeously appareled and live in luxury are in kings' courts (Lk 7:25; Mt 11:8).

Poverty characterizes Jesus' ministry. He explains to a potential disciple that his living conditions are worse than that of foxes and birds because he has nowhere to lay his head (Lk 9:58; cf. Mt 8:20). It was noted above that he invited to his banquet the poor, maimed, blind, and lame (Lk 14:21-24). Paul, in his speech to the Ephesian elders, discusses how he has sought no one's silver or gold or apparel but has worked with his own hands to support himself and others, and credits his actions to a saying of Jesus "It is more blessed to give than to receive" (Acts 20:35).

Jesus asks his disciples to adopt his posture toward

wealth and poverty. Only Luke includes the detail that Simon Peter, James, and John and Levi "left everything" (Lk 5:11,28) when they followed Jesus. Luke, in general, agrees with Mark in his report about Jesus' instructions to the Twelve, "Take nothing for your journey, no staff, nor bag, nor bread, nor money and do not have two tunics. And whatever house you enter, stay there, and from there depart" (Lk 9:3-4; Mk 6:8-10). However, Mark allows them to carry along a staff, Luke does not. Luke realizes if one makes an exception for a staff, total dependence on God is weakened. Both he and Mark warn a missionary not to move around to get better accommodations. Only Luke at the Last Supper returns to this passage and establishes that the Apostles at that time did not lack anything although they were going to enter more trying times (Lk 22:35-38); also only Luke repeats this instruction of Jesus to take nothing for the journey at the sending out of the Seventy (Lk 10:4-9). Lucan, too, is the directive that when they give a banquet the disciples like Jesus are to invite the poor, the maimed, the lame, and the blind (Lk 14:13; cf. v 21). All the Synoptics set down Jesus' directive to the rich young man, "Sell all that you have and distribute to the poor, and you will have treasure in heaven; and come, follow me" (Lk 18:22; par.).

A number of narratives in Luke-Acts illustrate the correct Christian use of wealth. The story of Zacchaeus (Lk 19:1-10) is proper to Luke. Zacchaeus was rich, but his wealth did not keep him from wanting to see Jesus. He gives half of his goods to the poor and will restore fourfold anything of which he has defrauded anyone. He is generous with his money, and, apparently has not defrauded many people. An even greater generosity is found in the poor widow (Lk 21:1-4) who out of her poverty put into the treasury everything she had to live on.

The first chapters of Acts present a picture of the ideal community. Ananias and Sapphira (Acts 5:1-11) did not have to sell their property, nor did they have to give the money which they got for it to the community. Moreover, since Barnabas is praised because he sold a field and gave the money to the apostles (Acts 4:36-37), probably not everyone did this or was required to do it. Luke idealizes the early Christian community. He presents Christians as sharing all things in common and selling their possessions and goods, and distributing the money to anyone who had need (cf. Acts 2:44-45; 4:32-34). The "fellowship" (Acts 2:42) which gives the community one heart and soul (Acts 4:32) is this attitude towards one's property. In this spirit Peter says to the lame man, "I have no silver or gold, but I give you what I have, in the name of Jesus of Nazareth, walk" (Acts 3:6). Luke proposes for the Christians a community in which no one is possessive. Their generosity should be such that they are of one heart and soul. No one will be needy. They realize that what they really possess is the presence of God, of the risen Christ, and of the Spirit among them. It is against this background that one must judge the gruesome story of Ananias and Sapphira. Their action, if tolerated, would destroy the fellowship of the community. They are possessive and have no concern for the needy they just want to look good in the eyes of the community. By their action they deny that God and the Spirit work in the community through the apostles. Satan has filled their hearts. Their tragic outcome mirrors the evil of their deed which would have destroyed the ideal Christian community.

The Ethiopian eunuch (cf. Acts 8:25-40) was in charge of the treasury of Candace, queen of the Ethiopians. His consequent personal wealth did not prevent him from coming up to Jerusalem to worship, nor diminish his interest in the prophet Isaiah. He hears the good news of Jesus and wonders what hinders his baptism. He is baptized, and as many who have truly heard the Christian message, goes his way rejoicing. The story discloses that Luke does not oppose wealthy people, and it argues that such a person can so love that his wealth does not blind him to the all-important message about Jesus. The same should be said of Lydia (Acts 16:14-15), whom we viewed above.

Cornelius, the first Gentile to be converted, gives alms liberally to the people (Acts 10:2). When the prophet Agabus at Antioch predicts a world famine, the disciples determine that everyone will send what he can to the Christians in Judea. Barnabas and Paul are to bring their collection to the elders there (Acts 11:28-30; cf. 12:25; 24:17). Finally, even the burning at Ephesus of the books on the magical arts (Acts 19:18-19) manifests the disciples' correct attitude toward wealth. The value of these books was fifty thousand pieces of silver. Yet, given their nature, these books could not be sold and the money used for charitable purposes. Since the books would only lead their possible readers away from Jesus, they had to be destroyed in one way or another.

Luke also supplies a number of examples of an improper use or attitude toward wealth. Luke unites the discourses against the Pharisees and lawyers (Lk 11:37-53), which Matthew locates in two places in his gospel (Mt 15:1-2; 23:4,6-7,13,23,25-32,34-36). Jesus brings the charge against the Pharisees that they cleanse the outside of the cup and of the dish, but inside they are full of extortion and wickedness; as a solution, he counsels them in what is admittedly an obscure verse, "But, as regard that which is written, give alms; and behold everything is clean for you" (Lk 11:41). Luke, in Jewish fashion, sees alms as a means of making retribution for sins. Matthew in his parallel (23:26) says nothing about alms. Both Luke and Matthew agree that the Pharisees have neglected essentials in that they tithe mint, rue, and every herb, but leave aside justice and the love of God (Lk 11:42; Mt 23:23). Both Luke (20:47) and Mark (12:40) condemn the scribes who consume the house of widows and who, for a pretense, make long prayers.

Luke alone has the parable of the dishonest steward and the Pharisees' reaction to it (Lk 16:1-15). This parable, as was noted above, advises Jesus' hearers that they cannot serve God and money. At this the Pharisees scoff at Jesus because they were lovers of money (Lk 16:14). They have been and want to continue to make the vain effort to serve both God and money. The parable of the rich man and Lazarus, once again proper to Luke, comes next in Lk 16. This parable does not explicitly condemn the rich man for any particular action. Abraham comments briefly "Son, remember that you in your lifetime received your good things, and Lazarus in like manner evil things; but now he is comforted here, and you are in anguish" (Acts 16:25). The rich man's fault lay in that his money only led to his being clothed in fine and costly garb and to having daily, sumptuous feasts. He was, at best, indifferent to Lazarus and to his desire to be fed with what fell from his table. His wealth had not led him to any love of his neighbor!

All the gospels grant that Judas agrees to betray Jesus for money (Lk 22:5; par.). Perhaps no more tragic example exists of how money can turn one away from the Lord. Money infects the integrity of a number of the characters in Acts. When they see that their hope of gain is gone (Acts 16:19), the owners of the slave girl, with the spirit of divination, seize Paul and Silas and drag them to the magistrates. At least in part the riot in Ephesus (Acts 19:23-41) is caused by the possible loss of business which the silversmiths may endure. A final example of how money can be of greater value to someone than the gospel message is Felix (Acts 24:24-27). He hopes to get money from Paul and even hears him speak about faith in Christ. But, when Paul makes known such practical aspects of Christianity as justice and self-control, Felix loses interest and tells Paul that he will hear him when an opportunity presents itself.

Luke, then, does place definite emphasis on wealth and poverty, and either of them for him can have a metaphorical meaning. There is no outright condemnation of wealth in Luke-Acts, but Luke is well aware of how treacherous any attachment to money can be for one's relationship with God, Christ, and the neighbor. Poverty, on the other hand, is more congruent with the insight that a Christian ultimately depends on God and Christ. Everything else being equal, Luke does show a preference for the poor. Jesus and the early Christians lived poorly, and the giving of alms in one form or another was commended. Finally, the preaching of the gospel message was not to be associated with being well equipped or haveing the best accommodations.

E. Jesus and the Persecuted

Should persecuted Christians be considered among the disadvantaged? Yes, and this understanding of the persecuted chiefly explains how Luke continues his theme of Jesus the savior of the disadvantaged in Acts, for he less often adverts to other kinds of disadvantaged. Next, it would be a one-sided presentation of the persecuted Christians in Luke-Acts to insist that Jesus always appears as their savior. At times, the Father (e.g. Acts 26:22; 27:23-25) and the Holy Spirit are the ones who are called or who come to the aid of these Christians. At other times it is not clear whether Luke refers to the Father or to Jesus (e.g. Acts 5:19-20; 12:6-11, 17). However, it should not be forgotten that for Luke the exact determination of who performs a given task is not always as important as the fact that salvation history persists.

Let us now look at those passages where Jesus appears as the savior of the persecuted Christians. One of the clearest is Jesus' prediction (Lk 21:12-19) of the persecution that the disciples will endure. People will lay hands on the disciples and persecute them. They will deliver them to the synagogues and prisons and will bring them before kings and governors because of Jesus' name. Christians will even be delivered up by parents and brothers and kinsmen and friends, and some of them they will put to death. They will be hated because of Jesus' name. This list of the ordeals that Christians will suffer leaves little doubt that the persecuted are to be numbered among the oppressed and disadvantaged. But what does Jesus say to his disciples when he gives this general description of persecutions which will come upon them? He assures them,

> "This will be a time for you to bear witness. Settle it therefore in your minds, not to meditate beforehand how to answer; for I will give you a mouth and wisdom, which none of your adversaries will be able to withstand or contradict" (Lk 21:13-15).

The Christians have a permanent guarantee that when they

are persecuted Jesus will be with them. Later, in the same passage, he continues, "But not a hair of your head will perish. By your endurance you will gain your lives" (cf. Lk 21:13-15, 18-19). This latter passage can hardly be understood literally since above it was said that some of the Christians would be killed. Rather, the meaning of this latter passage is the guarantee that each Christian has of a resurrection. The ultimate hope each Christian has is that there is a resurrection of the dead. Christ as the first to rise from the dead had led the way (Acts 26:23; cf. 3:15; 4:2).

This resurrectional understanding of Lk 21:18-19 finds support in the nearest Lucan parallel, Lk 12:4-12. This passage instructs the disciples not to fear those who kill the body and thereafter have no more they can do. Rather they should fear the one who has power to cast them into hell. Everyone who acknowledges Jesus before humankind, the Son of Man will acknowledge before the angels of God. But he who denies Jesus before humankind will be denied before the angels of God. Interestingly, when the disciples in this passage are brought before the synagogues and the rulers and the authorities, they are not to be anxious how or what they are to answer or what they are to say, for the Holy Spirit will teach them what they are to say. Luke sees no difficulty in substituting the Holy Spirit for Jesus because the Holy Spirit is one way the risen Christ is present. Consequently, Lk 12:4-12, as Lk 21:12-19, represents the persecuted disciples as disadvantaged and oppressed. They are not to fear. Christ or his Spirit will aid them, for they will tell them what to say. Their ultimate hope is that they will be raised from the dead as was their leader Christ.

The Christians at the "Little Pentecost" (Acts 4:23-31) pray in the midst of their persecution to the Father as follows:

> "And now, Lord, look upon their threats, and grant to your servants to speak your word with all boldness, while you stretch out your hand to heal, and signs and wonders are performed through the name of your holy servant Jesus" (Acts 4:29-30).

Their answer to this prayer is to be filled with the Holy Spirit and to speak the word of God with boldness. Certainly, the Christians addressed their prayer to the Father, and he granted their petition. However, Jesus enters the picture too, because through his name the Christians perform signs and wonders. In fact, the Father, the Son, and the Holy Spirit, according to this passage, all assist the Christians in their bold proclamation of the word in the midst of persecution.

Above it was established that Luke draws an extensive comparison between Stephen and Jesus. Most of the parallels or references are to Jesus' passion. These parallels draw attention to a number of things, but one of these has to be that Stephen in his suffering finds Jesus as his support. The Spirit allows Stephen to speak so that his opponents cannot withstand his wisdom. When his opponents are enraged and grind their teeth against him, Stephen gazes into heaven and exclaims, "Behold, I see the heavens opened and the Son of Man standing at the right hand of God" (Acts 7:56; cf. 7:54-55). Exactly why the Son of Man is standing remains vague. The vision certainly proves supportive to Stephen, so the Son of Man is standing probably to indicate that he is active on Stephen's behalf. Perhaps he stands to intercede for Stephen or to receive him into heaven. This latter interpretation would well correspond with Stephen's prayer which he addresses to Christ, "Lord Jesus receive my spirit." The next little prayer should also be understood as addressed to Jesus since the nearest referent for "Lord" is "Lord Jesus": "Lord do not hold this sin against them" (Acts 7:59-60). Luke, therefore, through an extensive comparison with Jesus, a vision, and two short prayers communicates to his readers that Stephen is sustained by Jesus and his Spirit.

Paul's conversion story supplies an excellent example of how Jesus assists persecuted Christians. Paul, after all, intends to persecute more Christians as he makes his way to Damascus. He has letters from the high priest which will permit him to bring anyone whom he finds belonging to the Way bound to Jerusalem. Since the details of the story are so familiar, no need exists to go into them here. The risen Christ turns a persecutor of the oppressed Christians into a proclaimer of the word.

The magician Elymas at Cyprus withstands Barnabas and Paul, and seeks to turn the proconsul Sergius Paulus from the faith. Paul curses him with the punishment that the hand of the Lord is upon him and he will be blind and unable to see for a time. Mist and darkness immediately fall on the magician, and he goes about seeking people to lead him by the hand (cf. Acts 13:11). Although "Lord" in this passage might refer to the Father, two solid reasons demonstrate that it refers to Jesus. Acts 13:12 reports that when the proconsul sees what happens to Elymas he believed, because he was astonished by the "teaching of the Lord." "Lord" here, most reasonably, is the same person as "Lord" in the previous verse. Luke never designates the Father as a teacher, nor does he ever write that the Father teaches. Secondly, the punishment that the Lord inflicts on Elymas recalls what happens to the persecutor Paul when he sees the risen Christ. Luke with the same Greek verb says that both were blind, and with the only occurrence in the New Testament of a Greek noun and of its cognate verb he specifies that each of them has to be led around by the hand (Acts 13:11; cf. 9:8; 22:11). Acts 9:8-9 constitutes the nearest parallel:

> ...; and when his (Paul's) eyes were opened, he could see nothing; so they led him by the hand and brought him into Damascus. And for three days he was without sight, and neither ate nor drank.

Jesus thus again blinds an opponent of the Christians, and brings the proconsul to faith.

Luke attests that during Paul's stay at Corinth Jesus is the savior of persecuted Christians. The Jews oppose and revile Paul because he witnesses to them that Jesus was the Christ. So, Paul moves to the house of Titius Justus, who lived next to the synagogue. Crispus, the ruler of the synagogue, his household, and many Corinthians listen to Paul, believe, and are baptized. At that time, the Lord encourages Paul in a vision:

> "Do not be afraid, but speak and do not be silent; for I am with you, and no man shall attack you to harm you; for I have many people in this city" (Acts 18:9-10).

In a context of persecution and witnessing which recall the predictions of Lk 21:12-19, the risen Jesus promises Paul his presence and protection. This promise is not one of a moment, for Paul stays a year and a half in Corinth and teaches the word of God.

Once, Paul upon his return to Jerusalem was praying in the temple, and the risen Jesus appeared to him. He advises Paul, "Make haste and get quickly out of Jerusalem, because they will not accept your witness about me" (Acts 22:18). Paul responds that the Jews know that in every synagogue he imprisoned and beat Christians, and that he approved and even watched the garments of those who killed Stephen. Nonetheless, the risen Lord insists, "Depart; for I will send you away to the Gentiles" (Acts 22:21). This pericope surely relates to the universal mission and, especially, to Paul's mission to the Gentiles. However, the context apprises the reader of the refusal of the Jews to accept Paul's witness, and so the situation is similar to the one considered in the above paragraph. The risen Christ is with his disciple, who witnesses to him amid opposition.

Later, in Jerusalem, the risen Christ again appears to Paul and encourages him, "Take courage for as you have witnessed about me at Jerusalem, so you must bear witness also at Rome" (Acts 23:11). Again, the risen Christ supports his witness. "Take courage" looks to every kind of opposition and oppression that Paul will incur on his journey and in his stay in Rome. Paul's arrest in Jerusalem, the threat of death and scourging, and the near riot among the members of the Sanhedrin, all the events which immediately precede this vision, likewise disclose why Paul needs to be encouraged.

Paul's appearance before Festus and Agrippa II provides

yet another example of Christ as the hope and savior of the oppressed and persecuted Christians. Paul defends himself as a Christian:

> "King Agrippa, do you believe the prophets? I know that you believe." And Agrippa said to Paul, "In a short time you think to make me a Christian!" And Paul said, "Whether short or long, I would to God that not only you but also all who hear me this day might become such as I am — except for these chains" (Acts 26:27-29).

Paul wants everyone to be like him, and Agrippa II recognizes Paul as a Christian. Paul with good humor grants that he does not want everyone to be a prisoner like himself. A second important factor is that in our studies of the parallels between Christ and his followers this passage (Acts 25-26) was seen to be the most extensive comparison between Jesus and Paul. So, as in the case of Stephen, these parallels show that Paul in his suffering and persecution finds an example in Jesus' passion. Moreover, the speech itself illustrates twice that Jesus is the hope and savior of the persecuted Christians. Paul claims that he is on trial for his hope in the promise made by God to our fathers that there is a resurrection of the dead (Acts 26:6-8), and this is Paul's claim in other passages (cf. Acts 23:6; 24:15, 21; 28:20), too. That this hope rests on Jesus' own resurrection is realized through a correct understanding of the relationship between Acts 26:6-8 and 26:22-23. Acts 26:4-23 forms a diptych: the first panel of the diptych tells us of Paul's life (Acts 26:4-5) and of the resurrection of the dead (Acts 26:6-8), and the second panel continues the first with further information on Paul's life (Acts 26:9-21) and Jesus' resurrection (Acts 26:22-23). The second part of each panel treats the resurrection. First, we are told that the hope of the promise made to our fathers consists in the resurrection of the dead; then this is further determined by the fact that Christ has risen first from the dead. Thus, the hope of all Israel, that is of all Christians, is that Christ rose from the dead and so fulfills the promise made to our fathers. Christ, as the first, will lead all the

Christians to their resurrection. The hope of the persecuted Christians, here represented by Paul, is ultimately in Christ and his resurrection.

Secondly, according to Luke's presentation of Paul's conversion story in Acts 26, the risen Christ speaks directly to Paul and gives him his mission. Some of Jesus' words bear on our present topic:

> "But rise and stand upon your feet; for I have appeared to you for this purpose, to appoint you to serve and bear witness to the things in which you have seen me and to those in which I will appear to you, delivering you from the people and from the Gentiles — to whom I send you to open their eyes,. . . ." (Acts 26:16-18a).

Christ will deliver Paul from the people and from the Gentiles. Paul, as portrayed by Luke, reminds one of Jeremiah to whom the Lord said:

> "Do not say, 'I am only a youth'; for to all to whom I send you you shall go and whatever I command you you shall speak. Be not afraid of them, for I am with you to deliver you says the Lord" (Jer 1:7-8; cf. 1:17, 19; 15:20-21; 20:13).

Both Paul and Jeremiah are sent to audiences who will not always be receptive, but they are not to fear because Christ and God, respectively, will deliver them. Consequently, Christ, who through his resurrection is the hope of Christians, promises Paul, who stands for all Christians, that he will deliver him. Luke enhances this message by drawing extensive parallels between Jesus' passion and Paul's defense before Festus and Agrippa II.

Jesus, then, during his earthly life, promised his followers that he would always be with them during their persecutions, and that he would tell them what to say. His resurrection is their hope because they will follow where their leader has gone. This promise and hope support Christians during their persecutions. Luke, through parallels drawn with

Jesus' passion, and through visions (Paul alone had four of them) and wonders, lets his readers see how Christ encourages and supports the persecuted Christians. Finally, the lot of these Christians is such that they merit inclusion among the disadvantaged, and as a result enjoy the particular favor of Christ.

F. Jesus and Other Disadvantaged People

Jesus interacts with other disadvantaged people. None of his immediate apostles or disciples is a particularly influential member of society, although the tax collector Levi probably enjoyed financial prosperity. The Jewish rulers, elders, scribes, and high priestly families all recognize that Peter and John were uneducated, common men (cf. Acts 4:13), and it does not seem rash to claim that this was true of the majority of the apostles and disciples.

Jesus and his disciples encounter and respond favorably to the Samaritans. Above it was noted that the Samaritans form part of Luke's theme of universality, but, as a people despised by the Jews, they were also disadvantaged. Everything that Luke says about the Samaritans is proper to Luke-Acts. A Samaritan village will not accept Jesus or his disciples because they were headed to Jerusalem. Even though James and John ask permission to bid fire to come down from heaven and to consume them, Jesus will have no part of it, and they move to another village (cf. Lk 9:51-56). In fact, Jesus even uses Samaritans as examples of how one is to respond to God's word and work. Everyone recalls that a Samaritan shows Jesus' Jewish audience what it means to be a neighbor to the man who fell among robbers (Lk 10:29-36). Jesus is so bold as to say to the Jewish theologian who placed the question, "Go and do likewise." An expert in the Jewish law is told that a half-breed Jew, a Samaritan, has a better understanding of Jewish law than does a priest, a Levite or the expert himself. He ought to take the Samaritan as a model. A Samaritan also shows the correct response to the healing activity of Jesus. Ten lepers, nine Jews and one Samaritan, meet Jesus as he enters a village and ask him to heal them (Lk 17:11-19). He orders them to show themselves to the priests. As they go, they are healed. Only the Samaritan returns to thank Jesus. The Jews had been healed too; "Were not the ten cleansed: Where are the nine?" Nonetheless, the foreigner demonstrates gratitude and faith, for Jesus also tells him ". . .your faith has made you well." Consequently, Jesus himself twice holds up a Samaritan as a model which Jews should follow if they really want to be a neighbor and to respond to the healing activity of Jesus. Today, these Samaritans can stir up some of our noblest convictions, but Jesus' Jewish audience must have felt degraded. Imagine, being told to imitate a Samaritan!

The risen Christ, before his ascension, informs the apostles that they will be his witnesses in Jerusalem, in all Judea, and Samaria, and to the end of the earth (Acts 1:8). Persecution in Jerusalem does lead the Christians to flee to Samaria. Philip proclaims Christ and works miracles there, and as a result the Samaritans listen to him and are baptized (Acts 8:1-24). The coming of Peter and John is not a condemnation of the quality of the faith of the Samaritans, rather Luke is concerned to establish that Philip's actions and the conversion of the Samaritans is God's will and has full church approval. Not even the conduct of Simon spoils the success of Philip and of the Christian message among the Samaritans. Peter and John themselves later preach the gospel to many villages of the Samaritans (Acts 8:25), and the church throughout all Judea and Galilee and Samaria has peace and grows in number (Acts 9:31). Paul and Barnabas pass through Phoenicia and Samaria; they recount for them the conversion of the Gentiles and bring the Christians there great joy (Acts 15:3).

Jesus, then, is the first to approach the Samaritans, and he even appeals to their ranks for examples of true understanding, gratitude, faith, and love of neighbor. They are the first non-Jews to hear the message, which they receive with joy. The two greatest Christian missionaries also speak to them. The church in Samaria prospers.

When Jesus answers Peter's question whether he told the

parable on watchfulness for the disciples or for everyone, Jesus proposes some reflections on the faithful and wise steward. Among these reflections stands the warning:

> "But if that servant says to himself, 'My master is delayed in coming,' and begins to beat the menservants and the maidservants, and to eat and drink and get drunk, the master of that servant will come on a day when he does not expect him and at an hour he does not know, and will punish him and put him with the unfaithful" (Lk 12:45-46; cf. Mt 24:48-51).

The reflection suits the probable living conditions in the early church as it awaited the coming of the Lord. Some Christians held higher positions than others. This reflection on their moral conduct, that is, on their watchfulness, reminds them that they are not to mistreat other Christians, for the Lord will come suddenly and punish offenders.

"Children" can represent Christians. When the disciples want to prevent some people from bringing children to the Lord, Jesus reacts with the words:

> "Let the children come to me, and do not hinder them; for to such belongs the kingdom of God. Truly, I say to you, whoever does not receive the kingdom of God like a child shall not enter it" (Lk 18:16-17).

Children, unlike adults, realize that they are receivers, and this is probably why Luke chose to put this story about them right after the parable of the Pharisee and the tax collector. The tax collector resembles the children in that he humbles himself, unlike the Pharisee who represents those who trusted in themselves that they are righteous (cf. Lk 18:9). Moreover, both Mark and Luke put the story about the rich young man right after that about the children. However, there is a significant difference. Mark (10:17) writes, "And as he was setting out on his journey, a man ran up and knelt before him, ..." while Luke (18:18) has "And a ruler asked him,..." Both basically agree that the young man's question is what should he do to inherit eternal life. However, since Luke joins this story directly to that of Jesus' reception of the children, the question of the rich young man prolongs the thought of the previous story, namely, children as recipients of the kingdom. The explanation occurs toward the end of the story. To the question, "Then who can be saved?", Jesus answers, "What is impossible with humans is possible with God" (cf. Lk 18:27). Entering the kingdom is less a question of our doing than it is of the power of God to do what seems impossible. Children, unlike the Pharisee and the rich young man, realize their dependence.

Christians are also viewed much as children in the passage:

> And he said to his disciples, "Temptations to sin are sure to come; but woe to him by whom they come! It would be better for him if a millstone were hung round his neck and he were cast into the sea, than that he should cause one of these little ones to sin" (Lk 17:1-2; Mk 9:42; Mt 18:6-7).

The first verse of this passage is Lucan. Jesus in this passage threatens those who would bring temptation to the weak members of the community. Mark and Matthew explicitly speak of "one of these little ones who believe in me." Though Luke omits this qualification, he surely sees the "little ones" as designating the disadvantaged members of the community.

The Ethiopian eunuch has already been adverted to in connection with the Lucan themes of universality and the rich and poor. But a eunuch, as a maimed, imperfect human being, was not to enter the assembly of the Lord. Isa 56:3-5 does moderate this position. The prophet advises the eunuch to say no more, "Behold I am a dry tree," for, if eunuchs keep the Sabbath and do what the Lord wants and hold fast to his covenant, he will give them an everlasting name and a monument better than sons and daughters. The author of the Wisdom of Solomon (3:14) promises the faithful eunuch special favor and a place of great delight in the temple of the Lord. It may be that in Acts 8:26-40 "eunuch" means an office, and so should not be taken literally. But Luke, from what we have seen thus far, would have had no hesitancy in making such an outcast of Jewish society the hero of his story. The fact remains that, if the Ethiopian was truly a eunuch, he could not be fully a Jew; but he does become a full-fledged Christian.

Most of the people Jesus called to follow him were uneducated. He and his disciples treat Samaritans favorably; nor are weaker, more humble Christians to be mistreated. An Ethiopian eunuch finds his answers in the correct understanding of Scripture and of the message about Christ. He is baptized and goes his way rejoicing.

G. Conclusion

In summary, although he found considerable material on the topic in his sources, Luke gives special attention to Jesus as the savior of the disadvantaged. Jesus and his followers make salvation available to disadvantaged persons. Jesus associates with and forgives sinners. Since Luke views women as among the disadvantaged, Jesus and his followers interact with them. Nor are widows overlooked, and parallels between men and women suggest an appropriate equality. Those who are disadvantaged because of sickness or the activity of the evil spirit find a savior in Jesus. Wealth and poverty can have a metaphorical meaning for Luke. There is no outright condemnation of wealth, but its treacherous nature is recognized. Poverty is more congruent with Christianity, and Jesus is especially sent to the poor. Jesus and the early Christians lived poorly. The persecuted, too, are included by Luke among the disadvantaged. Jesus promised persecuted Christians that he would be with them and tell them what to say. His passion and resurrection are the hope of Christians during times of persecution. Also, Jesus and his followers reach out to the Samaritans. In short, anyone who is disadvantaged receives favorable treatment from Luke. Finally, the universality of salvation probably belongs to the Lucan theme of Jesus, the savior of the disadvantaged. There is, after all, a certain elitism in insisting on membership in a given nation.

Luke's readers are to have Jesus' attitude toward the disadvantaged. If they themselves are among the disadvantaged, they have reason to take courage because Jesus brings salvation especially to them.

CHAPTER 6

DELAY OF THE PAROUSIA AND LUKE'S NOTION OF ESCHATOLOGY

Luke broadens the time schedule within which God continues to bring his salvation to Israel. He no longer speaks of an instant or imminent Parousia, second coming of the Lord. Nor does Luke identify the Parousia with eschatology, the end times. Rather, the Parousia for Luke is the end of the end times, it is the final establishment of the kingdom. But the end times according to Luke begin with the birth of Jesus.

John the Baptist goes before the Lord to prepare his ways (Lk 1:76; cf. 1:15-17; Mal 3:1); like Elijah, who will be sent before the great and terrible day of the Lord, John will turn the hearts of the fathers to the children (Lk 1:17; cf. Mal 3:1; 4:5-6). The day shall dawn on them from on high (Lk 1:78; cf. Mal 4:2; Isa 60:1-2). The messenger goes first to prepare the day of the Lord. Later, Jesus contends in the synagogue at Nazareth that the proclamation of the acceptable year of the Lord (cf. Lk 4:19) has been fulfilled for his hearers. Luke himself in his story of Pentecost inserts into the quotation from Joel, "...in the last days, God declares..." He thus makes Pentecost an event of the last days. Consequently, the last days should not be completely identified with the Parousia, which is really the last event of these days.

However, the question remains — does Luke see the Parousia as delayed or immediate, or at least imminent? Lucan scholars have dedicated no small amount of attention to the question, and they are by no means in agreement. However, most would side with H. Conzelmann's position that the Parousia according to Luke is delayed.

The correct answer to the above question depends on a number of accurate assumptions. One cannot, for instance, pick and choose which Lucan passage to consider. Every Lucan passage that bears on the topic must be considered. This means that one cannot dismiss the Infancy Narrative; insofar as it relates to the Parousia it, too, must be studied. Secondly, serious attention must be given to Acts. Luke in Acts depicts for us the risen Christ active in his Church. Acts would, therefore, be the most logical place to investigate how Luke interrelates the lives of Christians with Jesus' second coming, the Parousia. Finally, some Lucan passages are obviously more significant for establishing the Lucan understanding of the Parousia than others. The accurate identification of such passages is crucial for an interpretation of Luke's opinion on the matter.

The crucial passage in determining Luke's understanding of the Parousia is Acts 1:6-11. It is best to quote the passage in its entirety:

> So when they had come together, they asked him, "Lord will you at this time restore the kingdom to Israel?" He said to them, "It is not for you to know times or seasons which the Father has fixed by his own authority. But you shall receive power when the Holy Spirit has come upon you; and you shall be my witnesses in Jerusalem and in all Judea and Samaria and to the end of the earth." And when he had said this, as they were looking on, he was lifted up, and a cloud took him out of their sight. And while they were gazing into heaven as he went, behold two men stood by them in white robes, and said, "Men of

> Galilee, why do you stand looking into heaven? This
> Jesus, who was taken up from you into heaven, will come
> in the same way as you saw him go into heaven."

This passage calls for several observations. It is in a key
location. It is right at the beginning of Acts, and the disciples
have asked the question, when does God intend to restore
the kingdom of Israel through Jesus? They are asking about
the time schedule of God's salvation history. They are told
that they are not to know, but that the Father knows and has
fixed the time.

Next follows the mission of the apostles as Jesus' witnesses, and then Jesus ascends into heaven. The aspect of
Luke's description of Jesus' ascension in Acts which inter-
ests us is that, while the apostles are gazing into heaven, the
two men say that their gazing into heaven achieves nothing
and that Jesus will come in the same way as they have seen
him go into heaven. Luke informs his readers that an intense
anticipation of Jesus' second coming, this gazing into
heaven, pays no dividends. That the risen Christ will come
again is a surety, but the apostles must accept the reality that
they do not know when, and that their gazing into heaven
represents an unacceptable attitude. After all, they were just
told of their reception of the Holy Spirit and their missionary task as Jesus' witnesses to the end of the earth. The
Lucan description of the ascension in Acts is thus realistic
and challenging. It looks to the future and to the history of
the church. The scene does not create any expectation of an
instant or imminent Parousia.

Much the same should be claimed for Acts 3:19-21:

> "Repent, therefore, and turn again, that your sins may be
> blotted out, that times of refreshing may come from the
> presence of the Lord, and that he may send the Christ
> appointed for you, Jesus, whom heaven must receive
> until the time for establishing all that God spoke by the
> mouth of his holy prophets from of old."

Perhaps those who find traces of an early Christology in this passage are correct, but that Luke understood this passage of Jesus' incarnation and not of his Parousia is an untenable position. First of all, Acts 3:19-21 contains much Lucan terminology, and nowhere else in Acts does Luke bring up Jesus' earthly life toward the end of a speech. True, in Acts 2:22; 10:37-39; 13:23 Luke does speak of Jesus' earthly life; but the passages stand toward the beginning of their respective speeches, not at the end. In fact, Luke in Acts pays little attention to Jesus' earthly life. Toward the end of his speeches, Luke usually writes of God's raising Jesus from the dead (e.g. Acts 2:32; 4:10; 5:30; 10:40; 13:30, 34, 37; 17:31; 26:23). Besides, Acts 3:19-21 contains some parallels to the first passage studied in this section, Acts 1:6-11. The same Greek nouns appear for "time. . .times and seasons" (cf. Acts 1:6-7; 3:19, 21). Greek cognates express the notions of "restore" and "establishing" (Acts 1:6; 3:21), and God the Father determines the action: "which the Father has fixed by his authority" (Acts 1:7) and "may come from the presence of the Lord, and that he may send. . .appointed for you. . .whom heaven must receive. . .that God spoke by the mouth of his holy prophets" (Acts 3:20-21). Doubtless, the most telling argument that the latter passage cannot refer to the incarnation is that the time of the passage is the future. Even taking for granted that we readers must adjust to the temporal setting of the speech, the incarnation has already occurred, and the sending of Christ spoken of is best understood as a reference to the Parousia. Acts 3:19-21 does suggest the imminence of the Parousia more than does Acts 1:6-11, but the former passage sets the tone for the whole of Acts, and 3:19-21 remains vague as to any precise time. The prevailing message is that the Father knows and determines the time of which we are ignorant.

A. J. Mattill, Jr, contends that he can find an imminent hope of the Parousia in Acts 10:42; 17:31; 24:15, 25. Mattill's source for this understanding is the work of R. F. Weymouth. Acts 10:42 reads: "And he commanded us to preach to the people, and to testify that he is the one ordained by God to be judge of the living and the dead." The only way in which this passage can be interpreted as affirming an imminent Parousia is if one claims that the "living" refers to Peter's audience and the people alive at that time, and so Peter (and thus Luke) anticipates an imminent Parousia because Jesus would soon be functioning as judge of those who were alive at the time Peter gave this speech. The assumption in this interpretation is that Jesus functions as judge at his second coming, and this is reasonable enough. What is unreasonable is that one can so interpret "living" that its partial application to the members of Peter's audience and the people living at that time necessitates an imminent Parousia. Rather, Luke through Peter is asserting that Jesus will be judge of every human being who has ever lived or who will ever live. "Of the living and the dead" expresses the universal extent of Jesus' judging function; but it does not allow one to conclude as to the time of that judgment. Consequently, the time of the Parousia continues to be undetermined.

The other passages which Mattill adduces to prove that Luke held for an imminent expectation in Acts are:

> "The times of ignorance God overlooked, but now he commands all men everywhere to repent, because he has fixed a day on which he will judge the world in righteousness by a man whom he has appointed, and of this he has given assurance to everyone by raising him from the dead" (Acts 17:30-31).

> "...having a hope in God which these themselves accept, that there will be a resurrection of both the just and the unjust" (Acts 24:15).

> And as he argued about justice and self-control and future judgment, Felix was alarmed and said, "Go away for the present..." (Lk 24:25).

The weight of Mattill's argument for an imminent expectation in these verses depends on how one translates *mellein* in each of these passages. Again, Mattill follows the lead of Weymouth and translates *mellein* as "before long" or "soon." So, Weymouth translates the relevant words in each of these passages as "before long he will judge the world in righteousness," "that before long there will be a resurrection both of the righteous and the unrighteous," and "the judgment which was soon to come," respectively. However, Mattill and Weymouth are mistaken. As was pointed out above, *mellein* means "to be destined" and belongs to Luke's theological concern that God continues to bring his salvation to Israel. Consequently, although in English one may be inclined not to translate *mellein* at all, the correct translations of the relevant phrases would be: "on which he will (i.e. is destined to) judge the world," "that there will (i.e. is destined to) be a resurrection of both the just and unjust" and "the judgment which is destined to be." None of these passages, then, support Mattill's contention of an imminent expectation. The passages, on the contrary, determine that there will be a judgment and a resurrection, both of which are associated with the Parousia. However, they provide no definite idea as to when these things will happen.

A redactional study of the relationship of Luke's Gospel to Mark and Matthew also indicates that Luke maintains a delay of the Parousia. Here, I am following the lead of Conzelmann, but I depart from his interpretation in a number of passages. Only once does Luke insert something about the nearness of the kingdom (Lk 10:11). By adding John's reply to his questioners (Lk 3:10-14), Luke moves the eschatological call to repentance more to the background and introduces ethical instructions. It is true that both Matthew and Luke speak of "mysteries" while Mark has "mystery" in "And he said to them, 'To you has been given the mystery of the kingdom of God, but for those outside everything is in parables'" (Mk 4:11; cf. Lk 8:10; Mt 13:11), but this change does not really prove too significant. Luke and Matthew may have thought that the singular was too simplistic an interpretation of the kingdom, or perhaps, they wanted to express the timeless secrecy of the kingdom. Much more productive is a comparison of Lk 9:27 with Mk 9:1 (cf. Mt 16:28): "And he said to them, 'Truly, I say to you, there are some standing here who will not taste death before

they see that the kingdom of God has come with power.'"
Luke omits the phrase, "has come with power." He replaces
the idea of the coming of the kingdom with a timeless
conception of it, and in this way he makes the saying inde-
pendent of any definite time. "Some standing here" means
those who are standing by "at the time." From the life of
Jesus we can see what the kingdom is like, but when the
kingdom itself is to appear is not disclosed.

Lk 9:60 reads: "But he (Jesus) said to him; 'Leave the dead
to bury their own dead; but as for you, go and proclaim the
kingdom of God.'" Matthew (8:21) mentions nothing about
the kingdom of God. Very likely, Luke has taken a saying
which originally related to the nearness of the kingdom, and
united it with the notion of the supreme importance of
following Christ and of sharing in his mission of proclaiming the kingdom.

The instruction in Lk 12:35-40 on watchfulness is proper
to Luke, and directly touches upon the delay of the Parousia. The point of these instructions is that no matter how
long the delay is, one should be prepared. The suddenness
with which a thief can come stresses the urgency of being
watchful. Jesus in Lk 12:56 warns the multitudes, "You
hypocrites! You know how to interpret the appearance of
earth and sky; but why do you not know how to interpret the
present time?" The "present time" certainly looks to Jesus
and the difficult decisions that the Christians will have to
make even as regards members of his own family (cf. Lk
12:49-53). But this awareness of the present time most properly bears upon Jesus' previous instructions and parable on
watchfulness (cf. Lk 12:35-48), and their message is that one
must not be led astray by the delay of the Parousia.

The story about the narrow door includes the
exhortation:

> And someone said to him, "Lord, will those who are
> saved be few?" And he said to them, "Strive to enter by
> the narrow door; for many, I tell you, will seek to enter
> and will not be able. When once the householder has risen

and shut the door, you will begin to stand outside and to knock at the door saying, 'Lord, open to us.' He will answer you, 'I do not know where you come from'" (Lk 13:23-26).

The urgency in this passage concerns one's being among the few who will be saved. There is comparatively little stress on when the householder will close the door, for Luke only determines the fact that the householder will close it.

Luke 14:1-24, which is mostly Lucan (cf. Mt 22:1-14), takes place at a banquet to which a ruler of the Pharisees had invited Jesus. Two statements made during the course of this banquet could be interpreted in light of the Parousia. Jesus tells his host that when he gives a feast he ought to invite the poor, the maimed, the lame, and the blind; then he will be blessed because they cannot repay him. The host will be blessed in the resurrection of the just. Immediately after this, one of Jesus' table companions proclaims, "Blessed is he who shall eat bread in the kingdom of God" (Lk 14:13-15)! Jesus then tells the parable of the great banquet. It is from this parable that one can establish to what time Jesus refers. At first, one might be inclined to understand "Come; for all is now ready" (Lk 14:17) as an indication of an instant or imminent Parousia, but the force of this imperative depends on the time of the banquet. According to the parable, the man has already given the banquet! Consequently, the parable is speaking of the Parousia, but since it reports a banquet that has already taken place, it applies to the Parousia without determining its time. When the Parousia does happen, one should be ready to come. The end of the parable supports this interpretation:

> Then the householder in anger said to his servant, "Go out quickly to the streets and lanes of the city, and bring in the poor and maimed and blind and lame." And the servant said, "Sir, what you commanded has been done, and still there is room." And the master said to the servant, "Go out to the highways and hedges, and compel people to come in, that my house may be filled. For I tell

you, none of these men who were invited shall taste my banquet" (Lk 14:21-24).

This parable deals less with the Parousia than with what kind of people will partake in the messianic banquet. As already demonstrated, the parable portrays Jesus as the savior of the disadvantaged and universality.. Luke in this parable does not imply an immediate or imminent Parousia.

A comparison of "From the days of John the Baptist until now the kingdom of God has suffered violence, and men of violence take it by force" (Mt 11:12) with "The law and the prophets were until John; since then the good news of the kingdom of God is preached, and everyone enters it violently" (Lk 16:16) reveals that Luke prefers to speak of preaching about the kingdom, rather than to assume its presence. Needless to say, this statement is somewhat modified by the fact that Luke does write of people entering the kingdom. Although the parable of the rich man and Lazarus (Lk 16:19-31) does report an afterlife, this has been so individualized that we learn nothing about Luke's notion of the Parousia.

Luke communicates to us his general understanding of the Parousia or of the day of the Lord in his discussion of the end of the age (Lk 17:22-37; cf. 18:8, 30), which is mostly Lucan. The kingdom does not come with observable signs; in a sense, it is in the midst of Jesus' hearers. The day of the Son of Man will be like lightning which flashes and lights up the whole sky. First Jesus must suffer, but people will eat and drink and carry on their lives. The day of the Son of Man will take people unawares, but if they lose their life in Christ they will preserve it. Despite the mysterious nature of the day of the Son of Man, it will be as obvious as a dead body surrounded by vultures. Luke, in this discussion, furnishes us with no time schedule, however, he knows that the Parousia will come and that we will recognize it with ease when it does.

Only Luke introduces the parable of the pounds with the words, "As they heard these things, he proceeded to tell a parable, because he was near to Jerusalem, and because they

supposed that the kingdom of God was to appear immediately." (Lk 19:11). Obviously, Luke's intention in the parable is to inform us that before the kingdom comes Christians
must trade with the pounds they have received. Nonetheless, the king will most certainly return to claim his kingdom, and those who attempt to resist him are doomed to
failure. Thus, we are again certain that the kingdom will
come, but not immediately. Since no indication of time is
given about the king's return, any contention that the
Parousia will be imminent goes beyond the text.

Luke in Lk 21:5-36 makes clear that the end will not be at
once (Lk 21:9; cf. Mk 13:7; Mt 24:6) because he alone has
introduced "not. . .at once." Jesus cautions his hearers not
to be led astray by the many who will say, "I am he" and
"The time is at hand." First, there will be wars, earthquakes,
hurricanes, hunger (cf. Lk 23:28-31), heavenly signs, terror,
and persecutions during which the risen Christ will be with
Christians. Jerusalem will be destroyed, and her people will
be killed or carried off captive. The coming of the Son of
Man and the nearness of the kingdom will be as clear as
when a fig tree or any other tree comes out in leaf and lets us
know that summer is near. In brief, Lk 21:5-36 bears a
striking resemblance to Lk 17:22-37. Therefore, a number of
scholars have understood the difficult phrase "this generation will not pass away until all has taken place" (v 32) as the
generation which is alive when these signs happen (cf. Lk
9:27), and in view of what we have seen thus far of Luke's
notion of the Parousia, this understanding seems the most
reasonable. Luke as a second generation Christian (cf. Lk
1:1-4) knew that nobody of Jesus' generation had experienced the Parousia.

Jesus' puzzling statement, "For I tell you that from now
on I shall not drink of the fruit of the vine until the kingdom
of God comes" (Lk 22:18), parallels what he says in Lk
22:16: "For I tell you I shall not eat it (this Passover) until it
is fulfilled in the kingdom of God." Both passages are eluci-
dated by Lk 22:28-30:

"You are those who have continued with me in my trials;
and I assign to you, as my Father assigned to me, a
kingdom, that you may eat and drink at my table in my
kingdom, and sit on the thrones judging the twelve tribes
of Israel."

This passage is in the same pericope as the other two verses
(vv 16, 18). It brings up again the notions of kingdom and
eating and drinking at Jesus' table where it is reasonable to
assume that he too would eat and drink. Jesus' puzzling
statement looks ahead to the messianic banquet in his kingdom, which is also the kingdom of his Father. But none of
these three passages supply us with any idea of the time of
the Parousia or of the establishing of the kingdom.

Our study has now covered both Luke's Gospel and Acts
of the Apostles. The purpose of this study was to show that
Luke modifies his presentation of how God continues to
bring his salvation to Israel. Luke describes God's salvific
will as now happening in the end times between the life of
Jesus and his second coming or Parousia. Luke sees this
Parousia as delayed. To describe the Parousia as imminent
goes contrary to the important testimony of Acts, and does
not find much support in Luke's Gospel. God's salvation
through Christ now happens in these times, the end times,
and we live in ignorance of when Jesus will come again to
establish the kingdom.

CHAPTER 7

CHRISTIANS LIVE PEACEFULLY IN A ROMAN WORLD

Another Lucan specification of how the Christians experience God's salvation through Christ is that they live peacefully in a Roman World. Luke has certainly inserted Christianity into the world of his time, and, according to him, Christians are good citizens who violate no Roman law. Thus, the last words of Acts describe Paul as preaching and teaching in Rome, "quite openly and unhindered." The opponents of the Christians fare less well. They pay little or no attention to God's will and even fail to observe Roman law.

The governing authorities most commonly found in Luke-Acts are Jewish and Roman, and Luke treats them in radically different ways. Luke generally treats Jewish officials negatively. However, he makes a sharp and significant distinction between the high priest and the Sadducees on the one side and the Pharisees on the other. According to Luke, the Christians are the true Pharisees (cf. Acts 26:4-8, 28-29); so during Jesus' passion and throughout Acts, the Pharisees, at least by name, cease to be opponents of the Christians. In fact, the Pharisee Gamaliel defends the apostles; and Paul, too, finds defenders among the Pharisees (Acts 23:6-10). This reveals Luke's literary astuteness because the high priests belonged to the Sadducee party which was no longer influential in Judaism after 70 A.D. Christianity's opponents have practically vanished.

Luke furnishes a varied portrait of the Herodian treatment of Christ and the Christians. Herod Antipas is glad to see Jesus; however, when Jesus refuses to answer him, Herod and his soldiers treat Jesus with contempt and mock him. Yet Herod Antipas does not think that Jesus was guilty (Lk 23:8, 11, 14-15). Herod Agrippa kills James the brother of John; and, since this pleases the Jews, he arrests Peter (Acts 12:2-3). In contrast, Luke's treatment of Agrippa II (Acts 25:13—26:32) is gentle and favorable. Agrippa II wants to hear Paul's defense; pleasantly interacts with him, and twice affirms his innocence. In summary, Luke evaluates the Herodian princes in terms of their treatment of Christ and the Christians.

Was Jesus' cleansing of the temple a violation of Jewish and so of Roman law? His action resembles those of the prophets of the Old Testament. Jesus acts violently in the cleansing of the temple (Lk 19:45-48). According to Luke, Jesus reacts to the greed of the merchants who have turned God's house of prayer into a den of thieves. But Luke abbreviates and tones down Mark's account; he leaves out the buyers, the overturning of tables and chairs, and the preventing of anyone carrying things through the temple (cf. Mk 11:15-16). Lk 22:36-38, 49-52 do not advocate violence. Jesus' exhortation, "let him who has no sword sell his mantle and buy one" fulfills the scripture, "And he was reckoned with transgressors" (Lk 22:36-38). For this fulfillment two swords suffice, which hardly establishes the apostles as revolutionaries. The violence in Lk 22:49-52 belongs to one of Jesus' disciples; Jesus (only in Luke) heals the injured ear. Jesus' enemies have the swords and clubs. Luke has down played Jesus' violence in the temple; but he does not leave the event out of his Gospel. His report does not advocate violence in a Christian's life. But for Luke Jesus teaches and acts assertively and aggressively.

In the narrative of paying taxes to Caesar (Lk 20:20-26), Jesus' opponents are trying to entrap him; they have no real interest in establishing a norm for paying taxes to the Romans. Jesus recognizes their intention, and his answer avoids their trap. Jesus accepts Roman taxes as a reality —nothing more. Jesus' passion marks the first major encounter with the Romans. Pilate does not behave during Jesus' passion as a courageous official who defends the disadvantaged, but he does try to free him (Lk 23:16, 20, 22; Acts 3:13). The high priests and scribes force Pilate's hand; according to Luke the main blame for Jesus' death falls on them (cf. Lk 24:20). In several places (Lk 22:52; 23:4-5, 10, 13-16) during Jesus' passion, only Luke introduces the chief priests and rulers as Jesus' opponents and distinguishes them from the people (esp. Lk 23:25; cf. v 13). Jesus' innocence (Lk 23:4, 14-15, 22; cf. vv 41, 47-48; Acts 3:13-14; 13:28) constitutes Luke's main theological message during Jesus' passion. The last words at Jesus' passion are those of the Roman centurion: "Certainly this man was innocent" (Lk 23:47). Jesus' silence during his passion witnesses to his acceptance of his Father's will (cf. Lk 22:42) and to his feelings about the horrid miscarriage of justice (cf. Lk 22:68-71; 23:3). Nowhere does Luke ever say that Jesus has been condemned.

With modifications Luke (23:2, 3, 37, 38) takes over Mark's presentation of Jesus as King (Mk 15:2, 9, 12, 18, 26, 32). This title, surely not a political one for Mark or Luke, recalls Jesus' transcendence over any political force of this world:

> And he (the good thief) said, "Jesus, remember me when you come into your kingdom." And he said to him, "Truly, I say to you, today you will be with me in Paradise" (Lk 23:42-43).

Before Jewish officials Luke allows for civil disobedience. To the accusation of the Jewish officials who had governing authority in Jerusalem, Peter and John (Acts 4:19-20) and Peter and the apostles (Acts 5:29) retort that they have to obey God rather than man. Certainly, Luke thinks that the apostles are doing the right thing (cf. Acts 5:38-39); but, by any standards, the apostles are committing civil disobedience. For the Jewish officials had police authority in Jerusalem.

According to Luke, the Christians have quite amicable relations with the Romans. Roman laws and customs benefited them. The first Gentile convert is the Roman centurion, Cornelius (Acts 10:1—11:18). At Paphos, Sergius Paulus, the Roman proconsul, believes when he sees the results of Paul's curse on Elymas (Acts 13:6-12). Romans became Christians.

In Philippi, Roman customs and practices are at first used against Paul and Silas (Acts 16:21). But notice of their Roman citizenship causes the magistrates to fear because they beat and imprisoned them; the magistrates apologize, let them out of prison, and ask them to leave the city (Acts 16:35-40). The Jews create a riot at Thessalonica but cannot find Paul. The city authorities require bail of Jason and others and free them (Acts 17:1-9). In Corinth, Roman law again protects Paul. When the Jews bring Paul before the tribunal, Gallio, the proconsul of Achaia, reacts as follows:

> ...Gallio said to the Jews, "If it were a matter of wrong-doing or vicious crime I should have reason to bear with you, O Jews; but since it is a matter of question about words and names and your own law, see to it yourselves; I refuse to be a judge of these things" (Acts 18:14-15).

In Ephesus, the town clerk fears that Paul's opponents will be charged with rioting, for they cannot justify the commotion (Acts 19:40).

Claudius Lysias, a Roman tribune, rescues Paul from the Jewish mob in Jerusalem (Acts 21:27-36; 23:27). He allows Paul to speak to the people (Acts 21:39-40). Although Lysias had ordered Paul to be examined by scourging, Paul's appeal to his Roman citizenship spares him this humiliation and frightens Lysias because he had bound a Roman citizen (Acts 22:22-29). The high priest, contrary to the law, orders Paul to be struck (Acts 23:2-3); Lysias rescues Paul from the clamorous dissension of the Sanhedrin (Acts 23:9-10) and the ambush of the Jews (esp. Acts 23:12-22, 30). Two centurions and Roman soldiers provide Paul safe conduct to Caesarea (Acts 23:23-25, 31-32). Lysias writes his opinion about the whole affair to Felix, "I found that he was accused about questions of their law, but charged with nothing deserving death or imprisonment" (Acts 23:29).

The Roman procurator, Felix, has a rather accurate knowledge of the Way. Paul defends himself before him; according to Luke, Felix's greed for money (Acts 24:26) keeps him from freeing Paul. His conduct toward Paul confirms his realization that Paul was innocent. Paul remains in custody but enjoys some freedom; his friends are not to be prevented from attending to his needs.

Paul appears before Festus and then before Festus and Agrippa II. When Festus wants to do the Jewish leaders a favor and send Paul to Jerusalem for trial, Paul appeals to Caesar (Acts 25:11-12; cf. vv 21, 25; 26:32; 28:19). Again, Roman law protects a Christian, Paul's appearance before Festus and Agrippa II represents the climax of his defense, and this section (Acts 25-26) strongly parallels that of Jesus before Pilate. Festus' answer to the Jews exhibits how Roman customs protected the Christians:

> I answered them that it was not the custom of the Romans to give up any one before the accused met the accusers face to face, and had opportunity to make his defense concerning the charge laid against him (Acts 25:16).

In Agrippa II we find a man who knows Roman law and customs and the disputes of the Jews, yet this defense ends with a twofold declaration of Paul's innocence. Everyone says, "This man does nothing to deserve death or imprisonment"; then Agrippa II tells Festus, "This man could have been set free if he had not appealed to Caesar" (Acts 26:31-32).

The Lord had instructed Paul that he would have to witness about him also in Rome (Acts 23:11; cf. 19:21). The Roman centurion, Julius, conducts Paul to Rome (Acts 27:2); on the way, at Sidon, Julius treats Paul kindly and allows him to visit friends who care for him (Acts 27:3). When the soldiers plan to kill the prisoners lest any escape, the centurion, wishing to save Paul, prevents them from carrying out their purpose (Acts 27:42-43). Once again, a Roman provides a Christian with kind and fair treatment.

When they arrive in Rome, Paul is allowed to stay by himself with only a soldier to guard him. Paul reports to the local Jewish leaders that although he did nothing against the Jewish people or the customs of the fathers, he was delivered as a prisoner to the Romans. The Romans wanted to free him because they thought he did nothing worthy of death. However, since some Jews objected to this, Paul had to appeal to Caesar (Acts 28:17-19). Actually Paul endures imprisonment for the hope of Israel which is the resurrection of the dead (Acts 28:20; cf. 23:6; 24:14-15; 26:6-8, 22-23). Amazingly, the Jews in Rome had received no letters about Paul; and no Jew coming to Rome had reported any evil about him (Acts 28:21). An ideal situation for Paul (and Christians) ends Acts; for two whole years Paul lives at his own expense in Rome; he welcomes everyone who comes to him; he preaches the kingdom of God and teaches about the Lord Jesus Christ quite openly and unhindered (Acts 28:30-31). Once in Rome, Paul remains a prisoner but, thanks to the Romans, freely and without hindrance preaches and teaches.

Perhaps, Acts 4:27 constitutes the only negative statement about the relationship of a Roman official to Christianity: "For truly in this city there were gathered together against your holy servant Jesus whom you anointed, both Herod and Pontius Pilate, with the Gentiles and peoples of Israel." But here Luke relates an historical reality: Jesus had been crucified, and Pilate was among the perpetrators. In the context, Luke points out that even this crime was part of God's plan (Acts 4:28).

In summary, Luke advocates taking full advantage of the Roman policy. His principle would be: Christians should use every available legal means to protect themselves. Obviously, Luke is not facing a situation of the outright opposition of Roman officials to Christianity as does the author of the Revelation of John. For Luke, not all the Jews are opponents of the Christians; and, at least, one of the Herodians, Agrippa II, seems friendly. The Christians are the true Pharisees. Romans become Christians; Cornelius is the first Gentile convert. Roman officials treat the Christians kindly and fairly; they protect them from Jewish and other political abuse and intrigue. Roman laws and customs favor the Christians as they preach about Christ. To the Romans, Jewish religious questions and disputes are of no import. Jesus, unless one wants to make a case for the cleansing of the temple, and the Christians commit no crime; Paul's only "crime" is his belief in the resurrection of the dead. In the overall Lucan theology no political force, Roman included, overcomes God's plan. Most importantly, Paul (Christianity) at the end of Acts resides in the capital city of the world and preaches and teaches freely and without hindrance.

A corollary of the above would be something never explicitly stated by Luke. The activity of the Christians and the tenets of their religion create no difficulty for a sensible, reasonable system of government. Only an irrational government or people, led by religious prejudice and/or hatred, could find fault with Christianity. In any nation ruled by reason, Christians make good citizens.

This is the self-image that Luke wants us, his readers, to have.

CHAPTER 8

THE PERSONAL DIMENSION IN LUKE'S PORTRAYAL OF GOD'S SALVIFIC WILL

Often one hears the observation made that Luke assigns a personal dimension to his presentation of Israel's salvation history. "Personal" here means any enhancement of the dignity of human beings, of the significance of their actions and of the resultant care and concern due them. Sometimes, Luke achieves this scope through contrast. Certainly, Luke's themes of universality, of Christ as savior of the disadvantaged, of the appropriate personal response, and of joy, wonder, blessing, and praise *demonstrate* this personal dimension. These themes demonstrate God's openness in Christianity to everyone and how this affects people. But since each of these themes is considered elsewhere, no need exists to review them here. Nonetheless, the reader should not forget that they form the core of Luke's personal portrayal of God's salvific will. However, Luke has other ways in which he manifests this personal concern. This personal concern can best be seen in Lucan passages where he differs from Mark's Gospel. Luke's differences from Matthew's Gospel are less revealing since one cannot always tell whether one of them is following his own source or has changed Q. However, by attending to theological concerns we can sometimes determine who made the change. Material proper to Luke will not be studied here unless he has inserted or added a few verses or a phrase to a pericope which finds a parallel in Mark or Matthew. This does not mean that the extended material proper to Luke does not reveal his concern about the personal, rather the contrary. But this material is considered in other parts of this book. Here the scope is more to alert the reader to Luke's concern for the personal in the passages which parallel Mark and Matthew. When one views these passages together with the other themes which bring out the personal, it must be recognized that Luke has a notable personal dimension in his portrayal of God's salvific history.

Luke brings out this personal dimension in a number of ways. He intensifies the presentation of a person or of a situation in which a person is involved. For instance, he will build up a miracle or stress a given attribute. More personal information and details are communicated to the reader. Luke names persons, places, and the subjects of verbs. He directly addresses his audience and supplies data which correspond to their actual experience. He drops negative statements about Jesus and his disciples. Careful treatment of Peter is obvious. But, most of all, Luke reserves a special place for the person and character of Jesus.

A. Luke Intensifies the Presentation of a Person or of a Situation

Luke intensifies the presentation of individuals or of a situation in which they are involved. He characterizes the people's reaction to John the Baptist, "As the people were in expectation, and all questioned in their hearts concerning John..." (Lk 3:15). He specifies of Herod that he was "reproved" by John "...for all the evil things that Herod had done,...added this to them all, that he shut up John in prison" (Lk 3:19-20).

In the healing of the demoniac, Luke observes that the demon came out of him "having done him no harm" (Lk 4:35). This addition serves both to note the condition of the possessed man and the power of the cure. Luke moves the significant piece of information about the daughter of Jairus, "about the age of twelve" from the end of the story to the beginning, and thus, gains earlier the empathy of his reader for her and her father's sad plight (Lk 8:42; cf. Mk 5:42).

Luke personalizes a little more the description in the proverb, "from their fruit you will know them" by writing of the good man "out of the good treasure of his heart" and by his concluding generalization, "for out of the abundance of his heart his mouth speaks" (cf. Lk 6:45). The same can be said of the story of the healing of the possessed boy. Luke inserts into that pericope that the father of the boy, "cried ...I beg you look" and "I begged your disciples" to show the father's desperation and humility.

Luke stresses the radical commitment of a disciple. In Lk 9:60b-62, which are proper to him, Luke insists on the radical personal commitment of the follower of Christ who must subordinate any family concerns to the call to follow Jesus and proclaim the kingdom of God. The rich young man is designated a "ruler" (Lk 18:18). A discussion about riches and the rewards of discipleship follows the scene of the encounter between Jesus and the rich young man. When the discussion turns to the persons whom one has to leave to follow Jesus, Luke adds "wife" to the list and drops "lands" (Lk 18:29; cf. Mk 10:30). Apparently, Luke felt that a basic relationship had been overlooked and that "lands" should not be put on the same level with "wife," "brother," "parents," or "children" in this consideration of a disciple's commitment.

Luke develops the image that a Christian should have of God in prayer. The parable of the importunate friend at midnight, immediately following the Our Father, contends that the Father certainly surpasses any human father in giving good gifts to his children. Luke underlines the personal characteristics of the Father because he has added to

"What father among you, if his son asks for a fish, will instead of a fish give him a serpent" the further comparison, "or if he asks for an egg, will give him a scorpion" (Lk 11:12).

Luke intensifies the presentation of three scenes in which Jesus encounters and interacts with opponents. He augments Lk 11:45-54 with the notice that Jesus' proclamation of woes on the Pharisees and lawyers leads them to press hard to try to catch him in something he might say. Personal charges against those who misuse their office often lead to antagonism rather than conversion. Only Luke has the exclamation of the Jewish leaders in the parable of the wicked husbandman, for they realize that the parable relates to them, "When they heard this, they said, 'God forbid' " (Lk 20:16). Again, Luke introduces a personal expansion even though people reject Jesus. Finally, Luke has brought into the treatment of the Sadducees' question about the resurrection (Lk 20:27-40) a number of statements which touch on the personal:

> "The sons of this age marry and are given in marriage; but those who are accounted worthy to attain to that age... for they cannot die anymore,...and are sons of God, being sons of the resurrection...for all live in him." And some of the scribes answered, "Teacher, you have spoken well."

The Sadducees have simply misunderstood the nature of resurrected life. Marriage belongs to this world, not to the next. There no one dies, for they are sons and daughters of God and of the resurrection. Their life is for God.

Luke's report on the destruction of Jerusalem contains some personal expansion not found in the other Synoptics, some of which seem to relate to actual experiences. There will be "wrath upon the people; they will fall by the edge of the sword, and be led captive among all nations; and Jerusalem will be trodden down by the Gentiles,..." (Lk 21:23-24). The same holds for Luke's description of the coming of the Son of Man where he writes "..., and upon the earth distress of nations in perplexity at the roaring of the sea and waves, men fainting with fear and with the foreboding of what is coming on the world." Although all the Synoptics end this pericope on a positive note, Luke does not speak of the gathering of the elect but of "Now when these things begin to take place, look up and raise your heads, because your redemption is drawing near" (cf. Lk 21:25-26, 28). Lk 21:34-36, proper to Luke, continues this positive note. These verses encourage the *disciples* (Christians) not to be weighed down by anything but to watch at all times, and to pray that they will escape all these things and to stand before the Son of Man.

In the narrative about the last supper, Luke adds the understandable concern of the disciples about who will betray Jesus, "And they began to question one another, which of them it was that would do this" (Lk 22:23).

Judas receives special treatment from Luke in the scene of Jesus' arrest (Lk 22:47-53; cf. Mk 14:43-52; Mt 26:47-56). The Lucan phrase, "the man called Judas," implies distance and some contempt, and Luke also writes, "He drew near to Jesus to kiss him." Unlike Mark and Matthew, he does not explicitly say that Judas kissed Jesus. Judas' hypocrisy strikes Luke as insufferable. Jesus, then, for the only time in the whole New Testament, addresses Judas by name and thus demonstrates his own fidelity to personal relationships. Only Luke continues, ". . . do you betray the Son of Man with a kiss?" Judas' kiss ironically destroys rather than confirms any personal relationship with Jesus. Moreover, this is the only time that the second person, singular, present of *paradidōmi*, "I betray," occurs in the New Testament. The personal, yet hortative, value of this question for Luke's reader cannot be easily estimated. The disciples' words to Jesus, "Lord, shall we strike with the sword?" are likewise proper to Luke. "Lord" shows them to be aware of their relationship to Jesus. They look to him for directions.

B. *Luke Provides More Personal Information and Details and Expands on Personal Descriptions*

Luke is more personal than Mark and Matthew in other ways. For instance, he provides more personal information and details and expands on personal descriptions. The proverbial statement, "And no one after drinking old wine desires new, for he says 'The old is good,'" (Lk 5:39), shows Luke as alert to human tendencies. Moreover, Luke has inserted "kings" (Lk 10:24) alongside prophets as desirous of seeing what the disciples have seen. He expands on the persons and social positions included. Only Luke makes the narrative about a lamp more personal by giving the purpose of its being lit, "That those who enter may see the light" (Lk 11:33), and provides the personal application of the image of the light, "If then your whole body is full of light, having no part dark, it will be wholly bright, as when a lamp with its rays gives you light" (Lk 11:36).

When John the Baptist sends two of his disciples to inquire if Jesus is the one to come or shall they wait for another, Luke writes the more personal, "To what then shall I compare *the men* of this generation, and what are *they like*" (Lk 7:31) while Matthew pens "But to what shall I compare this generation" (Mt 11:16)? Also, in the healing of the Gerasene demoniac, Luke does not drop from sight the man out of whom the demon came (cf. Lk 8:33).

Luke continues this personal concern in his passion narrative. He adds the incident of Jesus' appearance before Herod Antipas (Lk 23:6-12). This encounter condemns false personal relationship with Jesus. Herod Antipas wants to see a miracle; he has no disposition whatsoever towards conversion. Jesus will not even answer his questions. The worth of Herod Antipas' recovery of his friendship with Pilate has little value since it results from his contemptuous attitude toward Jesus. After Jesus has entrusted his spirit to the Father, Luke writes that the people stood by "watching," while their rulers scoffed. He prepares us for the positive response of the crowd, "And all the multitude who assembled to see the sight, when they saw what had taken place, returned home beating their breasts" (Lk 23:48). Jesus' death provokes a number of personal and positive responses most of which are proper to Luke. The centurion praises God and exclaims, "Certainly, this man was a good man." Jesus' acquaintances and the women who followed him from Galilee stand at a distance and view these things. Their viewing is stressed. Joseph of Arimathea musters the courage to ask Pilate for Jesus' body. When he has wrapped it in a linen shroud, he lays it in a new tomb. Finally, the women from Galilee see the tomb and how his body was laid; they go home and prepare spices and ointments so that they can give Jesus a decent burial. The response of these individuals to Jesus finds expression in their declaration or indication of his goodness or innocence and in their providing for his burial (Lk 23:47-56).

C. Luke Addresses and Names Persons and Supplies the Subjects of Verbs

Luke addresses and names persons, and he supplies the subjects of verbs. At times, he directly addresses his audience; for instance, only Luke directs and dedicates his two volumes to a person, Theophilus (Lk 1:3; Acts 1:1). Granted that this dedication may be to a sponsor who will pay for the publication or symbolically may represent all of Luke's readers, nonetheless, it is an address and conveys a personal relationship. Luke renders the beatitudes more personal to his audience by introducing "you" and "yours"; for instance, "Blessed are you poor, for yours is the kingdom of God" (Lk 6:20; cf. 6:21-23; Mt 5:3-12). The same holds for Luke's woes (Lk 6:24-26). Probably, with the same intention Luke, in contrast to "What is the first of all the commandments?" (Mk 12:28; Mt 22:36), has the lawyer put Jesus to the test with the more personal questions, "Teacher, what shall I do to inherit eternal life?" (Lk 10:25). In Lk 17 a number of personal items are introduced. Twice (Lk 17:1, 22) Jesus addresses his disciples and tells them about temptations to sin, "Take heed to yourselves. . ." (Lk 17:3a), and about the coming of the kingdom, "behold, the kingdom of God is in the midst of you" (Lk 17:21).

Of course, in the scene of the last supper, "...which is given for you. Do this in remembrance of me" are due to Luke's source, but "for you" and "in remembrance of me" are certainly personal in nature. Moreover, Luke's less Aramaic "for you" is more universally personal than is Mark's and Matthew's "for many" (Lk 22:19-20; cf. Mk 14:24; Mt 26:28). Finally, in the scene of the betrayal and arrest of Jesus, Luke, in opposition to the other Synoptics, names "the chief priests and officers of the temple and elders" whom Jesus addresses (Lk 22:52).

D. Luke Addresses His Audience and Their Actual Experiences

On any number of occasions, Luke makes a pericope more relevant to the church's later experience. Thus, his gospel becomes more personal for his readers who live in that later church. In Jesus' instructions on love of one's enemies, Luke apparently expands Matthew's "and pray for those who persecute you" (Mt 5:44b) to "do good to those who hate you, bless those that curse you, pray for those who abuse you" (Lk 6:27b-28) and changes his "And if you salute only your brethren, what more are you doing than others? Do not even the Gentiles do the same?" (Mt 5:47) to:

> "If you love those who love you, what credit is that to you? For even sinners love those who love them. And if you do good to those who do good to you, what credit is that to you? For even sinners do the same. But if you lend to those from whom you hope to receive, what credit is that to you? Even sinners lend to sinners, to receive as much again...and lend, expecting nothing in return; and your reward will be great..." (Lk 6:32-35).

Luke has given more attention to how a Christian treats those who persecute him, and to the tendency to love, to do good, and to lend only to one's friends. Sinners do all of the latter. But Jesus' instructions call for great generosity towards one's fellow human beings. Doubtless this is why Luke concludes this pericope with the relational statement, "Be merciful, even as your father is merciful" (Lk 6:36) instead of "You, therefore, must be perfect as your heavenly Father is perfect" (Mt 5:48). Much the same attitude is reflected in Luke's insertion in the pericope about judging,

> "...condemn not, and you will not be condemned; forgive, and you will be forgiven; give, and it will be given to you; good measure, pressed down, shaken together, running over, will be put into your lap" (Lk 6:37-38).

Luke adjusts his description of discipleship to that of the later church. By moving from the twelve apostles (Lk 9:1, 10, 12) to the disciples (Lk 9:14), Luke extends the number of those who will set the blessed loaves and fishes before the crowd (Lk 9:16). Given the similarity of the passage to the Institution Narrative, the thought is that more persons than the Twelve will make the Eucharist available to Christians. Likewise, Luke's isolated sending out of the seventy by Jesus in Lk 10:1-16 demonstrates that in no way should this mission be limited to the Twelve. Although the Lucan addition, "...and salute no one along the way," seems harsh, its real purpose is to mark the urgency of the task, for the instruction to the seventy whenever they enter a house, "...first say, 'Peace be to this house,'" is gentle enough. Luke alone has expanded Jesus' prediction of his passion and call to follow him in suffering to "all" and speaks of taking up one's cross "daily" (Lk 9:23), and in the passion narrative he adds the phrase, "behind Jesus," to "to carry (the cross) behind Jesus," and thus establishes Simon of Cyrene as a disciple to be imitated by all (Lk 23:26). A passage with a similar message for Luke's reader is to be found in the narrative about the coming of the kingdom (Lk 17:20-37). The description of the days of Lot (Lk 17:28-30) repeats and expands on the human activity which occurred during the days of Noah (Lk 17:26-27). Luke means that

Christ must suffer, thereafter normal human activity will continue until suddenly the day of the Lord arrives. It will do no good at its arrival to attempt any human retrieval. A Lucan addition to the context of the pericope (Lk 17:20-37) echoes the Caesarea Philippi scene (cf. Lk 9:24) and supplies correct advice for one's personal conduct until the day of the Lord, "Whoever seeks to gain his life will lose it, but whoever loses his life will preserve it" (Lk 17:33; cf. Mt 10:39).

Only Luke introduces the Our Father with the request of one of Jesus' disciples, "Lord, teach us to pray, as John taught his disciples" (Lk 11:1; cf. Mt 6:6-8). The disciple realizes the importance of his and his fellow disciples' special relationship to Jesus whom, in anticipation of the resurrection, he names, "Lord." Luke's (11:3) "each day" instead of Matthew's "this day" in the phrase "Give us each day our daily bread" better describes the constant human need of the Father's support.

One definite experience of the later church was the persecution which its members had to endure. Luke addresses this problem for his readers. In Luke 11:45-54 he develops the thought with the insertions, "The wisdom of God said" and "apostles" in the statement, "Therefore also the wisdom of God said, 'I will send them prophets and apostles, some of whom they will kill and persecute,...'" The statement now applies to the later church and the persecution her prophets and apostles will have to endure. Luke has also heightened the personal interaction in the exhortation to fearless confession of the Son of Man (Lk 12:2-9) with: "I tell you my friends,...But I will warn you whom to fear:...yes, I tell you, fear him! And I tell you...the Son of Man." In the promise of the assistance of the Holy Spirit (Lk 12:11-12), Luke has introduced items which relate the pericope better to the later persecution of the early church, "...before the synagogues and the rulers and the authorities" and (how) "...you are to defend yourselves." Luke has adapted Jesus' predictions of persecution to the later experiences of the church. He has extended Mark's presentation with the following:

"...they will lay their hands on you and persecute you
...prisons...(before) governors...Settle it therefore in
your minds,...how to defend yourselves; I (will give you)
a mouth and wisdom, which none of your adversaries will
be able to withstand or contradict...But not a hair of
your head will perish;...you will gain your lives" (Lk
21:12-19; cf. Mk 13:9-13).

Luke has rendered Jesus' prediction more relevant and
personal because he has described the actual experiences
which the early Christians were having. The guarantee of
the risen Jesus' presence at such times encourages the persecuted. As was shown above, "But not a hair of your head
will perish" must look to the resurrection, and "By *your*
endurance *you* will gain *your* lives" proves a more personal
expression for the disciples and Luke's readers than "But he
who endures to the end will be saved" (Mk 13:13; cf. Mt
24:13).

In noting that faith in Jesus will cause divisions in households only Luke (Lk 12:49-53) affixes the statement, "...for
henceforth in one house there will be five divided, three
against two and two against three" and each time expands
the conflict by indicating that it can originate from either
side of the relationship noted.

Through Peter's question about the parable on watchfulness and faithfulness, "Lord, are you telling this parable for
us or for all?" (Lk 12:41), Luke applies the parable to
everyone who becomes a steward in the Lord's household.
The conclusion of this application, which is likewise proper
to him, makes the further point that one's punishment will
be in terms of one's awareness of the master's will; more
talent means that more will be demanded. Luke has a more
universal yet a more personal application of this parable.
Probably, he is thinking of the later community, too, when
he adds the following personal challenge to the story about
agreement with one's accusers, "And why do you not judge
for yourselves what is right?" (Lk 12:54-57).

Another Lucan passage seems to deal with community
relationships. Some of the material in Lk 22:24-34 which

immediately follows Luke's Institution Narrative is proper to Luke: the dispute over greatness and continuing with Jesus in his suffering. Surely, the other Synoptics report the dispute over greatness, but they do not place it in the context of the Institution Narrative. Luke's thought on service seems to flow from the Eucharist. Moreover, the disciples have remained with Jesus in his suffering. He covenants with them, as his Father did with him, a kingdom where they may eat and drink at his table. Disciples unite themselves with Jesus in his suffering and enjoy the covenantal promise of the messianic banquet.

Luke seemingly wants to address the later church in his sayings regarding anxiety about earthly things (Lk 12:22-32), since he speaks of "his disciples" as a "little flock." He has added some personal touches to these sayings. He alone begins the pericope with "And he said to his disciples, . . ." and in proverbial style generalizes Jesus' instruction to, "If then you are not able to do as small a thing as that (add a cubit to your stature), why are you anxious about the rest?" Luke's last statement in this pericope, "Fear not, little flock, for it is your Father's good pleasure to give you the kingdom" strikes a more personal note than Matthew's (6:34): "Therefore do not be anxious about tomorrow, for tomorrow will be anxious for itself. Let the day's own trouble be sufficient for the day."

E. Luke Drops or Modifies Negative Statements about the Apostles and the Disciples

Luke has dropped or modified Mark's negative statements about the Apostles and disciples so that they appear in a better light. Furthermore, he calls attention to them and even portrays Jesus as defending them. In fact, there is no trace in Luke of Jesus' admonition of the apostles for their failure to understand the parable of the sower, "Do you really not understand this parable? Then how are you going to understand all the other parables" (Mk 4:13)? This verse makes the apostles look ignorant. Luke also omits, from the story of the stilling of the storm, the apostles' reaction when Jesus is sleeping and they awake him with the words, "Teacher, do you not care if we perish?" (Mk 4:38), and their rebuke of Jesus in the cure of the woman with the flow of blood, "You see the crowd pressing around you, and yet you say, 'Who touched me?'" (Mk 5:31). The first of these shows the apostles as fearful, and the second as not being sufficiently respectful of Jesus. Similar reasoning on the part of Luke explains his omission of the apostles' response to Jesus' charge that they were to tell no one of the Transfiguration until the Son of Man should have risen from the dead, "So they kept the matter to themselves, questioning what the rising from the dead meant" (Mk 9:10). Likewise, Luke finds unacceptable Mark's (9:28-29) portrayal of the apostles after Jesus heals the boy possessed by a spirit, "And when he had entered the house, his disciples asked him privately, 'Why could we not cast it out?' And he said to them, 'This kind cannot be driven out by anything but prayer.'" The apostles again appear ignorant and, perhaps, weak because of their failure, and Luke sees no reason to present this. Naturally, Luke did not take over Mark's story of the sons of Zebedee and their desire to sit, one at Jesus' right and the other at his left when he comes into his glory (Mk 10:35-45). Finally, the flight of the apostles at Jesus' arrest struck Luke as misrepresenting them and not an appropriate action for followers of Jesus.

Luke's statement that Peter, John, and James during the Transfiguration were heavy with sleep certainly reveals their weakness, but his explanation of their fear in terms of entering the cloud proves more reasonable (cf. Lk 9:32, 34). In the second prediction of Jesus' passion, Luke modifies the ignorance of the disciples with, ". . . and it (the passion) was concealed from them, that they should not perceive it" (Lk 9:45). One can hardly attribute guilt to them if somehow God in his providence saw fit to conceal the passion from them. The third prediction of Jesus' passion provides two further indications of the personal dimensions of Luke's presentation of Israel's salvation history. Luke has dropped Mark's (10:32) notice that those who followed were afraid.

"Fear" is not the kind of response that an apostle or disciple should have. Moreover, Luke again excuses the disciples' misunderstanding, ". . .this saying was hidden from them, and they did not grasp what was said."

When the Pharisees ask Jesus to rebuke his disciples because of their conduct at his triumphal entry into Jerusalem, Jesus defends their actions, "I tell you, if these were silent, the very stones would cry out" (Lk 19:39-40). A little later, Luke alone, of the Synoptics, names Peter and John as the two disciples whom Jesus sends to prepare the Passover.

Luke has added a number of personal touches about discipleship to the Gethsemane scene (Lk 22:39-46; cf. Mk 14:32-42; Mt 26:36-46). He notes that it was Jesus' custom to go to the Mount of Olives and that the disciples "followed" him. Since he says that they followed at a distance, he infers that they are not that enthusiastic about this particular experience. Luke, earlier than Mark and Matthew, introduces Jesus' precept that the disciples are to pray "not to enter into temptation," but he drops their specification that Jesus took along Peter, James, and John, began to be greatly distressed and troubled, and said to them, "My soul is sorrowful, even to death, remain here and watch." In the long run, this knowledge about the three disciples would have been to the detriment of their spiritual presentations. Luke wants the disciples to make a good appearance as is confirmed by his contention that they were sleeping "from sorrow." He also does not mention that Jesus returned a second and a third time to the disciples who continued to sleep.

F. Careful Treatment of Peter is Obvious

Luke gives Peter special treatment. Some scholars prefer to regard Lk 5:1-11 as almost entirely proper to Luke. Whether this is the case or not, the fact remains that in this pericope Luke gives added attention to Peter whose name appears six times. To put Peter in a better light Luke, in the scene of Caesarea Philippi, omits Mark's (8:32-33): "And

Peter took him and began to rebuke him. But turning and seeing his disciples, he (Jesus) rebuked Peter, and said, 'Get behind me, Satan! For you are not on the side of God, but of men.' " Luke also eliminates from the scene on the Mount of Olives Jesus' questions, "Simon, are you sleeping? Could you not watch one hour?" (Mk 14:37; cf. Mt 26:40). Luke again gives special attention to Peter when he tells him how Satan has wanted to sift him like wheat. Jesus assures Peter that he has prayed for him lest he fail and enjoins on Peter the fraternal directive, "...and when you turn again, strengthen your brethren" (Lk 22:31-32). Peter is introduced by Luke earlier into the passion narrative (Lk 22:54-71; Mk 14:53-72; Mt 26:57—27:10), and nothing is said about Peter's cursing or swearing. Nor is Jesus mentioned by name during the denial scene. On the other hand, Jesus is named "Lord" when personal contact with him moves Peter to conversion (Lk 22:61-62), "And Jesus turned and looked at Peter, and Peter remembered the word of the Lord, how he said to him, 'Before the cock crows today, you will deny me three times.' And he went out and wept bitterly." This personal contact between Jesus and Peter is proper to Luke. Moreover, Luke has so located Peter's conversion that there is a break in thought between the denial and the subsequent mistreatment of Jesus. Consequently, Peter's denial should not be associated with this mistreatment.

G. Luke Reserves a Special Place for the Person and Character of Jesus

Luke gives special attention to the person and character of Jesus. For instance, he does not follow Mark's lead when he says things of Jesus which seem undignified. Luke has not taken over the report that Jesus' relatives thought he was crazy (Mk 3:21) nor that Jesus does not know everything (cf. Mk 13:32; 15:34).

He does not take over passages which too boldly express Jesus' human sensibility (cf. Mk 1:43) or anger (Mk 3:5; 10:14). Does this also explain why Luke does not speak of

Jesus' taking children in his arms (cf. Mk 9:36; 10:16) or of his looking on the rich young man with love (Mk 10:21)? Luke uses the verb, "crucify," only once of both Jesus and the two criminals. Others, not Luke, during Jesus' passion predicate "crucify" of Jesus alone. To Luke, the word must have represented a horrible miscarriage of justice. Luke described the mistreatment of Jesus in very general terms. He did introduce into the third prediction of Jesus' passion, "shamefully treated" (Lk 18:32), but he omits the spitting and blows which Jesus endures according to the other Synoptics. The scene before the high priest preserves Jesus' dignity better than it does in the other Synoptics. False witnesses are not sought, and there is no direct confrontation between Jesus and the high priest, for the whole Sanhedrin addresses him. The emphasis is on Jesus' personal testimony. Nothing is said about the high priest's tearing his garments nor is any condemnation delivered. Jesus does not blaspheme, his opponents do (Lk 22:65). Finally, Luke only alludes to the flogging (Lk 23:16, 22).

For Luke Jesus is very popular with the people. Luke, in the narrative about Jairus' daughter and the woman with the hemorrhage, informs his reader that the crowd "welcomed" Jesus, "for they were all waiting for him" (Lk 8:40). Luke emphasizes Jesus' popularity by introducing into his narrative the following: "When the crowds were increasing..." (Lk 11:29), "In the meantime, when so many thousands of the multitude had gathered together that they trod on one another" (Lk 12:1), and "And early in the morning all the people came to him in the temple to hear him" (Lk 21:38). Lk 23:27-32 appear only in Luke. According to this passage, a great multitude of people follows Jesus and thus verifies his personal attraction. The degree of their attraction reveals itself in the wails and laments of the women whose attitudes Luke might be recommending to his reader as the appropriate responses of disciples to Jesus' passion. Jesus' compassion, however, is for the women and their children. Jesus, with paradoxical feminine images, characterizes the coming catastrophe.

Jesus' popularity forces his enemies to deal with him by stealth. Only in Luke's Gospel, does Judas agree to betray Jesus, and he seeks to do so, but "in the absence of the crowd" (Lk 22:6).

Luke expands on who Jesus is, what he will do, and how the disciples are to relate to him. Only Luke records Herod's question, "Who is this about whom I hear such things?" and mentions that Herod sought to see Jesus (Lk 9:9). Doubtless, Luke is ironical when he places these words in Herod's mouth, but they are intended to direct Luke's reader's attention to the person of Jesus. Mention of Jesus' glory (Lk 9:31-32; cf. 9:26) stands only in Luke's account of the Transfiguration, and the unique reference to Jesus' "exodus which he was to accomplish at Jerusalem" unites his experience with that of Israel and summarizes well his subsequent death and resurrection. At the beginning of the story on faith, "The apostles said to the Lord, 'Increase our faith!'" (Lk 17:5). They recognize their weakness and Jesus as the Lord who can increase their faith. According to Luke, Jesus' disciples call him "teacher," and his instruction to them about those who claim to be him is more direct, "Do not go after them," than that in the other Synoptics (Lk 21:7-8; cf. Mk 13:3-6; Mt 24:3-5).

As was noted earlier, the emphasis in the appearance before the high priest is on Jesus' own personal testimony. This personal testimony marks the decisive moment of the pericope. It illuminates the person of Jesus and thus founds the dedication of his disciples. Luke, unlike Mark and Matthew, has distinguished two "questions": "If you are the Christ, tell us" (Lk 22:67a) and "Are you the Son of God, then?" (Lk 22:70a). Jesus' answer to the first question reveals that he is convinced that they will not believe him anyway nor answer any question which he might ask. Nonetheless, he states that from now on the Son of Man will be seated at the right hand of the power of God. This statement introduces their second question to which Jesus answers, "You say that I am." Their retort, "What further testimony do we need? We have heard it ourselves from his own lips" reminds Luke's reader that he needs no more than this testimony before he expresses his own personal response to Jesus.

Luke, as Mark, records that at Jesus' death the curtain of the temple was torn in two. What Luke says elsewhere leads to the interpretation of this event as an indication of Jesus' importance, for he displaces the temple because true worship recognizes Jesus and his resurrection as the fulfillment of the promises of the Old Testament. In addition, Luke omits Jesus' lament taken from Ps 22:2 because it gives the impression of a rupture in Jesus' relationship with his Father. On the other hand, "Father, into your hands I commit my spirit" (Lk 23:46; cf. Ps 30:6), which occurs only in Luke, confirms this relationship and the total confidence which Jesus has in his Father.

It might well be true to say that Luke has dropped some Markan passages which too boldly express Jesus' human sensibility. But this statement must be modified by the fact that Luke has a number of passages proper to himself, that show that Jesus is sensitive to the needs and feelings of people. In contrast to Mark, Luke in the story about the sick healed at evening accents Jesus' attention to individuals, ". . . he laid hands on every one of them" (Lk 4:40). A kind of identification of Jesus and his concern for the boy's father appear in the Lucan addition to the story of the cure of the epileptic boy, ". . . healed . . . and gave him back to his father. And all were astonished by the *majesty* of God" (Lk 9:42-43). After Jesus' prayer to the Father (Lk 10:21-22), Luke continues with the words, "Then turning to the disciples he said privately. . ." Luke pays attention to Jesus' audiences and his private interactions with them. Proper to Luke, too, is the answer of the lawyer, and Jesus' charges about their failures among which is loading people down with heavy burdens without giving them any assistance in carrying them (Lk 11:45-52). Jesus' weeping over Jerusalem (Lk 19:41-44) shows his humanity. The ignorance of her people of the time of their visitation and their future destruction by enemies provokes his tears. Certainly, Jesus acts violently in the cleansing of the temple (Lk 19:45-46), for the merchants have turned God's house of prayer into a den of thieves. But Luke abbreviates and tones down Mark's account; he leaves out the buyers, the overturning of the tables and chairs, and the preventing of anyone carrying things through the temple (cf. Mk 11:15-16). Thus, although Jesus performs a violent act of probable civil disobedience, his concern has a solid religious basis and his behavior in Luke is less outrageous.

Jesus' sensitivity, through his care for others, strong expressions and willingness to forgive, proves amazing. Luke, not Mark or Matthew, records Jesus' strong assertion, "I have earnestly desired to eat this Passover with you before I suffer," and that he will not eat it or drink of the fruit of the vine until the kingdom of God comes (Lk 22:15-18). Jesus' calm answer to those who want to seize him in the garden on the Mount of Olives discourages violence, yet one of the disciples does react violently. But Jesus corrects this, and only in Luke does Jesus heal the ear of the slave of the high priest, "And he touched his ear and healed him" (Lk 22:49-51). Jesus in his solicitude for this injured person follows his own instruction to love one's enemies (cf. Lk 6:27, 35). Jesus' prayer, "Father, forgive them; for they know not what they do" (Lk 23:34), although absent from some important manuscripts, is probably genuine and unfolds Jesus' relation to the Father and his magnanimity toward his executioners. Finally, the story of the two thieves (Lk 23:39-43) again exhibits Luke's concern for the personal. The one thief rails at Jesus in words which recall the mockery of the Jewish rulers (cf. Lk 23:35, 39). The other corrects him, accepts the reality of their guilt, and asserts that Jesus has done no wrong. He petitions Jesus to remember him when he comes into his kingdom. There follows Jesus' response to the thief's confidence in him, "Truly, I say to you, today you will be with me in Paradise."

Two Lucan additions bring out Jesus' wisdom. The concluding words, "And they were not able in the presence of the people to catch him by what he said; . . . they were silent" (Lk 20:26), to the pericope about paying tribute to Caesar stand only in Luke. These words describe Jesus' marvelous intelligence and ability to deal with malicious questions. So effective is he that his opponents are reduced to silence. This happens again when scribes grant the wisdom of Jesus' reply to the Sadducees' question about resurrection. After that, no one dares to ask him anything (cf. Lk 20:39-40).

Luke underlines Jesus' knowledge, especially, of what the Father wants him to do and his personal determination to do it. Only Luke points out Jesus' knowledge even of the argument of his disciples about greatness and the radical importance of every individual, "...for he who is least among you all is the one who is great" (Lk 9:47-48). Lk 9:51-56 is proper to Luke, who in these verses reports Jesus' personal determination to do the Father's will and his unwillingness to destroy the Samaritans who would not receive him. Besides in Lk 12:49-53, only Luke adds Jesus' words, "I came to cast fire upon the earth; and would that it were already kindled!" and "how I am constrained until it is accomplished!" At a minimum, these words demonstrate that the Lucan Jesus is aware of the task which he has received from the Father and wants to accomplish it. Something should be said about Lk 13:31-33, the Pharisees' warning against Herod. Much of Lk 13 is proper to Luke. Lk 13:31-33 reveals the Lucan Jesus as aware of his Father's will that he is to continue his ministry, yet, since he is a prophet, he cannot die outside Jerusalem. According to Luke, Jesus' death does not come upon him without his knowledge but as a part of what he realizes the Father asks of him. The reference to and necessity of Jesus' suffering and passion in Lk 17:25 are also unique to Luke, "But first he must suffer many things and be rejected by this generation." Consequently, Luke more than the other Synoptics points out Jesus' knowledge and acceptance of his Father's will.

Luke insists on Jesus' innocence (Lk 23:4, 14-15, 22, 41, 47-48; Acts 3:13-14; 13:28). For instance, Pilate does not ask about freeing a prisoner, as he does in Mark, but expresses his intention of freeing the innocent Jesus. Unlike Mark and Matthew, Luke does not connect the flogging with Jesus' condemnation to crucifixion, rather Pilate proposes this punishment to satisfy somewhat the opponents so that Jesus can be freed. Little attention is given to the undignified comparison of Jesus with Barabbas. Luke highlights the opposition between them, "He (Pilate) released the man who had been thrown into prison for insurrection and murder, whom they asked for; but Jesus he delivered to their will" (Lk 23:25). Luke cannot bring himself to write "delivered him to be crucified." The cross which Simon of Cyrene is to carry is not said by Luke to be Jesus' cross because he is innocent (Lk 23:26). Thus, for Luke, Jesus is surely innocent.

H. Conclusion

In conclusion, there is much in Luke-Acts that witnesses to Luke's interest in the personal. The universal extent of Jesus' mission, his saving of the disadvantaged, and the emphasis which Luke puts on one's response and reaction to the news of God's salvific will would alone prove this Lucan concern for the personal. But Luke provides many other indications of this interest in the personal. He intensifies the presentation of a person or of a situation in which a person is involved. He gives more information, names people, directly addresses his audience, and adapts material to his reader's experience. Special respect and attention is paid to the disciples and apostles and, particularly, to Jesus.

This brings us to the end of Part II. Although throughout both Parts I and II, many indications were given about how Luke wants his readers to respond to the experience of God's actions in history, nonetheless, the question of discipleship will be directly addressed in Part III. The descriptions which Luke gives of the early Christians show the way that he wants his readers to act in the presence of God's salvific activity.

PART III

DISCIPLESHIP: HOW CHRISTIANS ACT IN THE PRESENCE OF GOD'S SALVIFIC ACTIVITY

CHAPTER 9

THE DESIRED PERSONAL RESPONSE TO GOD'S SALVIFIC WILL

Actually, the events in Luke-Acts accord with God's salvific will. But Luke again and again lets his readers see how to respond to the continual activity of God in their lives. The free response to God's saving action in Luke-Acts follows from that of the Old Testament. When scholarly confusion arises in this area, it is frequently caused by the failure to realize that Luke has used this as an umbrella-concept under which he includes all correct religious responses. Luke has a great variety of ways of phrasing this response. These phrases will be italicized so that Luke's thought can be followed more easily. Not all of the negative phrasings will be considered. Although variety exists in how Luke words the desired response to God's salvific activity, the more important and the more frequent words in this Lucan thought-pattern are: "to receive" (*dechomai, paradechomai*), "to hear" (*akouō*), "to see" (*blepō, horaō*), "to believe" (*pisteuō, pistis*), "to follow" (*akoloutheō*), "to be baptized" (*baptizō*), "to repent" (*metanoeō, metanoia*), and "to turn" (*epistrephō, epistrophē*). *Metanoeō* (Mt 5xs; Mk 1x; Lk

9xs; Acts 5xs; NT 34xs), *metanoia* (Lk 5xs; Acts 6xs; NT 22xs) and *epistrephō* (Lk 7xs; Acts 11xs; NT 36xs) are used mostly by Luke in the New Testament. Other than the above, the Greek of a given phrase will be given for the sake of clarity. Any theory which calls for fine distinctions among Luke's terms for a response to God's salvific activity runs contrary to the fact that Luke seems willing to use any one of them to designate the whole event, and given terms can vary in meaning. For instance, "hearing" and "seeing" can merely refer to physical perception or to partial or complete receptivity.

Since his thought flows from the Old Testament, Luke, in his description of the Lycaonians' response to Paul's healing of the cripple from birth, can pen a general call to conversion, "Men, why are you doing this? We also are men, of like nature with you, and bring you good news, that you *should turn from* these vain things to a living God who made the heaven and the earth and the sea and all that is in them" (Acts 14:15). In fact, much of the evidence to be considered in this section shows up in what experts in literary forms call "conversion stories."

Luke is rarely this general (cf. Acts 14:15) in his sketch of the human response to God's salvific will. Two passages, the risen Christ's mission to Paul and the agony on the Mount of Olives, will serve to make this point. Luke's narrative, in which the risen Christ assigns a vocational mission to Paul, probably provides the best background for Luke's thinking on this point:

> "For I *have appeared* to you for this purpose to appoint you to serve and to bear witness to the things in which you *have seen me* and to those in which I *will appear to you*, delivering you from the people and from the Gentiles to whom I send you *to open their eyes*, that they *may turn* from darkness to light and from the power of Satan to God, that they *may receive* forgiveness of sins and a place among those who are sanctified by faith in me" (Acts 26:16-18).

Certainly, this description of Paul's ministry is general. "From darkness to light" parallels "from the power of Satan to God." More general descriptions of conversion or response to God's salvific will cannot easily be found. But the response also has a very definite and determining aspect, "by faith in me." The risen Christ asserts that it is by faith in him that one moves from the darkness and the power of Satan to the light and God. Nor is one surprised when he discovers that the phraseology of Acts 26:18, which basically describes conversion, reminds him of the baptism of John (Lk 3:3; Acts 13:24; 19:4) and that of the Christians (esp. Acts 2:38; 22:16; cf. 8:16; 9:18; 10:48; 18:8; 19:5).

Luke does two further things of interest to us in this last defense speech of Paul. He tells us that Paul *was not disobedient* to the heavenly vision. Paul declares "first to those at Damascus, then at Jerusalem and throughout all the country of Judea, and also to the Gentiles, that they should *repent and turn* to God and perform deeds worthy of their *repentance*" (Acts 26:19-20). The phrase, "turn to God," cannot mean only what the Jews would have meant by it; the implication must be that the way to turn to God consists of faith in Jesus Christ. This implication is, in fact, borne out by the rest of the speech, for Paul maintains that, with God's help, up to this very day he has said nothing but what the prophets and Moses have said would come to pass: "that the Christ must suffer, and that, by being the first to rise from the dead, he would proclaim light both to the people and to the Gentiles" (Acts 26:22-23). This statement testifies to the Lucan conviction that the faith called for is the faith of the Old Testament. The true faith of Israel is the faith of Christianity. This is why in the aftermath of this speech Luke can have Paul address King Agrippa II with the words, ". . . do you believe the prophets? I know that you believe" (Acts 26:27). To believe in the prophets is to accept Paul's above summary statement about the Christ. Agrippa II is well aware that this is the thrust of Paul's argument, for he says to Paul, "In a short time you think to make me a Christian." Paul's reply accepts the personal designation of Christian and in jocular fashion grants that he wants Agrippa II to be a Christian: "Whether short or long, I would to God that not only you but also all who hear me this day might become such as I am — except for these chains" (Acts 26:28-29).

The Father, in Luke's account of the scene on the Mount of Olives (Lk 22:39-46), is not asking Jesus to turn from darkness to light, but to drink the cup which symbolizes his death and the events which surround it. A specific event of salvation history must be realized. Luke drops the statements of Jesus' agitation and lessens the admonition of the disciples. He writes, "Father, if you are willing, remove this cup from me; *nevertheless not my will, but yours be done*" not Mark's "Abba, Father, all things are possible for you; remove this cup from me; yet not what I will, but what you will" (Mk 14:36; cf. Mt 26:39). Luke's phrasing stresses more the Father's will and that Jesus wants this will to be done. Luke's representation of the disciples also proves of interest. He has not limited himself to Peter, James, and John but has the other disciples present. Only Luke observes that the disciples *follow* Jesus (v 39). His inference seems to be that "follow" is what a disciple does. When Jesus departs from the disciples, he does not say, "Sit here while I pray" (Mk 14:32; cf. Mt 26:36) but "pray that you may not enter into temptation." Consequently, Jesus ultimately wants the Father's will to be done, and the disciples are to follow him, they are to pray that they may not enter into temptation, which from the context must be a lack of openness to the Father's will.

With the above observations in mind, the question of what Luke sees to be a proper response to the continual salvific activity of God can now be understood in more detail. It is important to bear in mind that at times the reader of Luke is dealing with receptivity toward an individual salvific action of God or of Christ, and at others of the full Gospel message. Also Luke uses a variety of expressions to designate acceptance of God's salvific activity. Some responses are imperfect; others are full-blown and contain almost every expression of the Lucan pattern of response. This section falls into three parts. The first treats passages which Luke has located in significant places in either of his two books. The second considers passages where various expressions of response are clustered, and the third part reviews the remaining passages.

A. Luke Has Significantly Located Certain Response Passages

Everyone grants that the beginning and end of a book constitute places of emphasis. Whether Luke added the Infancy Narrative later or not makes little difference; he still intended it as the beginning of his two volumes. Luke's Gospel begins with the story of Zechariah who will be silent and unable to speak until what Gabriel told him comes to pass, "because you *did not believe my words*, which will be fulfilled in their time" (Lk 1:20). His incorrect response is obviously contrasted with Mary's correct one, "Behold, I am the handmaid of the Lord: *let it be done to me according to your word*" (Lk 1:38). Elizabeth phrases it a little differently, "blessed is she who *believed* that there would be a fulfillment of what was spoken to her from the Lord" (Lk 1:45). The shepherds, who represent the disadvantaged and have heard the message that in the city of David a Savior is born who is Christ the Lord, respond as follows: ". . . glorifying and praising God for all they had *heard* and *seen*, as it had been told them" (Lk 2:20). Simeon and Anna also respond positively to what God has done in Jesus. Simeon *receives* the child in his arms, blesses God and recites the *Nunc Dimittis*; his eyes have *seen* the salvation that God has prepared in the presence of all the people (cf. Lk 2:25-32; 3:6). Anna gives thanks to God and speaks of Jesus to all who were looking for the redemption of Israel (Lk 2:38). Since Zechariah's initial response changes to his later yielding to God's will (cf. Lk 1:62-63), Luke's Gospel begins with a series of positive responses to God's salvific activity.

Luke strikes a significantly different note at the end of Acts. Historically, many of the Jewish people did not accept the Christian message (cf. Acts 28:24), but considerable success was experienced among the Gentiles. Luke relates this fact through most of Acts and at the end predicts that the Gentiles will listen. As in the gospels he employs Isa 6:9-10 (Acts 28:25-27) to explain how it was possible that the Jews could have rejected the gospel which fulfilled their hopes and promises. He strikes the positive note that the Gentiles will hear. More importantly, the openness of Christianity to anyone's positive response to God's salvific will forms the last words of Acts. Paul welcomes everyone who comes to him (cf. Acts 28:30-31).

At first glance, the end of Luke's Gospel and the beginnings of Acts seem to contribute nothing to an understanding of Luke's delineation of the Christian response to the continual salvific activity of God. Yet, the risen Christ does insist, "*See* my hands and my feet, that it is I myself; *handle me*, and *see*; for a spirit has not flesh and bones as you *see* that I have" (Lk 24:39; cf. vv 37, 42-43). The Eleven and those with them accompany Jesus to Bethany, are blessed by him, and witness his ascension. They return to Jerusalem with great joy, and their faith is evident in their worship of God in the temple. These same believers make up the group which is with Jesus at the beginning of Acts (1:1-11). They *see* the risen and ascending Christ. They are instructed and receive the promise of commission as witnesses. They are mistaken about the time of the second coming and of the establishment of the kingdom, but they are the nucleus of all who are to believe.

Luke emphasizes another passage which reports the appropriate reaction to God's salvific action in one's life. The section on "The Universality of Salvation" has shown how Luke developed this theme of universality, and it builds up to his key presentation of it in Acts 10:1—11:18. Cornelius obeys the angel and sends men to Joppa to bring Peter to Caesarea (Acts 10:3-8, 22, 32-33; 11:13-14), and Peter obeys the Spirit who tells him about their coming and that he should go with them (Acts 10:19-23; 11:12) because through his vision God has shown him that he should call no man common or unclean (Acts 10:28-29, 34; 11:4-9). Peter calls for further obedience to God's will when he asks, "Can anyone forbid water for baptizing these people who have received the Holy Spirit just as we have" (Acts 10:47; cf. 11:15-17)? He, then, orders the Gentiles to be baptized because as he later indicates, *"who was I that I could withstand God?"* The apostles and the brothers who are in Judea twice summarize the event in response terminology, "the Gentiles also had *received the word of God"* and "then to the Gentiles also God has granted *repentance unto life"* (Acts 11:1, 18). Needless to say, all the passages considered thus far except for the agony in the garden are proper to Luke.

B. Luke Has Clusters of Expressions of the Appropriate Response to God's Saving Action

There are a number of passages in Luke-Acts in which Luke has clustered experiences of his thought pattern of response. Lk 8:4-21 is the most extensive passage in his Gospel on receptivity toward Jesus and the word of God. Luke alone of the Synoptics makes of these verses one long scene. A glance at the vocabulary leaves no doubt that these verses stress receptivity: *"ears"* (Lk 8:8), *"hear"* (Lk 8:8, 10, 12, 14, 15, 18, 21), *"seeds"* (Lk 8:5, 11), *"word"* (Lk 8:11, 13, 15, 21), *"see"* (Lk 8:10, 16), *"understand"* (Lk 8:10), *"believe"* (Lk 8:12, 13), *"receive"* (Lk 8:13), *"manifest"* and *"come to light"* (Lk 8:17). The parable about the quality of the soil on which the seeds fall reinforces the idea of receptivity, which the growth and hundredfold yield at the end of the parable mark as fruitful. Jesus in his exhortation, "He who has ears to hear, let him hear" (v 8) already begins to determine the meaning of the parable.

The introduction to the explanation of the parable contains an abbreviated comment as to why some (cf. Acts 28:25-28) do not understand God's word. The exposition of the parable expands on this failure. *The devil takes God's word from the hearts of some.* Others start with joy but, since they have no depth, *fall away* when tempted. Cares, riches, and the pleasures of life *choke off* the possible productivity of others. But those who hear God's word with honest and good heart do bear fruit.

Luke's notion of receptivity continues to dominate the pericope. Given the context, the lamp in v 16 must stand for God's word which is now to be seen, for Luke in v 18 returns to his exhortation on *hearing*. If one hears, he will hear more, but he who does not will lose what he thinks he has. Luke concludes with the assertion that those who hear and do God's word are Jesus' true mother and brothers. Jesus does not downgrade the dignity of his mother or brothers, but reveals the dignity of hearing and doing God's word. Only Luke has added the pericope about Jesus' kindred right at the end of this series of statements on receptivity. This makes Luke's communication the more forceful. With Mark and Matthew, Luke speaks of different types of soil. By means of the parable he is then able to account for why some do not see and understand, and for what kind of soil prevents reception of God's word and what kind of soil bears fruit. With Mark, Luke speaks of lighting a lamp, and he returns to the quality of one's hearing. But only Luke in this context claims that hearing God's word is better than being Jesus' very mother or brother; moreover, in this verse only Luke speaks of "hearing the word of God" (cf. Mk 3:35; Mt 12:50) and thus again emphasizes receptivity.

Apparently, with the same emphasis in mind, Luke has made other changes. He adds "*seed*" in Lk 8:5. He writes only once of a hundredfold productivity (Lk 8:8). Was he not much satisfied with results which were a mere thirtyfold or sixtyfold? He clarifies that the word is the word "of God" (Lk 8:11; cf. Mk 4:14) and adds "in order lest by *believing* they be saved," (Lk 8:12) and "*believing*" (Lk 8:13). Finally, he alone specifies that a person should hold to the word "with an honest and good heart" and bring it forth "in patience" (Lk 8:15); and he specifies that the lamp is to be put on the stand "in order that those who enter *might see the light*" (Lk 8:16). Luke has surely stressed receptivity toward God's word.

All the other passages in Luke's Gospel, where expressions of the response to God's salvific activity are clustered, seem in one way or another to parallel Lk 8:4-21. The closest parallels are Lk 10:23-24; 11:27-28, 33-36.

Lk 10:23-24 reads:

> Then turning to his disciples he said privately, "Blessed are the eyes which *see* what you *see*! For I tell you that many prophets and kings desired to *see* what you *see*, and did not *see* it, and to *hear* what you *hear*, and did not *hear* it (cf. Mt 13:16-17).

Luke may have substituted "kings" for Matthew's "righteous man" and introduced the "you" which immediately follows, to accent the disciples' blessedness in contrast to that of the prophets and even kings. The emphasis paid to "seeing" and "hearing" in the passage can hardly be denied. In contrast to Matthew (13:10-17), Luke has located his passage right after the prayer in which Jesus thanks his Father that he has hidden these things from the wise and understanding and revealed them to babes. The Father has given everything to Jesus. No one knows the Son except the Father, nor who the Father is except the Son and to whom the Son chooses to reveal him. This prayer, because of its Johannine theology, has been called "the Johannine meteorite in the Synoptic skies." Important for our discussion is that Lk 10:23-24 follow immediately on a revelatory passage which relates that Jesus can choose to reveal the Father to whom he wishes. He has chosen the disciples, and so they are blessed.

Our next passage is proper to Luke:

> As he said this, a woman in the crowd raised her voice and said to him, "Blessed is the womb that bore you, and the breasts that you sucked!" But he said, "Blessed rather are those who *hear* the word of God and *keep it*" (Lk 11:27-28).

These latter two passages parallel the last three verses of Lk 8:4-21. Of interest is the question, what leads to the woman's exclamation. Prior to her exclamation, Jesus has only been reported as speaking. The most natural conclusion would be that his words move her to exclaim. This interpretation would square well with Jesus' return to the word of God in his response; this "word of God" would be what Jesus says. Likewise, the parallel in Lk 8:4-21 supports such an interpretation, for the concentration in that passage was on receptivity and hearing the word of God. There, too, the speaker was Jesus. Certainly, the woman has Jesus primarily in mind; she is praising the woman who gave birth to and nursed him.

Jesus, furthermore, is the point of emphasis in Lk 11:33-36,

> "No one after lighting a lamp puts it in a cellar or under a bushel, but on a stand, that those who enter may *see* the light. Your *eye* is the lamp of your body; when your *eye* is sound, your whole body is full of *light;* but when it is not sound your body is full of *darkness.* If then your whole body is full of *light,* having no part *dark,* it will be wholly *bright,* as when a lamp with its rays gives you *light.*"

Lk 11:33, 36 are proper to Luke and Lk 11:33 surely parallels Lk 8:16 (cf. Mk 4:21; Mt 5:15). The key to understanding Lk 11:33-36 depends upon determining what significance the lamp has. It helps to read Lk 11:33-36 in context, and so we look to the previous pericope which is about the "Sign of Jonah." According to this pericope, this generation is evil because it seeks a sign. The only sign that will be given is that of Jonah, for as Jonah was a sign to the men of Nineveh, so will the Son of Man be to this generation. The story then turns to judgment. The queen of the South who came to hear the wisdom of Solomon, and the men of Nineveh who repented at the preaching of Jonah, will condemn this generation, for something greater than Solomon or Jonah is here which this present generation does not see. It is possible to see the "lamp" of Lk 11:33 as corresponding to the "something greater" of 11:32. But what is this something greater? As "something greater" is neuter some scholars do not identify the "something

greater" as the person of Jesus; however, the crowds are told
that the Son of Man will be a sign to this generation as
Jonah was to the men of Nineveh. In view of this and what
was determined above about Lk 11:27-28, it seems more
reasonable to understand the lamp as a reference to Jesus.
But, of course, his words are not to be excluded since in the
previous pericope Luke does write of the "wisdom of
Solomon" and of the "preaching of Jonah."

"Lamp," then, in Lk 11:33 refers to Jesus and his words.
These are to be displayed so those who enter can see them.
After all, if it is true that one's eye lights one's body, when
the eye is healthy, one's whole body has light; if it is
unhealthy, one's body is in darkness. One should let the
lamp of Jesus and his words shine through one's whole body
so that it is full of light and has no darkness in it. A final
observation should be made about this pericope. Since there
is the contrast between light and darkness, healthy
(*haplous*) and unhealthy (*ponēros*, which regularly means
"evil"), Luke is talking about commendable and condemna-
ble responses to Jesus and his words.

This meaning for eyes and light helps the reader appre-
ciate what Luke means in three other passages. When John
the Baptist sends two of his disciples to ask Jesus "Are you
he who is to come, or shall we *look* for another?" both Luke
and Matthew report that Jesus' response was, "Go and tell
John what you have *seen* and *heard:* the blind receive their
sight, the lame walk, lepers are cleansed, and the deaf hear,
the dead are raised up, the poor have good news preached to
them. And blessed is he who takes no offense at me" (Lk
7:22-23; cf. Mt 11:4-5). The fact that John's disciples see and
hear what Jesus is doing serves as a response to their religious question. In no way does Luke's reader get the impression that Jesus' response indicates that he was not "he who is
to come." Rather the concluding verse (v 23) proclaims that
whoever does not fail to recognize this about Jesus is
"blessed."

Another quasi-confessional statement connected with
seeing is evident in the puzzling Lk 23:47: "Now when the
centurion saw what had taken place, he praised God, and

said, 'Certainly this man was just (*dikaios*)!'" Why should the centurion praise God because an innocent man had been killed? Moreover, Luke has clearly changed Mark's (15:39): "And when the centurion, who stood facing him, saw that he thus breathed his last, he said, 'Truly this man was the Son of God!'" To be sure, Mark's statement is confessional, but what did Luke have in mind when he changed Mark? The clue to Luke's purpose is to be found in Mark where what the centurion sees is how Jesus dies. Luke should be understood in the same way. It is because the centurion sees and hears that before Jesus dies he says "Father, into your hands I commit my spirit," that he praises God. Only Luke has this cry of Jesus. Whether "spirit" refers to the Holy Spirit (an interpretation I tend to favor) or not, Jesus demonstrates tremendous trust in his Father. As a result, the centurion praises God who can so inspire a person, and he knows Jesus is just because his behavior is not that of a criminal.

The account of the disciples on the road to Emmaus (Lk 24:13-35) proves to be much more straightforward. Jesus joins the two disciples. "But their *eyes were kept from recognizing him.*" They are talking about what had happened to Jesus, which they take to be common knowledge, and about their hope that he would redeem Israel. True, some of the women claimed to have *seen* angels who said Jesus was alive, and some of the men found the tomb as the women said, but they did not see Jesus. At this point, Jesus reacts and calls them "foolish." He shows from Moses and the prophets that all these things were to happen. Shortly therafter, he attempts to continue his journey, but they impose on them to stay. When he takes bread, blesses and breaks it, and gives it to them, "their *eyes were opened and they recognized* him; and he vanished out of their sight." When they report their experience to the Eleven and those with them, they describe "how he was *known* to them in the breaking of bread." The "opening of the eyes" obviously looks to the recognition of the risen Christ in the Eucharist and the correct interpretation of the scriptures concerning him. This recognition is not only intellectual, for normal sight contrasts with their present true vision and Jesus is named "Lord."

Lk 16:29-31, too, deals with the correct understanding of Moses and the prophets. Lazarus is comforted in the bosom of Abraham while the rich man is in anguish in Hades. The rich man tries to convince Abraham to send Lazarus to warn his five brothers, that they might not come to the place of torment. Abraham retorts, "They have Moses and the prophets; let them *hear* them." This solution does not satisfy the rich man who feels, "if some one goes to them from the dead, they will repent." But Abraham denies this assumption, "If they do not *hear* Moses and prophets, neither will they be *convinced* if someone should rise from the dead." The point of this parable is not that they have not physically heard Moses and the prophets but that they have not understood them correctly. This parable in its present context forms part of Jesus' interactions (Lk 16:14-31) with the Pharisees:

> The Pharisees, who were lovers of money, heard all this (the parable of the dishonest steward), and they scoffed at him. But he said to them, "You are those who justify yourselves before men, but God knows your hearts; for what is exalted among men is an abomination in the sight of God. The law and the prophets were until John; since then the good news of the kingdom of God is preached,... (Lk 16:14-16)

The hearing that Abraham demands in the parable is that in which one listens to the good news of the kingdom of God and does not love money nor justify himself before humankind. It is a matter of the right attitude of heart which hears the real message of Moses and the prophets, prime sources of God's salvific will.

Lk 10:16 (cf. Mt 10:40; Jn 13:20) marks the last passage in Luke's Gospel which contains a cluster of expressions of response to God's salvific will: "He who *hears* you *hears* me, and he who *rejects* (*atheteō*) you *rejects* me, and he who *rejects* me *rejects* him who sent me" (cf. Lk 9:4-5). This passage may originally stem from the early community where the duty of listening to the Christian missionaries would have been of paramount importance. Only Luke has expanded this verse by introducing "hearing," and he has preferred to express the receptivity negatively. Luke in this passage, for a certainty, treats receptivity of God's salvific will, for "him who sent me" must be the Father; and Luke has so set up the sequence that the one who rejects the Christian missionary rejects Christ and rejects the Father. Most authorities assume that Lk 10:1-16, "Mission of the Seventy," makes up a unit. So the verse being considered is the last verse of this unit. Luke, in 10:8 which is proper to him, informs us of Jesus' instructions, "Whenever you enter a town and they *receive* you, eat what is set before you," and the message of the Seventy is that "The kingdom of God has come near to you" (cf. Lk 10:9, 11). Most of the pericope (vv 10-16) warns those who do not *receive* the Christian missionaries. The dust from their city is to be shaken off against them; on judgment day their lot will be worse than Sodom's. If the mighty works done in Chorazin and Bethsaida had been done in Tyre and Sidon, they would have *repented* long ago. As noted above, Luke in v 16 carries over this antipathy toward the kingdom of God. After all, "rejecting" God forcefully makes Luke's point about what is really happening when one rejects a messenger of the kingdom.

Luke in Acts has clustered expressions of receptivity to God's salvific will in a number of passages. The reader will recall that, when it was asserted that the Christians are the true Israel, Acts 3:22-23 was cited:

> Moses said, "The Lord God will raise up for you a prophet from your brethren as he raised me up. *You shall listen to him* in whatever he tells you. And it shall be that every soul *that does not listen* to the prophet shall be destroyed from the people." (cf. Lk 9:35; Acts 7:37).

God raised up this prophet, and such weight is given to listening to this prophet that one cannot belong to the people if he fails to do so. This prophet, like all others, speaks the will of God. Through all the prophets God has foretold that his Christ should suffer, and so the Jews are now *to repent* and *turn again* that their sins be blotted out (Acts 3:18-19). Since Luke places no explicit limits on what one is to hear from the prophet, the natural inference is that one must hear at least the heart of Jesus' proclamation.

The Lucan qualifications for an apostle depend on an attitude of receptivity to Jesus' proclamation; otherwise,. he could not fulfill his task,

> "So one of the men who have accompanied us during all the time that the Lord Jesus went in and out among us, beginning from the baptism of John until the day when he was taken up from us — one of these men must become with us a witness to his resurrection" (Acts 1:21-22).

Of course, this passage bears on the interpretation of the witness activity of the apostles throughout Acts.

In general, Luke in the speeches of Acts calls for repentance and receptivity toward God's salvific will. Pentecost is no exception to this. The unity of Acts 2 has already been discussed. The sound of the mighty wind and the tongues as of fire bring in the concepts of hearing and seeing. Each member of the audience *hears* in his own language (vv 6, 8); they *hear* (v 11) the Christians telling of the mighty works of God. We readers can infer from the Joel quotation that one can designate their speaking as "prophecy" (vv 17, 18). Three times during the course of his speech, Peter alludes to the desired receptivity to his words: "Men of Judea and all who dwell in Jerusalem, let this be *known* (*gnōston*) to you, and *give ear to my words*," "Men of Israel, *hear* these words:...," "Let all the house of Israel therefore *know* (*ginōskō*) assuredly that God has made him both Lord and Christ, this Jesus whom you crucified" (vv 14, 22, 36). Luke attests to the common perception that Christ "... being therefore exalted at the right hand of God, and having received from the Father the promise of the Holy Spirit, has poured out this which you *see* and *hear*." (v 33).

Luke in the aftermath of the speech renders an account of their repentance. "Now when they *heard* this they were *cut to the heart . . .*," and Peter instructs them, "*Repent, and be baptized* every one of you in the name of Jesus Christ . . .," "Save yourself from this crooked generation" (vv 37-38, 40). The chapter concludes with "So those who received his word were baptized . . . And they *devoted themselves to the apostles' teaching* and fellowship . . . And all who *believed* were together . . . And the Lord added to their number day by day those who were being saved." (vv 41-42, 44, 47). All of these calls for or indications of receptivity look to God's salvific will. The apostles speak of God's mighty works, and the events of Pentecost fulfill scripture as does the resurrection of Jesus. This was all part of God's definite plan and foreknowledge, and God has made him Lord and Christ. It is the risen Christ who receives the Spirit from the Father and pours him out. The miracles that Jesus worked and the speaking of tongues and the mighty wind and tongues as of fire all witness God's activity. Even the increase in the numbers of the Christians ultimately comes from God.

Acts 13:13-52 and 19:1-7 (cf. 8:6, 12-16, 22) both parallel the Pentecost event and also detail incidents of response to God's salvific will. Let us take the latter of these passages first. The response of the disciples whom Paul finds in Ephesus is incomplete. They *believe* but have not even *heard* of the Holy Spirit. They have been *baptized*, but with John's baptism. John the Baptist, Paul apprises them, told the people to *believe* in the one coming after him, Jesus. "On hearing this, they were *baptized in the name of the Lord Jesus*." Since, when Paul lays hands on them, the Holy Spirit comes on them and they speak in tongues and prophesy, we are certain that this activity is of the saving God.

Imperfect response, miracles and the Holy Spirit further characterize Acts 8:4-24. Simon's response during the course of the story remains imperfect. Although Luke appears to portray the faith of the Samaritans as imperfect, his actual theological concern is to advert to the correctness of this mission and the significance of the Church in Jerusalem, represented by Peter and John. The Samaritans' reception of the Spirit marks the divine approval of Jerusalem leadership and of the mission to the Samaritans, and promotes harmony in the Church. Anyway, the Samaritans in the city *"gave heed* to what was said by Philip when they *heard* him and *saw* the signs which he did" (v 6). They *believe* and are *baptized*, both men and women. Because of the signs and great miracles, even "Simon himself believed, and after being *baptized* he continued with Philip." Jerusalem hears that Samaria "has *received* the word of God" and so they send Peter and John (vv 12-14). Since the Samaritans were only *baptized* in the name of the Lord Jesus (v 16), Peter and John lay hands on them and they *receive* the Holy Spirit. Later, when Simon attempts to obtain God's gift with money, Peter warns him, *"Repent,* therefore, of this wickedness of yours, and pray to God that, if possible, the intent of your heart may be forgiven you" (v 22). Simon has the good sense to ask Peter to pray that none of these threats come upon him. In addition to the miracles and the reception of the Holy Spirit, the prayer and Philip's good news about the kingdom of God and the name of Jesus Christ (v 12; cf. v 5) evidence God's salvific presence in this passage.

Luke sets forth another parallel to Pentecost in Paul's speech at Pisidian Antioch (Acts 13:13-52). The rulers of the synagogues with their question to Paul and Barnabas introduce the thrust of the speech, "Brethren, if you have any word or exhortation for the people, say it" (v 15). As in the Pentecost speech Paul three times alludes to the necessity of receptivity: "Men of Israel, and you that fear God, *listen,"* "to us has been sent the *message (word) of this salvation"* and *"Let it be known to you,* therefore, brethren..." (vv 16b, 26, 38). Luke has other calls to receptivity throughout this pericope. He seemingly directs the warning in vv 40 and 41 to those who are not disposed to listen. On the other hand, vv 42-43 gives the impression that some Jews did listen, for many Jews and devout converts to Judaism *follow* Paul and Barnabas. Acts 13:44 asserts that nearly the whole city gathered *"to hear the word of God."* As a matter of fact, the Gentiles are the ones who respond to Paul's challenge, "hear" (v 16b): "And when the Gentiles *heard* this, they were glad and glorified the word of God; and as many as were ordained to eternal life believed" (v 48). Note is made of John's baptism of repentance and his designation of the one who comes after him (vv 24-25). Finally, Paul refers to the witnesses who accompanied Jesus from Galilee and *saw* him after his resurrection. Paul himself now brings the good news that this promise of a resurrection has been fulfilled by raising Jesus from the dead (vv 31-33).

The non-receptive attitudes of the Jews heightens the seriousness of a correct response. They *did not recognize* Jesus *nor understand* the utterances of the prophets (v 27). Their jealousy leads them *to contradict* what is said by Paul; they revile him. They *thrust the word of God away from themselves* and *judge themselves unworthy of eternal life* (vv 45-46). They even incite some of the leading citizens, stir up persecution against Paul and Barnabas, and drive them out of their district. Finally, Paul and Barnabas follow Jesus' instruction and shake off the dust from their feet against them.

The response Luke wants in Acts 13:13-52 is to God's salvific activity. There is no need to prove this in detail. Suffice it to say, God in accord with his promise has given a savior, Jesus from the seed of David (v 23). Jesus must, then, be "the word of this salvation" (v 26) which Paul proclaims. Part of this proclamation is "that through this man (Jesus) forgiveness of sins is proclaimed to you, and by him everyone that *believes* is freed from everything from which you could not be freed by the law of Moses" (vv 38-39). Lastly, the Lord says to Paul, "I have set you to be a light for the Gentiles, that you may bring salvation to the uttermost parts of the earth" (v 47).

There are a number of other passages in which Luke has clustered expressions of response to God's salvific will. When the Jewish rulers, elders, scribes, and the high priestly family charge Peter and John not to speak or teach at all in the name of Jesus, Peter and John answer them:

> "Whether it is right in the sight of God to *listen* to you rather than to God, you must judge; for we cannot but

speak what we have *seen* and *heard* (Act 4:19-20; cf. 5:29-32).

This passage and its parallel in Acts 5 need no further explanation.

The mission to the Greeks in Antioch (Acts 11:19-26) provides an example of the correct response to God's salvific activity. The persecution that arose over Stephen caused the Christians to scatter. But they used this as an opportunity to preach to the Jews. Some from Cyprus and Cyrene even proclaim the Lord Jesus to Greeks in Antioch. "And the hand of the Lord was with them, and a great number that *believed turned* to the Lord." News of this reaches the church in Jerusalem, and they send Barnabas to Antioch. He saw the grace of God and "exhorted them all to remain *faithful to the Lord.* And a large company *was added to the Lord.*" The phrases, "And the hand of the Lord was with them," "turned to the Lord," "the grace of God," "faithful to the Lord," and "added to the Lord" unveil God's salvific activity in this pericope. Besides, Luke describes Barnabas as "a good man, full of the Holy Spirit and of faith."

The appropriate response to God's salvific activity is to be found in the "Controversy over Admission of Gentiles" (Acts 15:1-35). Peter defends their admission, "Brethren, you *know* (*ephistēmi*) that in the early days God made choice among you, that by my mouth the Gentiles *should hear the word* of the gospel and *believe*" (v 7; cf. v 3). God who knows the heart gave them the Holy Spirit just as he did to the Jewish Christian; he made no distinction between Jew or Gentile. He cleansed the Gentiles' hearts, too, *by faith.* They will be saved, just as the Jews, through the grace of the Lord Jesus (vv 8-9, 11). James supports Peter's position, "Brethren, *listen* to me. Simeon has related how God first visited the Gentiles to take out of them a people for his name. And with this the words of the prophets agree . . ." (vv 13:15; cf. Am 9:11-12). James judges that the Jewish Christians should not trouble those of the Gentiles "who *turn to* God" (v 19). The letter which the apostles, elders, and the whole church send has a different phrasing: "For it has seemed good to the Holy Spirit and to us to lay upon you no greater burden than these necessary things:. . . ." But none of these necessary things is circumcision. Luke does argue for the entry of the uncircumcised Gentiles into the Christian community, but he bases this on the Cornelius event. Since Luke contends that God brought about this conversion of the Gentiles by pouring out his Spirit on them, and that James sees their conversion as the fulfilment of scripture, the reader is not surprised by "it has seemed good to the Holy Spirit." Without dispute, God's salvific activity dominates the passages.

Paul's decision (Acts 16:6-10) to begin the Christian mission to Europe depends on God's will. Paul, Silas and Timothy pass through Phrygia and Galatia because the Holy Spirit forbade them to speak the word in Asia. Nor *did* the Spirit of Jesus *allow them to go in Bithynia.* When Paul sees the night vision of a Macedonian who says, "Come over to Macedonia and help us," they *seek to go to* Macedonia, for they conclude, "God had called us to preach the Gospel to them."

Both a woman and a man in Philippi show Luke's reader how to respond to God's salvific activity. Luke actually tells us very little about what Paul says to Lydia. But the Lord does open her heart *to give heed to what was said by Paul.* And when she was *baptized,* with her household, she besought them: "If you judge me to *be faithful to the Lord,* come to my house and stay" (Acts 16:14-15). After the experience of the earthquake and Paul's preventing his suicide, the jailer falls trembling before Paul and Silas, and wants to know what he must do to be saved. They tell him, "*believe* in the Lord Jesus, and you will be saved, you and your household"; and they speak the word of the Lord to them. After he washes their wounds, "he *was baptized at once,* with all his family." He then brings them into his house and offers them a meal; and "he rejoices with all his household that he *had believed in God*" (Acts 16:30-34). The Lord leads Lydia to faith, and the miracles of the earthquake and of Paul's apparent ability to see through prison walls to keep the jailer from suicide denote God's salvific activity.

Paul in Thessalonica argues in the synagogue from the scripture that the Christ had to suffer and to rise from the dead and that Jesus is the Christ. "Some of them *were persuaded, and joined* Paul and Silas; as did a great many of the devout Greeks and not a few of the leading women" (Acts 17:4). But the other Jewish people become jealous, and with the help of some rabble cause an uproar in the city and drag Jason and some of the Christians before the city authorities. So, the brethren send Paul and Silas by night to Beroea, where they again enter the synagogue. These Jews "*received the word with all eagerness*, examining the scripture daily to see if these things were so. Many of them therefore *believed*, with not a few Greek women of high standing as well as men" (Acts 17:12-13). But the Jews from Thessalonica come and stir up the crowds there too. The examination of scriptures in both cases evinces God's salvific activity.

It is probable that for the most part Paul's speech on the Areopagus might have been based on Jewish proselytizing. Nonetheless, the end of the speech and its aftermath are Christian. God has overlooked the times of ignorance and now commands everyone everywhere to repent. He has set a day on which he intends to judge the world in righteousness by a man whom he raised from the dead, and thus kept faith with everyone. The reactions of the audience (Acts 17:32, 34) portray the various responses to the Christian mission:

> Now when they *heard* of the resurrection of the dead, *some mocked;* but others said, "*We will hear you again* about this.". . . But some *joined* him and *believed*, among them Dionysius the Areopagite and a woman named Damaris and others with them.

The varied response of these three groups reminds the reader of the explanation of the parable of the sower. Only the last group merits imitation. Luke in this narrative sets forth God's salvific activity in creating and sustaining the whole world. As one of the Stoic poets has said, "In him we live and move and have our being." We are the offspring of this God who cannot be represented by our art or imagination. He has established a day of judgment and raised Jesus from the dead, a man destined to share in this judgment. God now calls for repentance and will no longer overlook ignorance.

Luke in the next pericope, the founding of the Church in Corinth (cf. Acts 18:1-17), again traces diversity in the receptivity toward God's salvific will. After Paul has taken up residence with Aquila and Priscilla, he argues in the synagogue every sabbath and persuades Jews and Greeks. The exact nature of this "persuasion" remains unclear, but in the very next verse Luke informs us that when Paul testifies to the Jews that the Christ was Jesus, the Jews *oppose* and *revile* him. At this, Paul *shakes out his garments* and goes to the Gentiles. However, after Paul has taken up residence in the house of Titius Justus, "Crispus, the ruler of the synagogue, *believed* in the Lord, together with all his household; and many of the Corinthians *hearing* Paul *believed* and were *baptized*" (v 8). The Lord (Jesus) appears to Paul and tells him not to be afraid but to speak and not be silent. He promises to be with him lest anyone harm him, "for I have many people in this city" (v 10). As a result, Paul stays there a year and a half teaching the word of God. The subsequent Jewish attempt to get Gallio to act against Paul fails, since the Romans are not interested in Jewish religious questions. Paul's message, that the Christ was Jesus and his teaching was the word of God, reveals that this pericope deals with God's salvific will. But the vision of the risen Christ provides the most visible manifestation of God's salvific activity. Doubtless, Luke intends Paul's shaking of his garments (cf. Acts 22:23) as a faithful carrying out of Jesus' instruction as regards those who refuse to hear about the kingdom of God (cf. Lk 9:5; 10:10-11; Acts 13:51).

Paul, in his speech to the elders at Miletus, supplies us with a summary (Acts 20:18-21) of his life among them. Among other things he did not shrink from testifying to

Jews and to Greeks of *"repentance to God* and of *faith in the Lord Jesus."* Most probably, Luke has here one of his favorite double expressions which functions much like Hebrew parallelism, and so "repentance to God" is the equivalent of "faith in the Lord Jesus." It makes little sense to contend that Paul was calling Jews to repentance to God without proclaiming Christ to them. Otherwise, the Jews would have had no reason to plot against him. Not only does this double expression ascribe Paul's action to God's salvific will, but Paul in the summary states of himself: "serving the Lord with all humility and with tears and with trials which befell me through the plots of the Jews..." Paul is doing the Lord's will.

Acts 22:14-16 conserves a last cluster of expressions of receptivity to God's salvific activity in Acts. It will be easiest to quote the relevant verses:

> And he (Ananias) said, "The God of our fathers appointed you *to know* his will, *to see* the Just One and *to hear* a voice from his mouth; for you will be a witness for him to all men of what you *have seen and heard.* And now why do you wait? Rise and be *baptized*, and wash away your sins, calling on his name" (Acts 22:14-16; cf. 9:18).

Although Luke does not explicitly report Paul's baptism in this pericope, the implication is that Paul experiences and lives these actions of God and Christ in his life. Luke illustrates this. Paul himself enlightens us about his appointment and present knowledge of God's will. He notifies us that he has seen and heard the risen Christ, and is now his witness.

C. Other Passages Portray the Correct Response to God's Saving Action

A number of passages which speak of receptivity to God's salvific activity have yet to be considered. Nothing has been said of the programmatic passage, Lk 4:16-30, which out-

214 *The Desired Personal Response To God's Salvific Will*

lines Luke-Acts. Jesus, the prophet, comes to his own, but his own do not receive him as the Christ who will save the disadvantaged, because they could not see in him anything more than a boy from the neighborhood. They are unable to recognize God's salvific activity in Jesus, who claims to fulfill the scriptures. So, Jesus like the prophets, Elijah and Elisha, has to go to the Gentiles to find acceptance. When the Jews in the synagogue hear all this of Jesus, they "were filled with wrath" (v 28). But Luke's thought in this pericope is that the lack of receptivity of the Jews to Jesus' "gracious words" should be an incentive to the Gentiles (and Luke's readers) to be receptive. Thus, one is not surprised when scholars of Luke-Acts affirm that a close parallel to Lk 4:16-30 is Paul's speech at Pisidian Antioch which was examined above.

Luke in several passages writes of following Jesus. The miraculous draught of fish (Lk 5:1-11; cf. Mk 1:16-20; Mt 4:18-22; Jn 21:1-14) in its present form is proper to Luke. The people are pressing on Jesus to hear the word of God, so Jesus enters Peter's boat, sits down and teaches the people. Afterwards, he directs Peter and his crew where and how to find a catch of fish. So many fish are caught that they have to beckon to their partners in the other boat to come and help them. Still both boats are so filled with fish that they begin to sink. Peter is greatly impressed by the miracle and falls at Jesus' feet with the words, "Depart from me, for I am a sinful man, O Lord." Jesus, addressed by the title, "Lord," which is most proper after the resurrection, encourages Peter, "Do not be afraid; henceforth you will be catching men." When the boats reach land, Simon Peter, James, and John "left everything and *followed him*." Luke has concretized God's salvific action in "God's word," the miracle and the call of the disciples by the risen Lord. These experiences lead to the disciples' following of Jesus.

All the Synoptics hand down the call of Levi (Lk 5:27-32; cf. Mk 2:13-17; Mt 9:9-13). Jesus says to him, " 'Follow me.' And he left everything, and rose and *followed him*." When the Pharisees and scribes murmur, "Why do you eat and drink with tax collectors and sinners," Jesus' answer discloses how God's salvific activity is present, "Those who are well have no need of a physician, but those who are sick; I have not come to call the righteous, but sinners to repentance."

Apparently, Luke and Matthew found the cure of the centurion's slave (Lk 7:1-10; cf. Mt 8:5-13; Jn 4:46b-54) in Q, and both agree that, when the centurion explains to the "Lord" his understanding of authority, Jesus "turned and said to the multitude that *followed him*, 'I tell you, not even in Israel have I found such *faith*.'" This faith has to be in Jesus and in his authority over illness. The naming of Jesus as "Lord" and the supposition of his power over illness, joined with the subsequent miracle, show us God's salvific activity. To be sure, in the multitude that is following Jesus there are many who have not yet come to the fullness of faith, but their following of Jesus has set them in the right direction.

The rich ruler (Lk 18:18-30; cf. Mk 10:17-31; Mt 19:16-30) asks Jesus, the "Good Teacher," what he must do to inherit eternal life. Jesus replies that only God is good, and then inquires if the ruler knows the commandments; but the ruler protests that he has observed all of them from his youth. Jesus then says to him, "One thing you still lack. Sell all that you have and distribute to the poor, and you will have treasure in heaven; and come, follow me" (v 22). At these words, the ruler becomes sad, for he is very rich. When Jesus sees this, he begins his discourse on the difficulty that the rich have in entering the kingdom of God. But Peter, concerned about the advantages of being a disciple, states, "Lo, we have left our homes and *followed you*" (v 28). Jesus assures him that those who have left home or family for the kingdom of God will receive manifold more now, and, in the age to come, eternal life.

Luke concludes the story of the healing of the blind man (Lk 18:35-43; cf. Mk 10:46-52; Mt 9:27-31; 20:29-34) with the words, "And immediately he received his sight and *followed him*, glorifying God; and all the people, when they saw it, gave praise to God." This miracle story requires several observations. The blind man's cry, "Jesus, Son of

David, have mercy on me" (vv 38, 39) contrasts strongly with the multitude's identification, "Jesus of Nazareth" (v 37). Moreover, the blind man also names Jesus "Lord" (v 41; cf. Mt 9:28; 20:30, 31, 33). These confessional statements make it very probable that Luke, like Mark, intends that this story should be understood metaphorically (cf. Jn 9). The blind man sees who Jesus is better than does the multitude. The miracle, the blind man's glorifying God, and the praise of God by the people demonstrate that God is acting through Jesus' cure.

After the chief priests, officers of the temple and the elders seize Jesus in the garden and lead him away, Peter *follows* at a distance (Lk 22:54; cf. Mk 14:54; Mt 26:58). Since subsequently Peter denies Jesus, "at a distance" means that his discipleship is at a weak point. On the other hand, the people and the women, who *follow* Jesus on the way of the cross and bewail and lament him (Lk 23:27), are more courageous in their stance toward Jesus. The latter passage is only in Luke, who does not explicitly tie either passage to discipleship. But, in view of what we saw in Lk 5:1-11, such a connection would be hard to deny in the case of Peter; nor does such an interpretation do violence to Lk 23:27.

Luke has another significant passage in Lk 9:7-9, of which v 9b is proper to him. The tetrarch Herod heard about everything that Jesus had done. Some are saying that John the Baptist has been raised from the dead, others that Elijah has appeared, and still others that one of the prophets has risen. But Herod retorts "'John I beheaded; but who is this about whom I *hear* such things?' And he sought to *see* him" (v 9). First, a clarification should be made on the Lucan treatment of the Herodian princes. The reference to Herod in Lk 9:7-9 looks to Jesus's death (Lk 13:31-33), and only in Luke's passion story does Jesus appear before Herod (Lk 23:6-13). In fact, the Herodian princes in Luke-Acts always appear in a context of Jesus' suffering or that of his followers. Agrippa I kills James and imprisons Peter (Acts 12:1-5), and Agrippa II hears Paul's defense (Acts 25:12—26:32) which was shown above to parallel Jesus' passion (Lk 23:1-

25). So, Luke through his presentation of Herod Antipas in Lk 9:7-9 points his readers toward Jesus' passion.

Although Herod's question and his eagerness to see Jesus should not be seen as the central point of Lk 9, these verses direct the attention of Luke's readers. This is not the first time that Luke has expressed people's interest in who Jesus is, as Lk 5:21; 7:20, 49; 8:25 (cf. 22:67, 70; 23:3) bear witness. Herod's question at first receives no immediate answer. The popular rumors do not satisfy him. But Luke keeps before his reader Herod's question because in the movement of Lk 9 he has arranged the questions about Jesus in step-parallelism. Jesus too asks, "Who do people say that I am?" But, since the popular rumors do not satisfy him either, Jesus again asks the question, this time with emphasis on the response of the disciples, "But who do you say that I am?" Peter identifies Jesus as "the Christ of God" (cf. Lk 9:18-20). Jesus immediately modifies this identification through the first prediction of his passion and resurrection and through his challenge to the disciples to suffer with him, "If any man would come after me, let him deny himself and take up his cross daily and follow me" (v 23). In Lk 9:1-50 two other explicit answers are given to Jesus' question. The emphasis falls on the transfiguration. It is only in the transfiguration story that a completely satisfactory answer is given to the question of who Jesus is: "This is my Son, my chosen; *listen* to him" (v 35). "Sonship," in the context of the transfiguration and of the structure of the chapter, has to mean more than "the Christ of God." After the transfiguration and the healing of the boy with an unclean spirit, only Luke observes that everyone was astonished at the majesty of God. Although Luke does not directly entitle Jesus "the Majesty of God," the expression is ascribed to Jesus because of the cure he worked. The pericope closes with Jesus' second prediction of his passion and the discussions about "who is the greatest?" and "he who is not against you is for you." The former discussion leads Jesus to take a child and put him by his side and to say, "Whoever *receives* this child in my name *receives* me, and whoever *receives* me, *receives* him who sent me" (v 48). The receptivity of the disciples toward one another is their receptivity toward Jesus and the Father. Luke returns to this theme of "receiving" in the next discussion where he observes, "Do not forbid him; for he that is not against you is for you" (v 50).

"Receiving" manifests itself again in the next pericope when the Samaritans would not *receive* (v 53) Jesus because he was going to Jerusalem. But Jesus' determination to go to Jerusalem corresponds to the Father's will because "the days of his being taken up were being fulfilled" (v 51). This pericope also lists the claims of discipleship. Although Jesus has nowhere to lay his head, *following* (vv 57, 59, 61; cf. v 11) him should not be subordinated to the sacred duty of burying one's father, nor to saying farewell to one's loved ones. No one *who puts his hand to the plow and looks back* is fit for the kingdom of God" (v 62). Vv 61-62 are proper to Luke.

Luke, by dropping out most of Mk 6:45—8:26, has brought Herod's question about Jesus into close contact with Jesus' own question about himself, and with the other christological statements of Lk 9:1-50 (62), all of which also touch on the nature of Christian discipleship. Luke's reader is exhorted to accept the true answers to who Jesus is, and so to the nature of his own discipleship. The transfiguration leaves no doubt that God's salvific will is present in Jesus whom the voice from the cloud instructs Peter, James, and John (and Luke's reader) to hear. The majesty of God works in Jesus, who preaches about the kingdom of God and cures those who have need of healing.

The story of Martha and Mary (Lk 10:38-42) was noted in the reflections on Luke's accounts of Jesus' interactions with women. Mary communicates an example of the ideal disciple who gives priority to *hearing* Jesus.

Jesus later chides the multitudes, ". . . *why do you not know how to interpret the present time?*" (Lk 12:56). They can perceive when a storm is coming and when it will be very hot. But they do not realize the significance of Jesus, for the "present time" refers to Jesus and the division that his message will bring to households because some will believe and others not. In this sense, Jesus has not come to give peace on earth. People will have to decide whether they will value faith in him over the basic family relationships (cf. Lk 12:49-53).

A similar passage occurs in Lk 21:28-33. Right after he has listed the events and signs which will characterize the end time, Jesus according to Luke alone observes, "Now when these things begin to take place, *look up* and *raise your heads*, because your redemption is drawing near" (Lk 21:28). He then tells them the parable of the fig tree and of all the other trees. As soon as they come out in leaf, summer is already near. "So also, you *see* for yourselves and *know* that when you *see* these things take place, you *know* that the kingdom of God is near. Truly, I say to you this generation will not pass away till all has taken place" (Lk 21:31-32; cf. 17:22, 24). The nearness of their redemption and of the kingdom, of which only Luke speaks here, pertains to God's salvific will. Their recognition of these events and signs should alert them about the nearness of their salvation.

Only Luke includes, "He who has *ears to hear* let him *hear*" (Lk 14:35) after the parable of salt. In itself, the image of salt is vague. But Luke has located this parable right after his discussion on the conditions of discipleship, much of which is proper to him (Lk 14:25-33; cf. Mt 10:37-38). The discussion ends with the words, "So therefore, whoever of you does not renounce all that he has cannot *be my disciple.*" These words repeat the idea at the beginning of the discussion:

> "If anyone *comes to me* and does not hate his own father and mother and wife and children and brothers and sisters, yes and even his own life, he cannot *be my disciple.* Whoever does not *bear his own cross and come after me, cannot be my disciple.*"

The point of all this is the radical importance of one's response to Jesus. No other relationship is to be put on the same level as that of our relationship to Jesus. Thus, Luke through his location of the parable of the salt ties its meaning to the supreme significance of following Jesus. This is what Luke exhorts his readers to hear, and hearing it gives one his true worth.

Lk 15, with its parables about the lost, involves the theme of repentance. In the next section this chapter will be discussed in more detail. Here, our attention rests on displays of repentance. All of these are proper to Luke. At the end of the parable of the lost sheep, Luke makes the practical application, "Just so, I tell you, there will be more joy in heaven over one sinner who *repents* than over ninety-nine righteous persons who need no *repentance*" (v 7). The parable of the lost coins ends with a similar statement, "Just so, I tell you, there is joy before the angels of God over one sinner who *repents*" (v 10). The word, "repentance," is not used of the prodigal son, but he surely repents. He *comes to his senses* and plans *to return to his father.* He even plans a little speech about his change of heart, *"Father, I have sinned against heaven and before you; I am no longer worthy to be called your son; treat me as one of your hired servants"* (vv 17-19, 21). His father characterizes him in terms of repentance, "for this my son was *dead*, and is *alive* again; he was *lost*, and is *found*" (v 24; cf. v 32). The nuance of "lost"(cf. vv 4, 6, 8-9. 17) in this chapter is "to be in need of repentance"; that of "found" (cf. vv 4-6, 8-9) is "to have repented." The father in this parable stands for the heavenly Father, and all three parables originate because of Jesus' effort to explain why he receives sinners. God's salvation is present in Christ, the savior of the disadvantaged.

Whether Luke wants his reader to join "Jesus blesses the children" (Lk 18:15-17) with the thought of the parable of the Pharisee and the tax collector is open to discussion. But both stories concern themselves with Jesus, the savior of the disadvantaged and the weak. In all the Synoptics Jesus tells his disciples not to prevent the children from coming to him, "Truly, I say to you, whoever does not *receive* the kingdom of God like a child shall not enter it." The correct attitude toward the reception of the kingdom of heaven is that of a child, who does not earn but instead receives.

Luke (19:37-38) furnishes a brief summary reaction to all

that God has done in Christ. The mere quotation of the passage, v 37 of which stands only in Luke, suffices to make the point:

> As he was now drawing near, at the descent of the Mount of Olives, the whole multitude of the disciples began to rejoice and praise God with a loud voice for all the mighty works that *they had seen*, saying, "Blessed is the King who comes in the name of the Lord! Peace in heaven and glory in the highest!"

Everyone admits that the parable of the vineyard is addressed to the Jewish leaders; the scribes and the chief priests perceived that Jesus had told this parable against them (Lk 20:19). The parable highlights the ingratitude of the Jewish leaders toward their God, represented by the owner of the vineyard who verges on the unrealistic when he sends his son, even though the tenants have beaten and treated his servants shamefully and given them nothing. Needless to say, the owner's son represents Jesus:

> Then the owner of the vineyard said "What shall I do? I will send my beloved son; *it may be they will respect him*." But when the tenants *saw* him they said to themselves, "This is the heir; *let us kill him*, that the inheritance may be ours." And they *cast him out* of the vineyard and *killed* him (Lk 20:13-15).

This sad and brutal rejection of Jesus does not destroy God's saving activity, for the vineyard will be given to others.

Two final passages from Luke's Gospel remain to be investigated. Both of them deal with Jesus' daily teaching in the temple, and with the positive reactions of the people to his words. After Jesus cleanses the temple, he teaches daily there. The leaders of the Jews want to do away with him but can do nothing, *"for all the people hung upon his words"* (Lk 19:48). At night, Jesus lodged on the Mount of Olives. "And early in the morning all the people came to him in the temple to *hear* him" (Lk 21:38). The latter of these passages shows up only in Luke (cf. Jn 8:1-2). As will be seen in the next paragraph, these two passages correspond with Luke's opinion that the temple only has true worth insofar as its use supports the acceptance of the coming of the just one, Jesus. Otherwise, its significance fades accordingly (cf. Acts 7:39-53). Assuredly, both of these passages encourage the chief characteristic of a disciple, "listening to Jesus" (cf. Lk 10:38-42).

Some further passages which address God's salvific activity can be found in Acts. At God's word, Abraham *leaves* the land of the Chaldeans and *lives* in Haran (Acts 7:4). When God gives him the covenant of circumcision and Isaac is born, Abraham circumcises him on the eighth day (Acts 7:8). The implication of Acts 7:44 is that Moses constructs the tent of witness according to the pattern which God had shown him. On the other hand, this speech of Stephen, in which Luke compares Jesus to Moses, contains a number of rejections of Moses. They *do not understand* that God was giving them deliverance by Moses' hands (Acts 7:25), and, when he tries to stop a quarrel, the guilty party exclaims, *"Who made you a ruler and a judge over us?"* (Acts 7:27; cf. v 35). Moses receives living oracles to give the Jews, but the fathers *refuse to obey him* and *thrust him aside.* They *return in their hearts to Egypt* and got Aaron *to make an idol, a calf to which they offer sacrifice* (Acts 7:38-41). Stephen summarizes the situation at the end of the speech:

> "You *stiff-necked* people, *uncircumcised in heart and ears*, you always *resist* the Holy Spirit. As your fathers did, so do you. Which of the prophets did not your fathers *persecute*? And they *killed* those who announced beforehand the coming of the Righteous One, whom you *have now betrayed and murdered*, you who received the law as delivered by angels and *did not keep it*" (Acts 7:51-53).

A harsher or more complete condemnation of the Jewish refusal to accept Jesus in Luke-Acts may be found only at the end of Acts (28:24-28).

D. Conclusion

Since he accepts Christianity as the true Israel, Luke's description of how one responds to God's salvific activity follows Old Testament patterns. As in the Qumran scrolls, Luke envisages a realm of light and one of darkness, and a disciple belongs to the realm of light because he or she responds to Gods' salvific action in his or her life. Of course, Jesus' own response to the Father's will in the scene on the Mount of Olives constitutes the model for everyone else's response. Yet the Christian response differs from all others because it ultimately is a response to Christ. Now, Christian faith is the true faith of Israel.

This section on the desired personal response to God's salvific will fell into three parts. The first treated passages which Luke locates in significant places in either of his two books. The second considered passages where various expressions of receptivity are clustered, and the third reviewed the remaining passages. At the beginning and the end of both his Gospel and Acts, Luke places narratives about receptivity to God's will; and this emphasis on the correct response persists throughout the whole of Luke-Acts. A key passage, to which those before it point, is the conversion of Cornelius in which the Gentiles receive the Holy Spirit just as the first Jewish believers did and God grants them repentance to life. Moreover, Acts ends with a call to the Gentiles to respond to God's salvific will, "Let it be known to you then that this salvation of God has been sent to the Gentiles; they will *listen*" (Acts 28:28).

Luke does not draw a fine distinction among the terms which he uses to designate response to God's salvific activity. His most frequent terms are: "to receive," "to hear," "to see," "to believe," "to be baptized," "to repent," and "to turn." Given an appropriate context, one or more of these terms can express incorrect, imperfect, or appropriate response. Other contexts are more full-blown and contain almost every expression of the Lucan pattern of response. Obviously, Luke's intention in all of these passages is to demand from his readers a corresponding receptivity toward God's salvific activity in Christ.

Careful attention to the above observations helps to solve the problem of how Jesus the preacher becomes the preached. Actually, Luke is probably more existential here than modern readers tend to be. For Luke, there is the historical moment when the earthly Jesus is preaching and has not yet been perceived or accepted as who he truly is. The experience and acceptance of Jesus as Lord and Savior is most properly post-resurrectional, and, although this confession and recognition can be read back into Jesus' earthly life, it really was only fully perceived and accomplished later in the early Christians' experience. In other words, God's salvific activity happens in time, and to demand of the participants of one moment of time the perception of those of a later moment is an error of the questioner, not of the biblical author.

CHAPTER 10

JOY, WONDER, BLESSING, AND PRAISE

The previous chapter discussed the extensive Lucan pattern of personal free response to God's salvific will. However, Luke has an at least equally extensive pattern about the reactions to the experience of God's salvific activity. The presentation will somewhat rely on the exposition of my friend and colleague, John Navone. But this study differs from his in a number of ways. Significantly, we do not agree on the words which Luke uses to express these reactions. For instance, *charizomai*, "I grant or bestow," does not belong to this pattern of expressions. On the other hand, the following words should be included: *gelaō*, "I laugh"; *diaporeō*, "I am very confused, I wonder"; *ekplēssomai*, "I am amazed"; *existēmi*, "I am amazed or surprised"; *laleō glōssais*, "I speak in tongues"; *phobeomai (phobos)*, "I am afraid or in awe"; *synchairō*, "I rejoice with or together"; and *thaumazō*, "I marvel, wonder." All the expressions of reactions to the experience of God's salvific will characterize the messianic or eschatological age, but, normally, Luke takes this for granted and only rarely explicitly points to the messianic age, which for him is the eschatological. Moreover the main interest here falls on God's salvific will, and it is, in fact, this aspect which most concerns Luke, for Luke wants his readers to understand these expressions as the correct reactions to God's salvific will.

The amount of data on this subject is considerable. In order to obtain some organization in this presentation, groups of these topics or expressions will be first considered, for Luke often places a number of expressions of joy, wonder, blessing, or praise in the same pericope or, at least, close together. Many of the readers of this book will not be interested in the original Greek, but for those who will find such information useful, I have given the Greek the first time it occurs. I have attempted to keep such references to a minimum, but those provided should give an idea of the Lucan word-pattern on which the themes presented here rely. The words or phrases which constitute the Lucan development of these themes will be italicized so the the thought may be followed more easily.

A. Groupings of Expressions of Joy, Wonder, Blessing and Praise

Luke's Infancy Narrative has four such groupings or clusters of these positive reactions to the experience of God's salvific will. Needless to say, they are all proper to Luke.

> And when Elizabeth heard the greeting of Mary, the babe *leaped* (*skirtaō*) in her womb; and Elizabeth was filled with the Holy Spirit and she exclaimed with a loud cry, "*Blessed* (*eulogēmenē*) are you among women, and *blessed* (*eulogēmenos*) is the fruit of your womb! And why is this granted me, that the mother of my Lord should come to me? For behold, when the voice of your greeting came to my ear, the babe in my womb *leaped* for *joy* (*agalliasis*). And *blessed* (*makaria*) is she who believed that there would be a fulfillment of what was spoken to her from the Lord." And Mary said, "My soul *magnifies* (*megalunō*) the Lord, and my spirit *rejoices*

(*agalliaō*) in God my savior, for he has regarded the low estate of his handmaiden. For behold, henceforth all generations will call me *blessed* (*makarizō*)...And his mercy is from generation to generation on those who *fear* (*phobeomai*) him" (Lk 1:41-50).

The passage itself explains the joy, blessedness, and praise. The child leaps in Elizabeth's womb because she has heard Mary's voice. Mary is the mother of Elizabeth's Lord and that is why she is blessed. Mary is also blessed because she believed what the Lord told her. In the *Magnificat* she reacts in praise and joy, for God has chosen her. Everyone will now bless her. Consequently, God's salvific action in Mary's motherhood leads to joy, blessing, and praise. God's mercy is on all who fear him.

The second group of expressions of joy, blessing and praise is found at John the Baptist's birth and Zechariah's Song of Praise.

And her (Elizabeth's) neighbors and kinsfolk heard that the Lord had shown great mercy to her and they *rejoiced* (*synchairō*) with her (Lk 1:58). And he asked for a writing tablet, and wrote, "His name is John." And they all *marvelled* (*thaumazō*). And immediately his mouth was opened and his tongue loosed, and he spoke, *blessing* (*eulogeō*) God. And *fear* (*phobos*) came on all their neighbors (Lk 1:63-65a)....*Blessed* (*eulogētos*) be the Lord God of Israel, for he has visited and redeemed his people (Lk 1:68)...to give light to those who sit in darkness and in the shadow of death, to guide our feet into the way of *peace* (*eirēnē*; Lk 1:79).

The last two verses show the reason for the joy and blessing. According to Lk 1:68, Zechariah blessed God because he has redeemed his people. God's salvific action calls forth this blessing. This is stated again in other words in Lk 1:79; "to guide our feet into the way of peace" parallels in Hebrew fashion "to give light to those who sit in darkness and in the shadow of death." Elsewhere Luke also uses "light" for

salvation (cf. Lk 2:29-32; Acts 13:46-48; 26:18, 23). The
other two passages, Lk 1:58 and 63-65a, are subordinate to
the main thought of salvation. Elizabeth's neighbors and
relatives rejoice with her because she has given birth to a
son, and everyone marveled. Zechariah's tongue was loosed
because he has followed the angel's instruction, and named
the child John (cf. Lk 1:14). All were fearful because of this
wonderful event. The child, John the Baptist, plays a role in
God's salvific plan. The *Benedictus* itself expressed this
succinctly "And you, child, will be called the prophet of the
Most High; for you will go before the Lord to prepare his
ways, to give knowledge of salvation to his people in the
forgiveness of their sins,..." (Lk 1:76-77). God's act of
salvation in Christ brings forth joy, wonder and praise.

The story of the shepherds and the angels supplies the
third grouping about joy, blessing and praise. The relevant
part of the passage reads as follows:

> ...and they were filled with a great *fear*. And the angel
> said to them, "Be not *afraid*; for behold, I bring you good
> news of *a great joy* (*chara*) which will come to all the
> people; for to you is born this day in the city of David a
> Savior, who is Christ the Lord..." And suddenly there
> was with the angel a multitude of the heavenly host
> *praising* (*aineō*) God and saying, "*Glory* (*doxa*) to God in
> the highest, and on earth *peace* among human beings
> with whom he is pleased" (Lk 2:10-11, 13-14)....and
> all who heard it *wondered* at what the shepherds told
> them...And the shepherds returned, *glorifying* (*doxazō*)
> and *praising* God for all they had heard and seen, as it had
> been told them (Lk 2:18, 20).

The encounter of the shepherds with the angels at first leads
to fear or awe. But great joy results from the good news that
the Savior, who is Christ the Lord, is born in the city of
David. This same event also explains why both the angels
and the shepherds praise and glorify God. This birth brings
peace on earth. Once again, God's salvific activity gives rise
to joy, wonder and praise.

The last grouping in the Infancy Narrative attends the encounter of Jesus and his parents with Simeon. The significant verses are:

> ...he (Simeon) took him up in his arms and *blessed* God and said, "Lord now let your servant depart *in peace,* according to your word; for my eyes have seen your salvation which you have prepared in the presence of all peoples, a light for revelation to the Gentiles, and for *glory* to your people Israel." And his father and mother *marveled* at what was said about him; and Simeon *blessed* them... (Lk 2:28-29, 32-34).

Simeon sees the baby Jesus as God's salvation for all peoples, and that is why he blessed God. This salvation is Israel's glory, the great marvel God has done for her. Thus, Simeon can depart in peace because his eyes have allowed that salvation to be his, too. Jesus' parents marvel at Simeon's words, and he blesses them because of the part that God has them play in salvation history.

The rest of Luke's Gospel comprises a number of groupings of expressions of joy, wonder, blessing and praise. Luke gives an instance in the healing of the paralytic (Lk 5:17-26; cf. Mk 2:1-12; Mt 9:1-8). Luke's expansion of Mark is easily detected. Mark concludes the pericope: "And he rose, and immediately took up the pallet and went out before them; so they were all *amazed (existēmi)* and *glorified* God, saying, 'We never saw anything like this'" (Mk 2:12)! Luke writes:

> And immediately he rose before them, and took up that on which he lay, and went home *glorifying* God. And *amazement (ektasis)* seized them all, and they *glorified* God and were *filled with awe (eplēsthēsan phobou)*, saying, 'We have seen *incredible things (paradoxa)* today" (Lk 5:25-26).

Luke first presents the paralytic himself as glorifying God. Moreover, he adds the notion that this experience was accompanied by awe and, doubtless, employs *paradoxa* to expand even further on the glorifying. The miracle marks an example of Christ as the savior of sinners who continues God's salvific activity. True, only God can forgive sins, but he has given the Son of Man authority on earth to do so.

Luke places the next expression of joy and blessing at the beginning of the sermon on the plain:

> "*Blessed* are you poor, for yours is the kingdom of God, *Blessed* are you that hunger now, for you shall be satisfied. *Blessed* are you that weep now, for you shall *laugh* (*gelaō*). *Blessed* are you when men hate you, and when they exclude you and revile you, and cast out your name as evil on account of the Son of Man! *Rejoice* in that day, and *leap for joy*, for behold, your reward is great in heaven; for so their fathers did to the prophets..." (Lk 6:20-23).

While Matthew (5:3-12) also has this passage, it is well known that he records more beatitudes than does Luke. Nevertheless, Luke, in what he does have, is in considerable agreement with Matthew. Yet he has either added "Blessed are you that weep now, for you shall laugh" or Matthew has dropped it. Since Matthew does not appear to be dropping beatitudes in this pericope, more likely, Luke has added it. Consequently, Luke in this pericope follows his source which treated blessing and joy. Probably, he added a beatitude which introduces laughing; but he does not explicitly make allusion to salvation. Still, as noted elsewhere, the resurrection was the aspect of salvation which Luke emphasized, and the relief to the disadvantaged reflects his theme of Christ the savior of such people. Thus, in this Lucan composition, too, blessing and joy occur in a salvific context.

The expressions of joy and blessings in Lk 6:20-23 resemble that of the return of the Seventy and of the rejoicing of Jesus (Lk 10:17-24). The relevant verses are:

> The seventy returned with *joy*, saying, "Lord even the demons are subject to us in your name!" And he said to

them, "...Nevertheless, do not *rejoice* in this, that the spirits are subject to you, but *rejoice* that your names are written in heaven."

In that same hour he *rejoiced* in the Holy Spirit and said, "I thank you, Father, Lord of heaven and earth, that you have hidden these things from the wise and understanding and revealed them to babes; yea, Father, for such was your gracious will..." Then turning to the disciples he said privately, "*Blessed* are the eyes which see what you see!..." (Lk 10:17-18, 20-21, 23; cf. Mt 11:25-27; 13:16).

The return of the Seventy with its expressions of joy is proper to Luke. Matthew does have Jesus' prayer of thanksgiving, but he says nothing of Jesus' rejoicing. Both Luke and Matthew report that the eyes of those who have seen what the disciples have seen are blessed. Lk 10:17-24, as 6:20-23, describes the disadvantaged and a resurrection, but the salvific context is clearer. Jesus prays, "...yea, Father, for such was your gracious will..." The Father willed that the revelation be to the disadvantaged. Moreover what have the eyes of the disciples seen of any import other than Jesus' making the Father's salvation available to these disadvantaged? Certainly, there was reason for the Seventy to rejoice in the miracles of control over the demons who oppressed people, but their own ultimate salvation was even a greater cause of rejoicing. Luke introduces the rejoicing into this salvific context.

The passage on true blessedness (Lk 11:28-29), which only Luke has, takes the thought discussed in the above paragraph and applies it to hearing. While Jesus is speaking, a woman in the crowd says to him, "*Blessed* is the womb that bore you, and the breasts that you sucked!" But he said, "*Blessed* rather are those who hear the word of God and keep it!" Hearing and keeping God's word is even a greater blessing than the physical reality of being Jesus' mother.

Luke speaks of blessedness in the parable of the watchful servants.

> *Blessed* are those servants whom the master finds awake
> when he comes;... If he comes in the second watch or in
> the third, and he finds them so, *blessed* are those servants!
> ...And the Lord said, "who then is the faithful and wise
> steward, whom his master will set over his household, to
> give them their portion of food at the proper time?
> *Blessed* is that servant whom his master when he comes
> will find so doing..." (Lk 12:37-38, 42-43; cf. Mt 24:45-
> 46).

Matthew relates only the last blessing. Luke either had
another source other than "Q," or constructed vv 35-38 from
the narration which he found there. Whatever be the case,
he certainly has noted that the servant who is alert and does
his duty is blessed. The story answers the question of how
the Christian should live until the Lord comes. Like the
story about true blessedness, it demands that disciples follow the Lord's instructions about their conduct. In addition,
the story proposes a judgment scene where the good will be
rewarded and the evil punished. Since the story flows from
the expectation of the Parousia, it deals with our being with
the risen Lord, and thus, with our salvation. The blessings
reflect the positive aspects of this salvation.

Perhaps nowhere else in Luke-Acts has Luke given as
much prominence to joy as in ch. 15. Other than Lk 15:4-7
(cf. Mt 18:12-14), the whole of this chapter is proper to
Luke; in the few verses that are in Matthew only one reference to joy occurs. Let us review the joy that Luke expresses
in this passage:

> And when he has found it (the sheep), he lays it on his
> shoulder, *rejoicing*. And when he comes home, he calls
> together his friends and his neighbors, saying to them,
> "*Rejoice with me*, for I have found my sheep which was
> lost." Just so, I tell you, there will be more *joy* in heaven
> over one sinner who repents than over ninety-nine right-
> eous persons who need no repentance (Lk 15:5-7). "*Re-
> joice* with me, for I have found the coin which I had lost."

Just so I tell you, there is *joy* before the angels of God
over one sinner who repents (Lk 15:9-10; cf. 19:9-10).
". . . and let us eat and make *merry (euphrainō)*; for this
my son was dead, and is alive again; he was lost, and is
found." And they began to make *merry* (Lk 15:23-24).
"Lo, these many years I have served you, and I never
disobeyed your command; yet you never gave me a kid,
that I might make *merry* with my friends (Lk 15:29). It
was fitting to *make merry* and *be glad*, for this your
brother was dead, and is alive, he was lost, and is found"
(Lk 15:32).

The elder brother's idea of making merry fits with the
others, for his selfish and alienating notion of merriment
("with my friends") heightens, by contrast, the nobility of
the father's invitation to make merry. Luke in this chapter
has also introduced a number of descriptive details which
expand on the joy. The shepherd puts the lost sheep on his
shoulder, and both he and the widow call together their
friends and neighbors. The father runs and embraces his son
and kisses him. He instructs them to dress him in the best
robe and to put a ring on his finger and shoes on his feet.
When the elder brother returns from the field, he hears
music and dancing. Luke three times (Lk 15:23, 27, 30)
informs us that the father brought out the fatted calf and
killed it. So joy surely permeates the whole chapter.

Luke introduces this chapter with Jesus' association with
tax collectors and sinners, and with the murmuring of the
Pharisees and scribes, "This man receives sinners and eats
with them" (cf. Lk 15:1-2). Thus, we have a context of
Christ, the savior of the disadvantaged and sinners. The
parables show that God (heaven) rejoices over one sinner
who repents, but the accent in the chapter falls on the
attitude of the elder son. Like the Pharisees and scribes he
does not rejoice over the repentance of a sinner even though
he is his brother just as the tax collectors and sinners should
have been regarded as their brothers. They were all Jews and
had the same God and Father. Therefore, the joy called for

in Lk 15 looks to Christ's saving of sinners, and summons us all to rejoice over the repentance of a sinner as does our Father.

The cleansing of the ten lepers (Lk 17:11-19), a miracle story proper to Luke, provides us with an example of Jesus, the savior of the disadvantaged. This story also attests that Luke feels praise of God to be the correct reaction to a miracle. The relevant verses are:

> The one of them, when he saw that he was healed, turned back, *praising* God with a loud voice; and he fell on his face at Jesus' feet giving him thanks (*eucharisteō*). Now he was a Samaritan. Then said Jesus, "Were not ten cleansed? Where are the nine? Was no one found to return and *give praise to God* except this foreigner?" (Lk 17:15-18).

Praise of God goes hand in hand with thanks to Jesus. The last words of this miracle story are Jesus' instructions to the Samaritan. "Rise and go your way; your faith has made you well." These words repeat the thought that Jesus saves the disadvantaged who believe. This proper reaction is gratitude.

Joy, peace, blessing and praise characterize Jesus' going up to Jerusalem:

> As he was now drawing near, at the descent of the Mount of Olives, the whole multitude of the disciples began to *rejoice* and *praise* God with a loud voice for all the mighty works that they had seen saying, "*Blessed* is the King who comes in the name of the Lord! *Peace* in heaven and *glory* in the highest!" And some of the Pharisees in the multitude said to him, "Teacher, rebuke your disciples." He answered, "I tell you if these were silent, the very stones would *cry out* (*krazō*)." And when he drew near and saw the city he wept over it, saying, "Would that even today you knew the things that make for *peace*! But now they are hid from your eyes. For the days shall come upon you, when your enemies . . . because you did not know the time

of your visitation" (Lk 19:37-44; cf. Mk 11:8-10; Mt 21:8-9).

Except for the indication of a crowd and for v 38, this passage is proper to Luke. Even in v 38 Luke has inserted "peace in heaven," and apparently changed Mark's "Blessed is the kingdom of our father David that is coming" to "the king." Luke placed these two words between the first "Blessed is the..." and "coming in the name of the Lord." Finally, he dropped the "Hosanna" from "Hosanna in the highest" (which both Mark and Matthew have) and replaced it with "glory."

Luke more than Mark and Matthew wants his readers to interpret this passage in terms of Zech 9:9: "Rejoice greatly, O daughter of Zion! Proclaim, O daughter of Jerusalem! Lo, your king comes to you; just and saving, he is humble and riding on an ass, on a young donkey" (cf. Lk 13:34-35; Ps 117:26). This Old Testament passage in part explains why Luke introduced joy into his scene; it also tells us that the king, according to Luke, is no warrior. His approach and demeanor is humble and peaceful. Nor has Luke rejected the Davidic background of this king even though he does omit Mark's "Blessed is the kingdom of our father David that is coming." Luke brings out Jesus' Davidic background by drawing a parallel between "Peace in heaven and glory in the highest" and "Glory to God in the highest, and on earth peace among men with whom he is pleased" (Lk 2:14). The angels sang this when they proclaimed the good news of great joy to the shepherds, "for to you is born this day in the city of David a savior, who is Christ the Lord" (Lk 2:11). That this parallel was intentional is obvious because, as noted above, Luke added "Peace in heaven" and substituted "glory" for "Hosanna." He has even developed what he means by peace. His lament over Jerusalem, "Would that even today you knew the things that make for peace," with the Lucan "today," points to the salvific moment that Jerusalem is experiencing with Jesus' approach. She does not know the time of her visitation; this truth is hidden from her eyes. Jerusalem has failed to realize who Jesus is and what he means for her. She has not accepted the peace of Jesus, but she will experience total destruction at the hands of her enemies.

Luke 19:37-44 says that the rejoicing, peace and praise are due to the mighty works and to the arrival of Jerusalem's king, which the disciples are witnessing. It does not seem unreasonable to see a parallel to Lk 7:18-23, where John the Baptist sends his disciples to Jesus to find out, "Are you the one *who is to come*, or shall we look for another?" The context of Lk 7:18-23 (cf. 4:16-20) is one of the mighty works of Christ, the savior of the disadvantaged. Jesus tells John's disciples to tell John what they have seen and heard: "... the blind receive their sight, the lame walk, lepers are cleansed, the deaf hear, the dead are raised and the poor have good news preached to them." Significantly, that scene ends, "And *blessed* is he who takes no offense at me" (Lk 7:23). The importance of the coming of her king to Jerusalem leads to the epithet "Blessed," and to peace and glory in heaven. That these ideas should be regarded as salvific is manifest from the parallel to the angel's praise at the birth of the savior, Jesus, and from the peace that Jerusalem's king brings with him.

Hence, Luke has introduced into 19:37-44 almost all the expressions of joy, peace, blessing and praise. The salvific nature of the passage lies in the mighty works that God has done in Jesus. These works merit joy, blessing, praise, and peace. Luke underlines this when Jesus answers some of the Pharisees who want him to rebuke his disciples, "I tell you, if these were silent, the very stones would cry out," and when he laments because Jerusalem did not know the things that make for peace.

The end of Luke's Gospel (Lk 24:32, 36-53) contains expressions of joy, wonder and blessing. Although the terminology of Luke 24:32 differs from that which has been dominating this presentation, nonetheless, the question, "*Did not our hearts burn within us* while he talked to us on the road, while he opened to us the scriptures?" betrays a tremendous personal joy and manifests God's salvific will which is found in the message of the scriptures.

Luke 24:36-53, which included Jesus' appearance, instructions about the scriptures, and ascension, forms a unified encounter with Jesus which happened within a day or a few hours. The relevant passages are:

> And as they were saying this, Jesus himself stood among them and said to them "*Peace* to you."... And while they still disbelieved for *joy*, and *wondered*, he said to them, "Have you anything here to eat?" (Lk 24:36, 41). Then he led them out as far as Bethany, and lifting up his hands he *blessed* them. While he *blessed* them, he parted from them, and was carried up into heaven. And they returned to Jerusalem with *great joy*, and were continually in the temple *blessing* God (Lk 24:50-53).

The presence of the resurrected Christ brings joy and wonder to the Eleven and to those who were with them. When Jesus opens the scriptures for them, he asserts, "Thus it is written, that the Christ should suffer and on the third day rise from the dead, and that repentance and forgiveness of sins should be preached in his name beginning at Jerusalem" (Lk 24:46-47). But for Luke, repentance and forgiveness of sins are another way of speaking of salvation, and so the context is one of salvation. This is further supported by the parallel to the risen Christ's blessing in Acts 3:26: "God, having raised up his servant, sent him to you first, *to bless* you in turning everyone of you from your wickedness." The blessing of the risen Jesus in this verse consists in turning the members of Peter's audience from their wickedness. Needless to say, this thought matches that of Lk 24:46-47. Consequently, at the end of Luke's Gospel, the risen Christ (and the preaching in his name of forgiveness of sins to all nations) moves the Eleven and those with them to joy, wonder and blessing. The risen Jesus' blessing of them prompts their blessing of God.

Acts 2 should be taken as a unit. Within this unit and at its end are found expressions of speaking in tongues, joy and praise. Let us look at the Pentecost event itself:

> And they were filled with the Holy Spirit and began *to speak in other tongues*.... And they were *amazed (existēmi)* and *wondered*, saying, "Are not all those who are speaking Galileans?...Cretans and Arabians, we hear them *telling in our own tongues the mighty works (ta megaleia)* of God." And all were *amazed* and *perplexed (diaporeō)*, saying to one another, "What does this mean?" (Acts 2:4, 7, 11-12).

The Pentecost event belongs to God's plan of salvation. Peter affirms that it fulfills what the prophet Joel foretold (Joel 3:1-5; cf. Acts 2:17-21). Once they have received the Spirit, the Twelve and those with them speak in tongues about the mighty deeds of God. Even though they apparently speak in Aramaic, the devout Jews who are gathered in Jerusalem from everywhere in the world are amazed because they can understand them. Their amazement grows since they do not know the meaning of the event.

Next, Peter gives the Pentecost speech. Within the speech, Acts 2:26-27 reads "...therefore my heart was *glad*, and my tongue *rejoiced*; moreover my flesh will dwell in hope. For you will not abandon my soul to Hades, nor let your Holy One see corruption." Luke proceeds to argue that these words, which are from Ps 15, cannot refer to David but must refer to Jesus, who was raised from the dead and did not see corruption. Therefore, the gladness, joy and hope expressed in this psalm belong to Jesus. But Jesus' resurrection is the aspect of salvation that Luke stresses in the greater part of the Pentecost speech (Acts 2:24-36). Naturally, we, like Jesus, should have gladness, joy and hope in our own resurrection.

Acts 2:42-47, which has been called Luke's first major summary, concludes Acts 2. Acts 2:43, 46-47 are of interest here: "And *awe* came upon every soul; and many wonders and signs were done through the apostles. And day by day, attending the temple together and breaking bread in their homes, they partook of food with *glad* and generous hearts, *praising* God and having favor with all the people." This Christian living causes awe in those who behold it, and the salvific action of Jesus working through the Spirit in the community leads to the partaking of food with glad and generous hearts, and to the praising of God. The rest of v 47 confirms this interpretation because it states: "And the Lord added to their number day by day those who were being *saved*." Pentecost happens in accord with God's salvific will, and the recipients respond with joy and praise.

Acts 3:1—4:31 contains a group of expressions of joy and praise. Most scholars grant that Acts 3:1—4:31 is a unit, since a major summary comes before (Acts 2:42-47) and after (Acts 4:32-37) it. Moreover, Luke builds Acts 3:1—4:31 around the story of the healing of the lame man at the Beautiful Gate; and, as a matter of fact, the examples of joy and praise are related to that miracle. The pertinent verses are:

> And *leaping up* he stood and walked and entered the temple with them, walking and *leaping* and *praising* God. And all the people saw him walking and *praising* God, and recognized him as the one who sat for alms at the beautiful Gate of the temple; and they were filled with *wonder* (*thambos*) and *amazement* (*ekstasis*) at what had happened to him.

> While he clung to Peter and John, all the people ran together to them in the portico called Solomon's, *astounded* (*ekthambos*). And when Peter saw it he addressed the people, "Men of Israel, why do you *wonder* at this, or why do you stare at us, as though by our own power or piety we had made him walk? The God of Abraham and of Isaac and of Jacob, the God of our fathers, *glorified* his servant Jesus whom you delivered up and denied in the presence of Pilate,..." (Acts 3:8-13). "You are the sons of the prophets and of the covenant which God gave to your fathers, saying to Abraham, 'And in your posterity shall all the families of the earth be *blessed*.' God having raised up his servant, sent him to you first, *to bless* you in turning everyone of you from your wickedness" (Acts 3:25-26). Now when they saw the boldness of Peter and John, and perceived that they were

> uneducated, common men, they *wondered*; and they rec-
> ognized that they had been with Jesus (Acts 4:13).
>
> And when they had further threatened them they let
> them go, finding no way to punish them because of the
> people; for everyone *praised* God for what had happened
> (Acts 4:21).

The reader will recall that the cure of the lame man at the
Beautiful Gate pictures the risen Christ as the one who
brings salvation through the disciples' use of his name. Luke,
from this one instance of a physical healing, generalizes in
that he says there is salvation in no other name (cf. Acts
4:12). That is the context in which these passages of joy and
praise appear. The six verses (Acts 3:8-13) which immediately follow on the cure are a concentrated Lucan demon-
stration of what kind of reception Christ's bringing of the
Father's salvation should have. In six verses, Luke speaks of
"leaping," "leaping up," "praise," "wonder," "amazement,"
and "being astounded."

The blessing which the risen Christ brings in Acts 3:25-26
fulfills God's covenant to Abraham that in him all the
nations of the earth would be blessed. The blessing consists
in being turned from one's wickedness. This whole speech of
Peter resulted from his concern to explain the cure of the
lame man. Although many scholars have rightly pointed to
Acts 4:12 as the generalization about salvation in Jesus'
name that Luke draws from this cure, the fact is that Luke
has already begun this generalization in Acts 3:25-26.

The Jewish rulers, elders and scribes notice the boldness
of Peter and John and their lack of education right after
Peter has proclaimed that there is no other name than Jesus'
by which a human being must be saved. They know, too,
that Peter and John had been with Jesus. Besides, Luke has
so structured the story that the healed man is standing right
there; there is no way that the miracle can be denied. So,
after they confer with one another, they threaten them, for
they cannot do anything else since everyone is praising God
because of what had happened.

The Cornelius event has statements of fear or awe, joy, amazement, and praise:

> At Caesarea, there was a man named Cornelius..., a devout man who *feared* God with all his household, gave alms liberally to the people, and prayed constantly to God (Acts 10:1-2). Now while Peter was inwardly *perplexed* (*diaporeō*) as to what the vision which he had seen might mean,... (Acts 10:17) ...And they said, "Cornelius, a centurion, an upright and *God-fearing* man,... was directed by a holy angel to send for you to come to his house (Acts 10:22) ...And Peter opened his mouth and said: "Truly, I perceive that God shows no partiality, but in every nation any one who *fears* him and does what is right is acceptable to him (Acts 10:34-35). You know the word which he sent to Israel, preaching *good news of peace* by Jesus Christ (he is Lord of all) (Acts 10:36) ...And the believers from among the circumcised who came with Peter were *amazed*, because the gift of the Holy Spirit had been poured out even on the Gentiles. For they heard them *speaking in tongues* and *extolling* God (Acts 10:45-46) ...When they heard this they were silenced. And they *glorified* God saying, "Then to the Gentiles also God has granted repentance unto life (Acts 11:18).

The man who fears God prays and is acceptable to him and suited for his service. The Cornelius event was certainly due to God's salvific will, for Peter saw a vision and later says, "If then God gave the same gift to them as he gave to us when we believed in the Lord Jesus Christ, who was I that I could withstand God?" (Acts 11:17). The Gentiles have their own Pentecost! Good news always brings joy, and so it did in the case of the good news of peace which Peter discloses in his speech. "Peace" in Acts 10:36 is an equivalent of salvation. The Gentiles who receive the Holy Spirit speak in tongues and praise God, and their experience leads to the amazement of the believers who are present (Acts 10:44-46).

Moreover, when the Jewish Christians in Jerusalem hear that God has granted the Gentiles repentance unto life, they likewise glorify God (Acts 11:18). The statements of fear or awe, joy, amazement and praise in the Cornelius event, then, correspond to all that we have seen thus far, that is, they relate to God's salvation.

Paul's activity at Pisidian Antioch parallels the Pentecost event. Thus, one is not surprised when he discovers that it contains further expressions of joy.

> "..., and you *that fear God*, listen...and those among you *that fear God*, to us has been sent the message of this salvation. Behold, you scoffers, and *wonder*, and perish; for I do a deed in your days, a deed you will never believe, if one declares it to you."... For so the Lord has commanded us, saying, "I have set you to be a light for the Gentiles, that you may bring salvation to the uttermost parts of the earth." And when the Gentiles heard this, they were *glad* and *glorified* the word of God; and as many as were ordained to eternal life believed.... And the disciples were filled with *joy* and with the Holy Spirit (Acts 13:16, 26, 41, 47-48, 52).

Acts 13:13-52 earlier served to show us that Luke saw a connection between Jesus' resurrection and our own. Salvation plays a significant role (Acts 13:23, 26, 38-39, 47) in this unit, but Luke puts weight on one aspect of salvation, eternal life (cf. Acts 13:46, 48). The wonder that Luke has Paul speak of in v 41 hardly presents the proper response to the speech. The quotation Paul employs contends that the scoffers wonder but perish, they cannot believe the great deed that God has done. Nonetheless, this unworthy wonder of the Jews contrasts strongly with the correct response given by the Gentiles, who are glad and glorify God's word that salvation, the light, will be brought to them. These Gentiles, who probably include the God-fearers, are ordained to eternal life. Luke concludes Acts 13 with the report that the disciples who remain in Pisidian Antioch are filled with joy and the Holy Spirit. Naturally, this joy of the disciples results from the message of Paul's speech and its aftermath. In fact, Acts 13:52 may well contain an hendiadys, for the meaning of "were filled with joy and with the Holy Spirit" may well signify "with the joy of the Spirit." However, one should not so associate joy with the Holy Spirit that he fails to realize that it is always the appropriate reaction to God's salvific action, whether or not the Holy Spirit is explicitly designated in the context.

The controversy over the admission of Gentiles into the Christian community (Acts 15:1-35) includes expressions of joy:

> ...they (Paul and Barnabas) passed through both Phoenicia and Samaria, reporting the conversion of the Gentiles, and they gave *great joy* to all the brethren...And when they read it (the letter from the church in Jerusalem) they *rejoiced* at the exhortation...And after they (Judas and Silas) had spent some time, they were sent off in *peace* by the brethren to those who sent them (Acts 15:3, 31, 33).

Almost all scholars will grant that Acts 15:1-35 can reasonably be considered a unit. Luke develops what he established in the Cornelius event. Luke's references to the Cornelius event and God's salvific will are unmistakable. Peter, according to Luke, reminds the apostles and elders that God determined that the Gentiles should hear the word of the Gospel and believe. God gave the Gentiles the Holy Spirit just as he did to the Twelve and those with them at Pentecost. James corroborates Peter's reminder with a citation from Amos 9:11-12 which shows that God has willed that the Gentiles believe.

Against this background, the great joy that the Phoenicians and Samaritans display over the news of the conversion of the Gentiles sets the model for the response which for Luke is the only suitable one. This is the response which the decision of the "Jerusalem Council" should confirm.

The letter of the apostles, elders, and church of Jerusalem sent to the Gentile Christians in Antioch, Syria, and Cilicia is read with rejoicing. Of that letter we are told that it seemed good to the Holy Spirit and to the apostles and elders that the Gentiles abstain only from the necessary things. The specification about the Holy Spirit assures us that the customs requested are what God wants observed.

Finally, Judas and Silas are sent off in peace by the Christians in Antioch. Up to this point, we have been able to relate "peace" with salvation, but this relationship has remained somewhat vague. Acts 15:1-35 offers an opportunity to flesh out some of the Lucan dimensions of peace. The debate in Acts 15 centers on whether or not God intends circumcision as something the Gentile Christians must submit to in order to be saved. Peter comments that they should not make trial of God by putting a yoke upon the neck of the disciples which neither their fathers nor they have been able to bear. Whatever one might want to say about Peter's historical accuracy on this point, to require the Gentiles to be circumcised is called an unsupportable yoke. James continues this reflection with the judgment that they should not trouble the Gentiles who have turned to God, but from the letter we know that this judgment does not allow every burden to be removed. The necessary things cannot be bypassed. However, the letter says that the apostles and elders of the church of Jerusalem had given no instructions to the persons who troubled or unsettled the minds of the Gentile Christians. Consequently, "peace" in this passage includes the assumption of those burdens that somehow are required by God for harmonious Christian living. Anything beyond this is viewed as a needless trouble and burden.

B. Other Examples of Joy, Wonder, Blessing and Praise

Luke writes still more of joy, wonder, speaking in tongues, blessing and praise in Luke-Acts. "Joy" belongs to salvific contexts. Of course, Zechariah is troubled when he sees the angel, and *fear* falls on him. But the angels say, "Do not be *afraid*, Zechariah, for your prayer is heard, and your wife will bear a son, and you shall call his name, John. And you will have *joy* and *gladness* (agalliasis), and many will *rejoice* at his birth" (Lk 1:12-14). Zechariah need not fear. Gabriel identifies himself in this passage and declares that he was sent by God in answer to Zechariah's prayer, so the context recounts God's salvific will. Gabriel greets Mary with the words, "*Hail* (chairō), O favored one, the Lord is with you. Do not be *afraid*, Mary, for you have found favor with God" (Lk 1:28, 30). Doubtless, Mary is to rejoice because she has received the Lord's favor; but the main reason has to be her motherhood of God's Son. Later, the people *rejoice* at the *glorious* (endoxos) things which Jesus does (Lk 13:17). This rejoicing occurs at the end of the miracle story in which Jesus cures the woman who had the infirmity for eighteen years. Zacchaeus likewise *joyfully* receives Jesus (Lk 19:6). Jesus comments on this event: "Today salvation has come to this house, since he is a son of Abraham. For the Son of Man came to seek and to save the lost" (Lk 19:9-10).

The apostles in Acts, after they have been beaten and charged not to speak in Jesus' name, leave the council, *rejoicing* that they were counted worthy enough to suffer dishonor for the name (Acts 5:41). They were punished because they were teaching and preaching Jesus as the Christ. Earlier, in a brief speech, Peter justifies their action with the observation, "We must obey God rather than human beings" (Acts 5:29). There is *much joy* in the city of Samaria when Philip proclaims the Christ and works signs (Acts 8:8). After he embraced the good news preached to him about Jesus and asked Philip to baptize him, the Ethiopian eunuch goes his way *rejoicing* (Acts 8:39). When they heard that a great number had believed and turned to the Lord, the church in Jerusalem sends Barnabas to Antioch. When he arrives and sees the grace of God, he is *glad* (Acts 11:23); and he encourages them all to remain faithful to the Lord.

The joy is not always that which is appropriate to Christians. Sometimes it is immature. The seeds which fall on the rock are those who, when they hear the word receive it with *joy*; but these have no root, they believe for a while and in time of temptation fall away (Lk 8:13). Worse still is the situation of Herod Antipas who was *very glad* when he saw Jesus (Lk 23:8). However, his interest was mere curiosity and the desire to see some miracle. Luke may well be ironical when he writes of Herod being joyful. Worst is the attitude of the chief priests and officers who *were glad* to give Judas Iscariot money to betray Jesus.

Another word for joy is *agalliaō* of which we have seen almost all of the examples. The jailer at Philippi *rejoices* with all his household that he had believed in God (Acts 16:34). The jailer had asked Paul and Silas what he must do to be saved. They told him to believe in the Lord Jesus and he and his household would be saved. He and all his family were baptized, and so, Luke speaks of joy.

The only examples that remain for *euphrainō* are two inappropriate Christian responses. The rich fool plans to build bigger barns and to lay things up for many years. He assures himself, "take your ease, eat, drink, be *merry*" (Lk 12:19). Luke's condemnation at the announcement of the fool's death runs, "So is he who lays up treasure for himself, and is not rich toward God" (Lk 12:21). Along the same lines, Luke describes the rich man in the parable of the rich man and Lazarus, "There was a rich man, who was clothed in purple and fine linen and who feasted (*euphrainomenos*) sumptuously every day" (Lk 16:19). He simply did not care about Lazarus.

All of the positive examples of joy seen thus far were in passages that illustrate God's salvific activity among Christians. The reader will have already realized that Luke in many passages has associated joy with amazement and wonder. Frequently, these latter expressions characterize the reaction to miracles (e.g. Acts 7:31), but, like all the expressions studied thus far, they have to deal with God's salvific will for Israel.

Some examples of *existēmi*, "I am amazed," have already been considered. Everyone who hears the answers of the child Jesus, who sat among the teachers in the temple listening to them and asking them questions, was *amazed* at his understanding and his answers. His parents were *astonished* (*ekplēssomai*) when they saw him (Lk 2:47-48). The child Jesus and his wisdom may be the center of the story. Yet, Jesus' excuse to his parents points to the Father's will, ". . .I must be in my Father's house." Later the parents of the twelve year old girl are *amazed* when Jesus raises her from the dead (Lk 8:56; cf. Mk 5:42). Mark has the same expression, nonetheless, the passage is a Lucan example of Jesus, the savior, for when someone tells Jairus that his daughter is dead, Jesus says, "Do not *fear*, only believe, and she will be saved" (Lk 8:50). Luke alone in this verse adds "salvation." In Acts of the Apostles, Simon who had previously created considerable *amazement* (Acts 8:9, 11) among the Samaritans, is himself *amazed* when he sees the signs and great miracles which Philip performs (Acts 8:13). Later, Luke's reader learns that Simon has much to learn; one cannot obtain the gift of God with money. However, Philip's miracles do denote God's salvific activity, and Simon grants that they are greater than he can achieve. After he was converted to Christianity, Paul enters the synagogues in Damascus and proclaims Jesus as the Son of God. All who hear him are *amazed* (Acts 9:21), for they know he came to Damascus to arrest the Christians. Their amazement is caused by Paul's sudden conversion, which Christ achieved because Paul is his chosen instrument to carry his name before the Gentiles and kings and the sons of Israel (cf. Acts 9:15). Later in Acts, when Peter has been freed from prison and they finally open the door to his knocking, they see him and are *amazed* (Acts 12:16). The amazement results from the miracle for which they were praying, but whose actualization they believed in less strongly. At all events, the Lord sent his angel and rescued Peter from the hands of Agrippa I, and from the expectations of the Jewish people. Perhaps this interpretation also means that the *joy* in Acts 12:14, where Rhoda recognizes Peter's voice but is so joyful she does not open the door, should be understood as a normal response to the experience of God's saving action. God truly hears the prayers of his people and protects those in his service. His actions bring them joy and amazement.

Another word for "amazement" or "wonder" is *thau-*

mazō. The people *wonder* at Zechariah's delay in the temple
(Lk 1:21). When he finally does come out and cannot speak,
they know he has seen a vision in the temple. Luke's reader
knows that Zechariah has seen Gabriel, who was sent to him
by God to bring him the good news that he and his wife
would have a son who will have a special task from the Lord.
During Jesus' appearance in the synagogue at Nazareth,
Luke summarizes the reaction of the audience, "And all
spoke well of him and *wondered* at the gracious words
which proceeded out of his mouth. . ." (Lk 4:22). When the
activity of the risen Christ was discussed above, the position
was defended that this verse means the resurrected Christ
fulfills scripture and becomes present in his word which can
be termed "gracious" because the Father and Christ grant
their salvific grace to those who hear. If this be the case, it is
not surprising that Luke feels that "speaking well of" and
"wonder" constitute appropriate attitudes toward Jesus'
words.

The centurion, in the miracle story of the healing of his
servant, so explains his concept of authority that Jesus
marvels and communicates this to the crowd: "I tell you not
even in Israel have I found such faith" (Lk 7:9). Matthew has
this miracle story and the fact that Jesus marvels at the
centurion's faith, but the story still belongs to the long list of
activities of Christ, the savior of the disadvantaged. Jesus
marvels at the response to salvation.

When Jesus calms the wind and the raging sea, his disciples are *afraid* and *marvel* to one another with the question,
"Who then is this, that he commands even wind and water,
and they obey him" (Lk 8:25). Although all of the Synoptics
have the story of stilling the storm (Lk 8:22-25; cf. Mk
4:35-41; Mt 8:23-27), only Matthew and Luke note that the
disciples marvel. Luke alters Mark's "And they feared a
great fear" to "are afraid and marvel." This Lucan attitude
toward the miraculous shows itself again in the Beelzebub
controversy. When the demon was gone out, the dumb man
speaks, and the people *marvel* (Lk 11:14; cf. Mt 12:22). Both
Matthew and Luke refer to marveling here, but Luke uses

thaumazō (which he tends to prefer) rather than *existēmi*, which is found in Matthew.

At first one gets the impression that Luke has nothing more than the other Synoptics in the story of paying tribute to Caesar. They all speak of *marveling* at the end of the story (Lk 11:14-23; cf. Mk 3:22-27; Mt 12:22-30). But Luke has made some changes at the end of this pericope. He is clearer than both of the other Synoptics on the point that those who are marveling are his opponents. He intensifies their wonder because he repeats what he said at the beginning of the pericope, "And they were not able in the presence of the people to catch him by what he said" (Lk 20:26; cf. v 20). For Luke, "marveling" becomes a participle, and the main verb is "they were silent." So wise and forceful has Jesus proven to be that his opponents must marvel and be silent.

Luke makes no change in Mark's report that everyone *marveled* at Jesus' healing of the demoniac in the synagogue, other than that he employs the noun, not the verb (Lk 4:36; cf. Mk 1:27). However, the miraculous draught of fish, during which Jesus calls Peter, is proper to Luke (see Jn 21:1-14). *Astonishment* seizes Peter, and all who were with him, at the catch of the fish which they had made at Jesus' word (Lk 5:9). Peter says that Jesus should, "Depart from me for I am a sinful man, O Lord."

Another word for amazement or astonishment is *ekplēssomai*. Jesus teaches in the synagogue in the pericope which immediately precedes the miracle story of the healing of the demoniac. All the Synoptics affirm that everyone was *astonished* at his teaching (Lk 4:32; cf. Mk 1:22; Mt 7:28), for he taught with authority. But Luke has two other examples of astonishment, which are proper to him. When he comes down from the mountain after the Transfiguration, Jesus cures the epileptic child whom his disciples could not cure, and everyone is *astonished* at the majesty of God (Lk 9:43a). The second part of this verse (which introduces Jesus' second prediction of the passion) repeats the idea. "But while they were all *marveling* (*thaumazō*) at everything he did, he said to his disciples . . ." (Lk 9:43b). Astonishment appears in Acts when Barnabas and Paul are in Cyprus. Elymas the magician seeks to turn the proconsul from the faith, but Paul curses him, "And now behold the hand of the Lord is upon you..." He is immediately blinded and has to be led around by the hand. The proconsul believes as a result, since he was *astonished* at the teaching of the Lord (cf. Acts 13:11, 13).

Four instances of *diaporeō*, "I wonder, am perplexed," are to be found in the New Testament all of which belong to Luke. Two of these are yet to be considered. All the Synoptics narrate the pericope of the opinions regarding Jesus (Lk 9:7-9; cf. Mk 6:14-16; Mt 14:1-2). Only Luke in this pericope portrays Herod as explicitly *perplexed* at the various interpretations as to who Jesus was. Then, also only in Luke, Herod asks a question which, although it should not be judged as central to Lk 9, nonetheless sets the direction of the chapter which seeks to answer Herod's Christological question, "but who is this about whom I hear such things?"

When the captain of the temple and the chief priests hear that the doors of the prison were securely locked but that the apostles were not inside, they are *perplexed* as to what this might mean (Acts 5:24). An angel of the Lord has opened the prison door and brought the apostles out, and instructed them to stand in the temple and speak to the people all the words of this life. "Words of this life" may mean the words which lead to life or which speak of life, perhaps, as realized in Jesus' resurrection. Both meanings point to the salvific nature of the Gospel message.

The final word which should be mentioned here is *phobeomai* (*phobos*), "I am afraid or *in awe*." Generally, in a religious context, the latter is the better translation. At times, Luke simply speaks of the human emotion of fear (Lk 20:19; 22:2; Acts 5:26; 16:38; 22:29; 23:20; 27:17). But "fear" expresses a correct attitude toward God (Lk 23:40; cf. 18:2-4; Acts 9:31; thus, we have the "God-fearers"(Acts 13:16, 26). That fear or awe is a proper reaction to God's activity in our lives is further supported by remarking what the Christians are not to fear. Christians are not to *fear* because the Father's good pleasure is to give them the kingdom, so they should not worry about clothes or what they are to eat or drink (Lk 12:32; cf. 12:28-31). When Paul is in danger of shipwreck, an angel of God tells him, "Do not be *afraid*, Paul; you must stand before Caesar; and lo, God has granted you all those who sail with you." Paul urges them to take heart because he has faith in God that it will be exactly as he was told (Acts 27:23-25).

In particular, Christians are not to fear those who persecute them. The risen Lord tells Paul one night in a vision, "Do not be *afraid*, but speak and do not be silent, for I am with you, and no man shall attack you to harm you; for I have many people in this city" (Acts 18:9). After all, fear is a proper Christian attitude toward God, not toward those who attempt to work against God's plan. The same truth is found in Lk 12:4-7:

> "I tell you, my friends, do not *fear* those who kill the body, and after that have no more that they can do. But I will warn you whom to *fear*; *fear* him who, after he has killed, has power to cast into hell, yes I tell you *fear* him! Are not five sparrows sold for two pennies? And not one of them is forgotten before God. Why, even the hairs of your head are all numbered. *Fear* not; you are of more value than many sparrows" (Lk 12:4-7; cf. Acts 9:26).

Those who kill the body, and who after that can do no more, are the persecutors of the Christians. However, Christ is to be feared because he can cast one into hell. Now Christians stand within God's providence, they have no need to fear.

The story of the widow's son of Nain (Lk 7:11-17) is proper to Luke. Luke in this pericope gives Jesus the title "Lord" (v 13) because the story shows us Jesus as the savior of a widow and her only son. "Lord" reminds Luke's readers that the risen Christ is also among them. When Jesus raises the dead young man, and returns him to his mother, *fear* seizes everyone and they *glorify* God. "A great prophet has arisen among us!" and "God has visited his people!" (v 16). Jesus' action is viewed as God's visitation of his people, and so they are in awe and glorify God. All of the Synoptics report the miracle of the Gerasene demoniac. But Luke has some significant additions. Both he and Mark write "they were *afraid*." But Luke adds the data that the "saved" man sits at Jesus' feet and that "all the people of the surrounding country of the Gerasenes... were seized with great *fear*" (Lk 8:35-37; cf. Mk 5:15-17). Luke repeats "fear" and points out that the man was saved. Jesus' saving power becomes manifest in the posture of the cured man at his feet.

Only Luke of the Synoptics adverts to the *fear* of apostles as they entered the cloud at Jesus' Transfiguration. All the Synoptics recognize the divine presence who proclaims "This is my Son, my Chosen, listen to him" (Lk 9:34-35; cf. Mk 9:7; Mt 17:5). Luke blends fear or awe with God's presence. Luke also associates fear with the coming of the Son of Man, "... and upon the earth distress of nations in *perplexity* (*aporia*) at the roaring of the sea and the waves, men fainting with *fear* and with *foreboding* (*prosdokia*) of what is coming on the world" (Lk 21:25-26). The parable of the pounds likewise depicts the coming of the Son of Man. Luke (19:21) and Matthew (25:25) in this parable both record the fear of the man who received one pound, for he knows his Lord to be a severe man.

Luke in the story of Ananias and Sapphira leaves no doubt about the connection between fear or awe and the action of God. Most authorities grant the parallel between Acts 5:1-6 and 5:7-11. Each of these sections ends with the death of the guilty party. These deaths lead to a *great fear* (Acts 5:5, 11) in the whole church and among all who hear of these things. Peter had informed Ananias, "Ananias, why has Satan filled your heart to lie to the Holy Spirit and to keep back part of the proceeds of the land...? You have not lied to men but to God," and to Sapphira, Peter says, "How is it that you have agreed together to tempt the Spirit of the Lord?" (Acts 5:3-4, 9). Finally, the action of Paul and those on shipboard with him once again betrays that fear most properly relates to God, "And *fearing* that we might run on the rocks, they let out four anchors from the stern, and prayed for day to come" (Acts 27:29).

All of the passages which disclose some element of amazement or wonder highlight aspects of salvation. Most frequently amazement and wonder result from miracles happening in salvation history. But wonder also follows on the word and deeds of Jesus and of his disciples. Questions arise about who Jesus is, and Jesus himself even marvels at the faith of the centurion. God's deeds, too, cause amazement or awe. Generally, Luke has expanded on the notion of wonder in Mark or in the Q. A number of the occurrences are his own.

Acts 19:1-17 was treated in the previous chapter as a parallel of Pentecost, and a narrative about the free response to God's salvific will. It fits in here, too, because when the disciples at Ephesus are baptized and Paul lays hands on them, "they *speak in tongues and prophesy*" (v 6). "Prophesy" should probably also be underlined since, from the Pentecost event on, it seems that the experience of the reception of the Holy Spirit leads the Christians to prophesy (cf. Acts 2:17-18). In the Pentecost event and in Acts 19:1-7, "to prophesy" is joined with "to speak in tongues" and is more associated with the marvelous and wondrous than with proclamation.

The reception and the living of the Christian message are for Luke a blessing. A number of passages which verify this Lucan position have already been adduced; however, other passages ought to be considered. There are two other examples of Luke's use of *makarios*. Jesus says at a banquet at the house of a Pharisee:

> "... But when you give a feast, invite the poor, the maimed, the lame, the blind, and you will be *blessed*, because they cannot repay you. You will be repaid at the resurrection of the just." When one of those who sat at the table with him heard this, he said to him, "*Blessed* is he who shall eat bread in the kingdom of God" (Lk 14:13-15).

Although Matthew (22:1-10) does have the parable of the great supper he does not have the Lucan teaching on humility (Lk 14:7-14) nor Lk 14:15; these are proper to Luke.

Also, in the parable of the great banquet, only Luke writes that the Lord (Matthew calls him a king) commands his servant, ". . . bring in the poor and maimed and blind and lame" and mentions, "my banquet" (cf. Lk 14:21, 24). The Lord in this parable behaves like Jesus, the savior of the disadvantaged. In fact, there is little doubt that Luke intends his readers to understand "the Lord" as Jesus. Luke, in his teaching on humility, directs the Pharisee who gave the banquet to act like Jesus and to invite the disadvantaged.

Jesus does not object to the exclamation of his table companion that he is blessed who eats bread in the kingdom of God. Rather he begins to determine who these are. Those who were invited originally refuse to come; none of them will taste the Lord's banquet. But those who will partake of the banquet, which the man's exclamation invites us to identify with the kingdom of God, are named: the poor, the maimed, the blind, and the lame. These, then, are the blessed. Luke draws the logical conclusion that the disadvantaged are the favorites of our savior, Jesus.

Paul, at the end of his address to the elders at Miletus, alleges that "It is more *blessed* to give than to receive" (Acts 20:35) are the words of the Lord Jesus. Paul remembered these words when he worked with his hands to see to his own needs and the needs of those with him. In every way he was showing the Ephesian elders that by toiling one must help the weak. Paul acts like Jesus, the savior of the disadvantaged, and so is blessed.

In addition, Luke used *eulogeō* for "blessed." Above it was remarked that the risen Christ blessed the Christians; the only other blessings by Jesus are in passages which Luke associates with the Eucharist. Of course, Christ saves in the Eucharist because his body is given for us, and the cup is the new covenant in his blood. But the blessing in Lk 9:16 is itself salvific. The people are hungry and need something to eat. The disciples cannot feed them. So, Jesus *blesses* the five loaves and the two fishes, and all eat and are satisfied. The *blessing* that Jesus gives in the Emmaus story leads the two disciples to recognition of him in the breaking of bread

(Lk 24:30). The risen Christ who fulfills the scriptures will always be present to the Christians in the breaking of bread. The hope of the disciples was not misplaced; Jesus did redeem Israel (cf. Lk 24:21).

"Peace" (*eirēnē*) for Luke can mean salvation or it can describe the results of salvation in the believer. True, at times "peace" signifies peace in this world (cf. Lk 14:32; Acts 12:20; 16:36; 24:32); a strong man, fully armed, does keep his possessions in peace (Lk 11:21). Both Luke (12:51) and Matthew (10:34) write of a "peace" that Jesus did not bring, for people may have to choose Jesus over their own relatives.

Two Lucan passages, one of which is proper to him, connect salvation with peace. Luke and Mark both agree that, after Jesus cures the woman with the flow of blood, he orders her, "to go in peace because your faith has saved (*sōzō*) you" (Lk 8:48; cf. Mk 5:34). "Peace" in this verse cannot be explained without bringing in the cure, the saving. The woman is at peace because her flow of blood, which lasted twelve years and could be cured by no one, was healed. The same must be said about Luke's conclusion to the narrative of the woman who was a sinner, "And he said to the woman, 'your faith has saved you; go in peace'" (Lk 7:50). We have already discovered that this passage, although parallels exist in Mark and Matthew, is largely due to Luke. Here, too, the woman's peace comes from her saving, which is the forgiving of her sins. Her strange behavior comes from her attempt to deal with the lack of harmony that her sinful life has brought upon her.

When he sends out the Seventy, Jesus instructs them, "Whatever house you enter, first say, 'Peace be to this house!' And if a son of peace is there, your peace shall rest upon him; but if not, it shall return to you" (Lk 10:5-6). "Peace" in this passage is not simply a form of greeting; this becomes more certain when Luke's reader observes the curse that Jesus orders for the town that does not receive the Seventy. As they shake its dust off their feet against that town, they are to announce, "... nevertheless know this, that the kingdom of God has come near!" (Lk 10:11). In a city that does receive them, the Seventy are to eat what is set before them; heal the sick, and proclaim "The kingdom of God has come near you" (cf. Lk 10:8-11). "Peace" relates to reception of the Seventy, their healing ministry, and the nearness of the kingdom. That is why those who do not receive the Seventy are more cursed on that day than Sodom. The peace greeting of the risen Christ (Lk 24:36) could be perceived the same way. This peace calms the startled and frightened Eleven, and those who are with them. They are troubled, and questions arise in their minds; they do not believe. The risen Christ brings peace to all these misplaced actions.

Finally, when we in the summary statement learn that the church throughout all Judea and Galilee and Samaria had *peace* and was built up and walking in "the *fear* of the Lord and in the comfort of the Holy Spirit and growing in number" (Acts 9:31), we are somewhat taken aback because the last news we had about Judea was that the Christians were being persecuted (Acts 9:26-30; cf. 8:1b-3). An understanding of peace in Acts 9:31 can be gained because Luke combines it with "built up," "walking in fear of the Lord," "comfort of the Holy Spirit" and growth of the community. "Peace" is another positive attribute of the community. Paul and the Greek-speaking Christians are not in Jerusalem any more, the persecutions have ceased; even Christians in Jerusalem know a peace.

Christians, therefore are blessed when they act like Jesus and receive the disadvantaged at their banquets. It is a real blessing to share in the messianic banquet; this blessing will be particularly extended to the disadvantaged. Jesus' blessing of the Eucharist brings nourishment and the realization that the risen Christ is present to his community. Peace, itself a blessing, flows from the saving acts of Christ in this world and from the nearness of the kingdom. Peace for the Church is the harmony that comes from an absence of persecution, and it is the quieting of the results of ignorance and sinfulness.

C. *Further Expressions of Praise of God*

Expressions of praise of God have already been seen along with joy, wonder, and blessing. The purpose of this section is to consider a few additional expressions of praise. These expressions, too, will bear upon God's salvific will. "Glory" (*doxa, doxazō*) expresses praise.

Luke, in a summary statement about Jesus' teaching in the synagogues of Galilee and the surrounding country, lets us know that Jesus was being *glorified* by everyone (Lk 4:14-15). Although Mark and Matthew have parallels to this Lucan passage and specify that the content of Jesus' preaching was repentance and the drawing near of the kingdom, neither of them say anything about teaching in the synagogues or about Jesus' being glorified at all. So, Luke alone has everyone glorify Jesus when he teaches. His teaching is more reasonably of the coming of the kingdom and of God's salvific will.

A similar result follows in a story which is proper to Luke, the cure of the infirm woman. She, too, *praises* God when Jesus frees her from her infirmities (Lk 13:13). This passage could well have been included among those about joy, amazement, blessing, and praise, for Luke ends it with "...and all the people *rejoiced* at all the *glorious things* (*endoxos*) that were done by him" (Lk 13:17).

All of the Synoptics (Lk 18:35-43; cf. Mk 10:46-52; Mt 20:29-34) relate the healing of the blind man. But only Luke at the very end of the story adds that the blind man, when cured, followed Jesus, "*glorifying* God; and all the people, when they saw it, gave *praise* (*aineō*) to God." Again the praise is given to God, although Jesus performed the miracle. Luke, as Mark, designates the man's faith as the reason why he has been saved. All of the Synoptics mark the presence of a centurion at Jesus' crucifixion (Lk 23:47; cf. Mk 15:39; Mt 27:54). Both Mark and Matthew record that the centurion confesses (or shares in the confession) that Jesus was truly the Son of God. Luke, on the other hand, writes, "...he *praised* God, and said, 'Certainly, this man was just...'" His words, to be sure, belong to Luke's theme of Jesus' innocence, but they fit here because they are the last words spoken at Jesus' crucifixion, and they are words of praise. The centurion, with the Christian insight of Luke, praises God for what he has done in the crucifixion of the innocent Jesus. The centurion is certainly not praising God because of the crucifixion of an innocent man, but because of Jesus' confidence in his Father.

Another praise of God is found in Acts 21:17-20. Paul has come up to Jerusalem where the Christians receive him *gladly* (*asmenōs*). The next day Paul visits James and the elders, and Luke depicts the scene as follows:

> After greeting them, he (Paul) related one by one the things God has done among the Gentiles through his ministry. And when they heard it, they *glorified* God.

Luke has obviously connected their praise of God with what God has done through Paul among the Gentiles. This praise of God reminds the reader of the passages we have just seen, where God is praised because of what Jesus has done. Moreover, the Christians in Jerusalem receive Paul gladly. As Luke sees it, the Jewish Christian leaders are in no way upset by the success that Paul has been having among the Gentiles. Rather, their warm reception of him testifies as to how Christians should always receive one another.

There are two examples of *megalunō* ("to magnify" or "to extol") which remain to be examined. When, in what is called the third major summary, the apostles work many signs and wonders, none dare join them, but the people *held them in high honor* (Acts 5:13). Luke intends his readers to see the passage as part of God's answer to the prayer of Peter, John and their friends:

> And now, Lord, look upon their threats, and grant to your servants to speak your word with all boldness, while you stretch out your hand to heal, and signs and wonders are performed through the name of your servant Jesus (Acts 4:29-30).

Assuredly, the miracles are performed by the apostles and especially by Peter; but Luke holds that these signs and wonders continue God's saving action in Christ, and in his followers. This is why the people hold the apostles in high esteem.

The other passage of import here is the story of the sons of Sceva (Acts 19:11-20). This passage parallels the third major summary where the emphasis falls on Peter's great miraculous powers. Here, however, the extraordinary miracles of Paul are accentuated. The story tells of how the seven sons of Sceva try to perform the same kind of miracles as did Paul in the name of the Lord Jesus. Instead, the evil spirit overpowers them, and they flee naked and wounded. This event becomes known to all the residents of Ephesus, both Jews and Greeks. They are *awestruck*, and the name of the Lord is *extolled* (v 17). Luke, in this pericope more definitely than in the third summary, attributes the miracle to Jesus and to God's salvific will. He concludes the passage with "So the word of the Lord grew and prevailed mightily." Luke has highlighted the reaction of the residents to this event, because a number of believers confessed their magical practices and some even burned their books on magic.

These further examples of praise lead to several conclusions. Generally, the Father is praised even though the action may have been by Jesus or by a disciple. But Jesus and the apostles can be praised also. Some salvific event always constitutes the ultimate reason for the praising; and finally, Luke frequently has expanded on the praise found in his sources, or has in some other way enhanced it in the context.

D. Conclusion

This consideration of joy, wonder, blessing and praise in Luke-Acts has been like a long journey. But this journey confirms that Luke describes how the various experiences of God's salvific will should be received. True, Luke's sources initially suggested to him these attitudes towards God's work in human history, but Luke has taken them over and made them a major theme in his double work. No one can deny that Luke has developed and creatively expanded what he found. His ability at storytelling allows him to move from the one parable about a lost sheep to the masterpiece, ch. 15 of his Gospel. It is this literary skill which actually draws Luke's reader to participate fully in the joy and wonder of the experience of being blessed because of what God has done, and in the summons to praise God. Finally, Luke sets this whole pattern of acceptance of God's salvific will against the backdrop of the end times which have arrived with Jesus, the Christ.

CHAPTER 11

CHRISTIANS ARE TO IMITATE THE FATHER AND JESUS

It is not always easy, in Luke-Acts, to distinguish between God's and Jesus' acting in the disciples and the fact that the Christians are to imitate the Father and Jesus. Very likely, Luke did not intend us to distinguish between them. Nothing has been said thus far about God who works in the disciples or whom the disciples are to imitate.

Two Lucan passages stress the close relationship between God and human beings. The first passage occurs in Paul's speech on the Apeopagus, "...as even some of your poets have said, 'For we are indeed his offspring.' Being then God's offspring, we ought not to think that the Deity is like gold, or silver, or stone, a representation by the art and imagination of man" (Acts 17:28b-29). Perhaps an even closer relationship between God and Christians is found in the story of Ananias and Sapphira. Although Ananias has obviously lied to Peter and the Apostles, Peter says to Ananias, "You have not lied to men but to God" (Acts 5:4) and to Sapphira, "How is it that you have agreed together to tempt the Spirit of the Lord?" (Acts 5:9). "Lord" in this latter passage most reasonably refers to God. To lie to Peter and the Apostles is to lie to God. Everyone is like God, but he particularly joins himself to the Christian Community.

Jesus in Luke (6:35b-36; cf. Mt 5:45, 47) says to his disciples,

> "But love your enemies, and do good, and lend, expecting nothing in return; and your reward will be great, and you will be sons of the Most High; for he is kind to the ungrateful and selfish. Be merciful, even as your Father is merciful."

The disciples are to imitate the mercy of the Father. This same imitation of the Father's mercy appears in the parable of the prodigal son (Lk 15:11-32). Imitation of God also appears in the conversion story of Cornelius. When Peter in a trance sees something like a great sheet descending from heaven and all kinds of animals and reptiles and birds of the air in it, a voice urges him to kill and eat, but Peter is unwilling to eat anything that is common or unclean. But the voice says to him a second time, "What God has cleansed, you must not call common" (Acts 10:15; cf. 11:8-9). This happened three times. Peter, according to Luke, twice rephrases this thought, "You yourself know how unlawful it is for a Jew to associate with or to visit anyone of another nation; but God has shown me that I should not call any man common or unclean. So, when I was sent for, I came without objection" (Acts 10:28-29) and "Truly I perceive that God shows no partiality, but in every nation anyone who fears him and does what is right is acceptable to him" (Acts 10:34). Peter's actions and treatment of Cornelius and his associates demonstrate that he has taken God as his model in openness to all those who fear God and do what is right. Moreover, Christians are to be merciful as God is merciful.

It was noted above that the risen Christ acts in his disciples. Peter speaks in the name of Jesus, the prophet like Moses (Acts 3:22-23); and, although Paul is the one who actually proclaims light to the Gentiles (cf. Acts 13:46-48), nonetheless, this activity is predicated of the Christ (Acts 26:23). Besides, the risen Christ identifies himself with the persecuted Christians (cf. Lk 21:14-15; Acts 9:4-6; 22:7-8; 26:14-15).

Luke does not often explicitly write of Christians' imitation of Jesus. He, as Matthew, recognizes "A disciple is not above his teacher, but everyone when he is fully taught will be like his teacher" (Lk 6:40; cf. Mt 10:24-25). Luke's clearest expressions about imitation of Christ occurs in the passage:

> And he said to all, "If any man would come after me, let him deny himself and take up his cross daily and follow me. For whoever would save his life will lose it, and whoever loses his life for my sake, he will save it. For what does it profit a man if he gains the whole world and loses or forfeits himself? For whoever is ashamed of me and of my words, of him will the Son of Man be ashamed when he comes in his glory and the glory of the Father and of the holy angels" (Lk 9:23-26; cf. 14:27; 17:33; par.).

Daily the Christian is to follow Jesus in his suffering. This following of Jesus will give life, whereas if one tries to save himself, he loses his life. A Christian who does not confess Jesus and his message will not be recognized by Jesus at the judgment. Probably, with reference to the above passages and as an example to Christians, all the Synoptics mention that Simon of Cyrene carries the cross behind Jesus (Lk 23:26; par.). Only Luke reports that Jesus at the last supper acknowledges of the apostles, "You are those who have continued with me in my trials. . ." (Lk 22:28).

Only Luke, of the Synoptics, during the last supper, tells us that Jesus instructs his disciples, "Do this in remembrance of me" (Lk 22:19). True, this instruction belongs to the tradition (cf. I Cor 11:24-25), but the fact remains that Jesus calls for imitation of his actions at the last supper and Luke notes this.

Three other passages in Luke's Gospel suggest that the

disciples are to imitate Jesus. At the beginning of Jesus' journey to Jerusalem, someone says to him, "I will follow you wherever you go." But Jesus explains to him that, although foxes have holes and birds of the air their nests, he himself has nowhere to lay his head (Lk 9:57-58; cf. Mt 8:18-20). The implication is that a disciple will have to imitate Jesus' lack of an abode. Only Luke introduces the pericope about the Our Father with, "He was praying in a certain place, and when he ceased, one of his disciples said to him, 'Lord, teach us to pray, as John taught his disciples'" (Lk 11:1). This disciple, who as the later Church addresses Jesus as "Lord," wants to do what he has seen Jesus doing. All the Synoptics record the story of the rich young man. In the course of this story, Jesus tells him, "One thing you still lack. Sell all that you have and distribute to the poor, and you will have treasure in heaven; and come follow me" (Lk 18:22; par.). Earlier it was pointed out that "riches" in this passage is used metaphorically and includes leaving one's house, wife, brothers, parents, and children for the sake of the kingdom of God (cf. Lk 18:29). Again, the story implies that Jesus himself has left all of these, and his disciples must do the same.

A passage in Acts introduces Luke's reader to his presentation of the imitation of Jesus by his disciples. Above, it was demonstrated that Paul's defenses before Festus and Agrippa II reveal many similarities to Jesus' passion in Lk 23:1-25. So, Luke pictures Paul like Jesus. Yet, in the dialogue after Paul's defense before Agrippa II, we read:

> And Agrippa said to Paul, "In a short time you think to make me a Christian!" And Paul said, "whether short or long, I would to God that not only you but also all who hear me this day might become such as I am—except for these chains" (Acts 26:28-29).

The significance of Paul's assertion that he would like Agrippa II to be like him is that Paul stands not only for himself but for Christians. But Paul, the Christian, in Acts 25-26 is extensively compared to Jesus during his passion.

In other words, Luke does not often speak of Christians carrying their crosses behind Jesus, rather he shows us Christians having the same experiences as Jesus had. That is why in the section, "The Disciples Continue the Work of Jesus" so many similarities were able to be found between Jesus and Stephen, between Jesus and Paul, and between Jesus and all of the disciples. There is no need to repeat all of those passages here. Nonetheless, they not only demonstrate the continuity between Jesus and his disciples but their imitation of him. Jesus and his disciples do or endure the same things. They are associated with the same places. Luke predicates the same words and descriptions of them. Finally, the disciples appear most like Jesus during his passion.

CONCLUSION

Like every book, this one has its presuppositions and methodology. The methodology, a kind of redaction criticism, might more properly be called composition criticism. Because both exegete and reader have the same main task of listening to what Luke has to say, a definite effort has been made to base the presentation and arguments on Luke's text.

I contend in this book that Luke's main reason for writing Luke-Acts is to show that the God of the Old Testament continues to bring his salvation to Israel which is now the Christians. Once one realizes that Luke addresses his readers who are the Christians as Israel, he or she can see how naturally Luke's thought flows. Luke has various ways of portraying the continuation of God's salvific will. The scriptures (the Law, Prophets, and Psalms) surely indicate that a person or action participates in God's salvation history; and, of course, the same would hold true of any mention of God's foreknowledge, will, plan, or purpose. Moreover, certain verbs reveal that God continues to bring salvation to the Christians. The Holy Spirit, angels and visions also make this clear. Needless to say, Jesus, especially as savior, is the main instrument of continuing God's salvific will. Not only does the earthly Jesus through his actions, teachings and miracles save, but the risen Jesus continues to save. The risen Jesus is Lord of the community. At times, he is present to the community through the Spirit, his name or his witnesses. He manifests himself in the Eucharist to the Christians. The disciples continue Jesus' work of salvation, for he works through them. Thus, Luke has continuity among Israel, Jesus, and the disciples or Church. Luke can write of disciples who either speak for Jesus or do what can be predicated of Jesus himself. The most extensive way in which Luke reports that the disciples carry on Jesus' salvific activity is that he describes them as he describes Jesus. They act and have the same experiences as the earthly Jesus does.

Other Lucan theological themes relate to the continuation of God's salvific will for Israel in that they describe how this salvation is present. This salvation is universal; it reaches out to everyone. Jesus specifies this salvation because he saves the disadvantaged, the outcasts. Certainly, salvation is for all, but sinners, women, the sick, the poor, the persecuted and everyone else who is an outcast enjoy a divine preference. Luke does believe that the Christians are living in the last days, but no definite time is given for the Parousia, Jesus' second coming. The Parousia will happen. Yet Christians should not distract themselves with the constant question of "when"; they are to carry on Jesus' teaching and activity. The Romans create no problem for the Christians. In fact, the Romans frequently defend the Christians from their unreasonable and less law-abiding foes. There is nothing in Christianity which should cause the Christians or the Romans any concern about the possibility of their harmonious coexistence. Christians make good citizens. Finally, Luke gives a more personal dimension to the presence of God's salvific will than do the other Synoptics. This personal dimension is clear from the Lucan themes of universality, of Jesus as the savior of the disadvantaged, of the required personal response and of joy, wonder, blessing and praise which Christians experience when they hear the message. But Luke also emphasizes the personal dimension by intensifying the presentation of a person or situation in which a person is involved. He provides more information, names people, directly addresses his audience, and adapts material to his readers' experience. He gives special respect and attention to the disciples and apostles and, particularly, to Jesus.

Disciples, according to Luke, are characterized by their receptivity toward God's salvific activity. To belong to the realm of light, and not that of darkness, one must respond to God's salvific action in his or her life. Luke does not draw a fine distinction among the terms which he uses to designate this response. Given the right context, one or more terms can express incorrect, imperfect or an appropriate response. Other contexts are more full-blown and contain almost every expression of this Lucan response-pattern.

Luke, likewise, has an extensive pattern about how one should react to the experience of God's salvific history. The whole of this pattern stands against the backdrop of the end times which have arrived with Jesus the Christ. All of these appropriate reactions to the experience of God's salvation history can be summarized under the headings of "joy," "wonder," "blessing" and "praise." Initially, Luke's sources suggested these reactions to him as appropriate, but he has creatively expanded on them.

Christians are to imitate Jesus (and the Father). Luke calls Christians to be like the Father and like Jesus. The Christians are God's offspring and should be merciful and regard no one as common just as he does not. Luke identifies anyone's treatment of the leaders of the community as the treatment of God and of the Spirit. So closely do the disciples imitate Christ that he can be said to work through and in them. They are to take up their cross and follow him and to celebrate the Eucharist in his remembrance. But, most of all, Luke shows us the Christians doing the same things and having the same experiences as Jesus. They are associated with the same places as Jesus is. Finally, they appear most like Jesus during his passion.

Luke, throughout Luke-Acts, establishes for his readers the truth of the above themes. He calls them as the true Israel to benefit from their faith in the continuation of salvation history. For them, God works, especially through Jesus, his salvation. His salvation reaches out to all of them in a personal and practical manner. Luke addresses those who live in a Roman world and will profit little from an over-emphasis on the Parousia. Their every weakness simply recommends them the more to their savior. The disciples, on their part, are to be receptive. The proper reactions toward God's saving actions are: joy, wonder, blessing and praise. In short, their lives should be imitations of Jesus.

BIBLIOGRAPHY

A number of my own publications appear in this bibliography because they present the arguments which stand behind many of the positions taken in this book and because they provide the reader with extensive bibliography for the various points discussed. Other citations given here were also used in the preparation of this book. Finally, some further readings in Luke-Acts are suggested.

Cadbury, Henry J., *The Making of Luke-Acts* (London, S.P.C.K., 1958-revised edition).

Conzelmann, H., *The Theology of St. Luke* tr. G. Buswell (New York, Harper & Row, 1960).

Lohfink, G., "Hat Jesus eine Kirche gestifet?" *TQ* 161 (1981) 81-97.

_____, *Die Sammlung Israels: eine Untersuchung zur lukanischen Ekklesiologie* (München, Kösel, 1975) 61-62, 91-99.

Navone, J., *Themes on St. Luke* (Rome, Gregorian University Press, 1970) 71-87.

O'Toole, R. F., "Why Did Luke Write Acts (Lk-Acts)?" *Biblical Theology Bulletin* 7 (1977) 66-72.

_____, *The Christological Climax of Paul's Defense* (Analecta Biblica 78, Rome, Pontifical Biblical Institute, 1978)

_____, "Luke's Notion of 'Be Imitators of Me as I Am of Christ' in Acts 25-26" *Biblical Theology Bulletin* 8 (1978) 155-161.

_____, "Christ's Resurrection in Acts 13, 13-52," *Biblica* 60 (1979) 361-372.

_____, "Activity of the Risen Jesus in Luke-Acts," *Biblica* 62 (1981) 471-498.

_____, "Luke's Position on Politics and Society in Luke-Acts," *Political Issues in Luke-Acts* (Maryknoll, Orbis Books, 1983) 1-17.

_____, "Luke's Notion of Worship and Paul's Stay at Athens," *Revue Biblique* 89 (1982) 185-197.

_____, "Acts 2:30 and the Davidic Covenant of Pentecost," *Journal of Biblical Literature* 102 (1983) 245-258.

_____, "Parallels between Jesus and His Disciples in Luke-Acts: A Further Study," *Biblische Zeitschrift* 27 (1983) 195-212.

Richard, E., "Luke—Writer, Theologian, Historian: Research and Orientation of the 1970's," *Biblical Theology Bulletin* 13 (1983) 3-15.

Vanhoye, A., *Structure and Theology of the Accounts of the Passion in the Synoptic Gospels*, tr. C. H. Giblin (Collegeville, The Liturgical Press, 1967).

Other Suggested Readings:

Crowe, Jerome, *The Acts*, (Wilmington, Michael Glazier, 1983).

Danker, Frederick W., *Jesus and the New Age* (St. Louis, Clayton Publishing House, 1976).

Fitzmyer, Joseph A., *The Gospel according to Luke* (Garden City, Doubleday, 1981) 143-258.

Juel, Donald, *Luke-Acts: The Promise of History* (Atlanta, John Knox, 1983).

Karris, Robert J., *Invitation to Acts: A Commentary on the Acts of the Apostles with Complete Text from the Jerusalem Bible* (Garden City, Image Books, 1978).

_____, *What Are They Saying About Luke and Acts* (New York, Paulist Press, 1979).

Kurz, William, *Following Jesus: A Disciple's Guide to Luke and Acts* (Ann Arbor, Servant Books, 1984).

LaVerdiere, Eugene, *Luke* (Wilmington, Michael Glazier, 1982).

Maddox, R., *The Purpose of Luke-Acts* (Edinburgh, T. & T. Clark, 1982).

Talbert, Charles H., *Literary Patterns, Theological Themes and the Genre of Luke-Acts* (Missoula, Society of Biblical Literature and Scholars Press, 1974).

_____, *Reading Luke: A Literary and Theological Commentary on the Third Gospel* (New York, Crossroad, 1982).

INDEX OF SELECTED TOPICS

This list is not exhaustive. It is designed to assist the reader in locating topics considered more than briefly in this book. If a topic is noted in the "Table of Contents", it will not be repeated here unless it appears again in another section of the book. So one may have to use both the table of contents and this index to find the complete consideration of a give topic. Of course, a complete understanding of a given topic can only be obtained by a reading of the entire book.